Canada and Quebec

Robert Bothwell

Canada and Quebec: One Country, Two Histories

REVISED EDITION

UBC PRESS / VANCOUVER

To Gail

© UBC Press 1998
First edition 1995

Printed in Canada on acid-free paper

ISBN 0-7748-0653-2

___

Canadian Cataloguing in Publication Data

Bothwell, Robert, 1944-
            Canada and Quebec

    Includes bibliographical references and index.
    ISBN 0-7748-0653-2

    1. Canada – English-French relations. 2. Quebec
(Province) – History – Autonomy and indepen-
dence movements. 3. Canada – Politics and govern-
ment. I. Title.
FC144.B66 1998   971.4   C97-910919-1
FC1027.B66 1998

___

UBC Press gratefully acknowledges the ongoing
support to its publishing program from the Canada
Council for the Arts, the British Columbia Arts
Council, and the Department of Canadian Heritage
of the Government of Canada.

UBC Press
University of British Columbia
6344 Memorial Road
Vancouver, BC V6T 1Z2
(604) 822-5959
Fax: 1-800-668-0821
E-mail: orders@ubcpress.ubc.ca
http://www.ubcpress.ubc.ca

Contents

Preface to the Revised Edition

THIS BOOK was first published in the lead-up to the Quebec referendum of 1995, in which the separatist side was narrowly defeated. The federalist victory undoubtedly saved Canada from immediate disruption, but the narrowness of the margin did not satisfy either side. As of early 1998, the separatist government of Quebec was still leading in opinion polls in that province, while the federal Liberal government had not improved its standing in Quebec sufficiently to make a third referendum unlikely. Canada thus continues to live under the gun of the possible departure of Quebec, with all that a split would entail. This edition of *Canada and Quebec* reviews and updates events since 1994 from the performance of Jacques Parizeau as premier of Quebec, through the narrow defeat of his cause in the 1995 referendum, to the federal election of June 1997 and beyond. None of these events has proved to be definitive, and the issue of Canada's future continues to hang in the balance.

Preface to the First Edition

THIS BOOK HAD ITS ORIGINS in the summer of 1994. With a Quebec provincial election impending and the victory of Jacques Parizeau and the Parti Québécois practically assured, it seemed evident that Canada would once again confront the twin questions of Quebec's relations with Canada and Canada's relations with Quebec – very soon. For Mr Parizeau promised that, if victorious, he would hold a referendum on the unambiguous question of Quebec's sovereignty – yes or no – within a year.

At the suggestion of May Maskow, the director of Open College at radio station CJRT, Toronto, I undertook to create a series of programs on Canada-Quebec, for broadcast in the winter and spring of 1995. Open College CJRT agreed to find the funds, somehow, for the enterprise, and work on Canada-Quebec proceeded from late August 1994 into February 1995. I owe May and her staff, especially Elizabeth Barry, my long-suffering producer, and Jeff Zabudsky, who handled many of the long-distance interviews, special thanks. Meanwhile Mary Alice Stuart set out to raise the requisite funds, which she did, to use a phrase from the program, 'with honour and enthusiasm.' The following organizations contributed to the station for this purpose: The Ondaatje Corporation, Bank of Montreal, The Bank of Nova Scotia, CIBC, Royal Bank of Canada, The Toronto-Dominion Bank, Camdev Corporation, The Henry R. Jackman Foundation, S.M. Blair Family Foundation, The Burton Charitable Foundation, The Eaton Foundation, and other generous supporters. Des Glynn slogged away at the thankless task of actually rounding up interviewees. In the process he met a largish selection of press secretaries, some helpful and cooperative – and some not. Joan McCordick explored on my behalf the byways of the Quebec bureaucracy, an instructive if not always fruitful task. To them I owe many thanks.

I explored the possibility of converting the radio scripts into a book with Laura Macleod of UBC Press. This was a novel undertaking. It is true, as Molière once observed, that we all speak prose, but *writing* prose is a little more specialized. The rhythms and continuity of written and spoken discourse are different, as many 'you knows' and 'I thinks' and 'so forths' and 'et ceteras' attest, not to mention 'and ... and ... and.' What is good and fluent in voice can be tedious and irritating on paper and, of course, vice versa. But Laura was also enthusiastic, and UBC Press committed itself to work within unusual time constraints in order to get the book out, if possible, before Mr Parizeau's mental clock ticked 'referendum time.'

With the indispensable help and sage counsel of Rosemary Shipton, my editor for the past twenty-five years, the project lurched forward over grammatical hills and down syntactical dales. Ken McRoberts took time out, in addition to an interview, to help with facts. Dave Bercuson paused in the middle of moving house to help arrange Calgary interviews, and Jim Miller provided help and hospitality in Saskatoon. Gretta Chambers assisted in a guided tour of improbable country roads, and furnished food and drink besides. Guy Laforest and Jim Miller actually submitted to a second round of interviews, when the first round suffered, as we might say, terminal handicaps.

Across Canada, many people paused in busy schedules to speak into my microphone, including two premiers and the prime minister of the country. I am grateful to all my interviewees for their time, their patience, and their candour. Not everybody had the time or the patience, naturally enough, and inevitably there were omissions. The omissions are the responsibility of the author, while the occasional refusals are, often enough, the result of what we may call a 'media strategy.'

Lastly I would like to thank my wife, Gail Corbett, who little thought that marrying a historian would involve packing up and heading for the hills of Quebec to interview subjects in improbable places. The adventure included an evening spent dutifully listening to tapes and preparing questions for the next day while the Brome Lake duck-pluckers, oblivious to the great Quebec Question, caroused beneath. Perhaps the duck-pluckers had it right.

Chronology

1869-70   Red River Rebellion under Louis Riel; Manitoba becomes a
           province

1885   North-West Rebellion under Louis Riel; Riel is hanged

1890-6   Manitoba Schools' question

1896-1911 Sir Wilfrid Laurier, prime minister of Canada

1914-18   First World War

1917-18   Conscription crisis

1921   Mackenzie King first becomes prime minister of Canada

1936   Maurice Duplessis first becomes premier of Quebec

1939-45   Second World War

1942   Conscription plebiscite

1944   Allied invasion of France; conscription crisis in Canada

1948-57   Louis St-Laurent, prime minister of Canada

1957-63   John Diefenbaker, prime minister of Canada

1959   Death of Duplessis

1960   Liberals under Jean Lesage elected in Quebec

1962   Lesage re-elected on hydro nationalization issue

1963-8   Lester B. Pearson, prime minister of Canada

1964   Canada Pension Plan

1965   Canada-US Autopact
           'Umbrella agreement' (accord cadre) between Canada and
           France authorizing Quebec-France agreement on culture
           Federal election in which Pierre Trudeau, Jean Marchand, and
           Gérard Pelletier are elected Liberal MPs

1966   Lesage government in Quebec is defeated by Union Nationale
           under Daniel Johnson, Sr

1967   French president Charles de Gaulle shouts 'Vive le Québec
           libre!' in Montreal and is invited to leave Canada
           René Lévesque quits Liberal Party and founds 'Mouvement
           Souveraineté-association'

1968
February Constitutional conference in Ottawa
April   Pierre Trudeau becomes Liberal leader and prime minister

June	Trudeau wins federal election with majority
September	Death of Daniel Johnson; Jean-Jacques Bertrand becomes Quebec premier
October	Foundation of the Parti Québécois (PQ)

1970
April	Robert Bourassa and the Liberals defeat Bertrand government in Quebec election
October	Kidnapping of British trade commissioner in Montreal; kidnapping and murder of Pierre Laporte; War Measures Act proclaimed

1971
June	Victoria constitutional conference

1973
February	Gendron report on language in Quebec
October	Bourassa is re-elected in Quebec; PQ becomes official opposition

1974
May	Bourassa government introduces 'Bill 22,' promoting the use of French in education and business in Quebec

1976
June	Bilingualism in the air dispute
November	René Lévesque and the PQ defeat Bourassa

1977
August	'Bill 101,' further restricting English in Quebec, is passed by the Quebec assembly

1979
May	Joe Clark and the Conservatives win the federal election and form a minority government
December	Clark defeated in parliament

1980
February	Trudeau and the Liberals win the federal election and form a majority government
May	Quebec referendum: separatism is defeated, 60 per cent to 40 per cent
September	Trudeau government proceeds unilaterally with constitutional reform

1981
November	Trudeau and nine provinces reach agreement on a constitution; Lévesque is isolated

1982
April	Trudeau's amended constitution is proclaimed

1984
June   Trudeau resigns
September Brian Mulroney and the Conservatives win the general election;
                  Mulroney becomes prime minister

1985
June   Lévesque retires
December Bourassa and the Liberals win the Quebec election

1987
April   Meech Lake preliminary agreement on the Constitution
June   Final agreement on the constitutional revision   .
October   Free Trade Agreement signed between Canada and the United
                  States
                  New government elected in New Brunswick

1988
April   New government elected in Manitoba
November Mulroney wins the federal election
December Bourassa uses the 'notwithstanding' clause to override the
                  Supreme Court decision on language

1989
April   Clyde Wells and the Liberals win Newfoundland election
September Bourassa re-elected in Quebec

1990
June   Meech Lake accord fails

1992
October   Constitutional referendum fails

1993
October   Conservatives overwhelmed in the federal election;
                  Jean Chrétien forms a Liberal government

1994
September PQ under Jacques Parizeau defeat the Liberals in the Quebec
                  election; Parizeau becomes premier

1995
October   Quebec referendum on sovereignty; the 'No' side wins narrowly;
                  Parizeau announces resignation

1996
January   Lucien Bouchard becomes premier of Quebec

1997
June   Liberals under Jean Chrétien win re-election nationally and
                  marginally improve their standing in Quebec

Canada and Quebec

Introduction

The Sense of
History

Tʜᴇ ʜɪsᴛᴏʀʏ of Canada and Quebec
is in reality many histories. It is the history of historians, the product of
learned study and reflection and, occasionally, dialogue among the professionals whose task it is to study and interpret Canada's past. It is the history
of nations – of the Aboriginal nations, who inhabited this continent before
the coming of the Europeans, of the British and the French, the Americans,
and, eventually, the Canadians, in their English- and French-speaking varieties. It is the history learned in schools, or passed down from generation
to generation. It is written history or it can be, as in this book, oral history.

This oral history of Canada and Quebec is the product of more than
one hundred interviews conducted in the autumn and winter of 1994-5. The
interviews were commissioned by radio station CJRT-Open College in
Toronto, which for many years has broadcast university-level courses to listeners and students across southern Ontario. Historians, economists, political scientists, politicians, and public servants, past and present, were asked
to reflect on what they knew and understood of the history of Canada and
Quebec. This history was broadly interpreted. It was the distant past – what
most historians understand by history; and it was the recent past – what
used to be dismissed as current events.

The two are of course related, but they are not often linked in people's minds. In the case of Canada and Quebec, however, the linkage was crucial. In Quebec in 1995 political actors are playing out a script bequeathed them by the past. At hearings across Quebec in the winter of 1995, witness after witness came forward before Quebec government commissions to bear explicit witness to one version or another of Quebec's history. It might be a history of injustice or oppression, the French done down by their immemorial enemy, the English, and surviving in the teeth of persecution. Or it might be a history of opportunity and cooperation, in which the two language groups have united so as to prosper materially and spiritually. There were those who did not appear: the First Nations of Quebec, who held to their own history and saw no necessity to expound it in a political forum sponsored by a government with a different agenda from their own. And there were those who could not appear: inhabitants of the Rest of Canada, whose fate, national and political, was nevertheless bound up with the decisions to be made in Quebec, in that province's forthcoming referendum.

The interpretation of the history of Canada and Quebec has changed considerably over the past few decades. Professional historians have for the most part concentrated on the more distant past, leaving the events of the 1960s or 1970s or 1980s to journalists, political scientists, or the participants. Pierre Trudeau, prime minister for sixteen years and leader of the struggle against separatism in the 1970s, has been memorialized, interpreted, and reinterpreted – by journalists and academics, by nationalists of the Canadian and Quebec varieties, and, of course, by himself. These interpretations are reflected in the interviews presented here.

But Trudeau and his record are not the only subject of debate. Robert Bourassa, the federalist premier of Quebec, is also a subject of controversy. Bourassa's record became a lively issue in the Quebec provincial election of September 1994, and an immense and expensive book critical of the former premier actually became a best seller in Quebec. That book, by one of premier Jacques Parizeau's current advisers, condemned Bourassa's insufficient Quebec nationalism; but other critics have damned Bourassa for his lack of commitment to Canada, and his mishandling of the Meech Lake constitutional reforms of the late 1980s.

Meech Lake itself still excites rage inside and outside Quebec. Meech meant 'we love you,' one Quebec interviewee explained; but Canada rejected the gesture. It was an act of statesmanship, some say. It marked a stage in the disintegration of Canada, according to others.

All these topics, all these views are represented here.

This oral history owes a great deal to the many people who agreed to be interviewed, sometimes at tedious length, about their knowledge and experiences. Every effort was made to include representative points of view, though, inevitably, in a country as big and diverse as Canada, there are gaps. The prime minister of Canada, two provincial premiers, the vice premier of Quebec, and a galaxy of other citizens found the time in busy schedules to say something into a microphone. Others, including the past and present premiers of Quebec, Messrs Johnson and Parizeau, and the premier of New Brunswick, did not find the time. Their absence is regretted. Negotiations to interview Lucien Bouchard were aborted by his tragic but fortunately not fatal illness in December 1994.

What emerges clearly is a divergence on the meaning of the events of the recent past. The roots of the divergence go much further back, as far as the seventeenth century. That divergence, from three centuries and more ago, is fundamental to understanding the different interpretation of Canadian history by the First Nations of Canada, as compared with the views of the majority of citizens inside and outside Quebec. That legacy is very much with us as Quebec contemplates its future.

In the present Canadian debate there is also fundamental disagreement about older events such as the settlement of the West or the fate of Louis Riel, and about recent symbols, such as the Quebec referendum of 1980, the Trudeau constitution of 1982, and the Meech Lake fiasco of 1987-90. What these events mean and have meant strikes at the heart of the relationship between English- and French-speaking Canadians. And what that relationship has been will determine, ultimately, what the connection between Quebec and Canada will be.

Chapter 1

From Conquest
to Rebellion

A<small>T THE BEGINNING</small> of the 1990s, a new bumper sticker appeared on Canadian cars. 'My Canada includes Quebec,' it read. Sometimes, in French-speaking areas, or if the car owner wanted to demonstrate extra sensitivity, it gave the French translation: 'Mon Canada comprend le Québec,' a very clever translation, which actually conveys a double meaning: Canada includes Quebec, the English version, but also Canada *understands* Quebec. Both ways, the message is comforting, reassuring. Quebec should stay in Canada because Canada not only includes, but understands, Quebec. But is it true? And if Canada includes Quebec, and Canadians understand Quebeckers, does Quebec include Canada, or do Quebeckers understand Canadians? Most important, do Canadians and Quebeckers understand themselves?

The evidence is decidedly mixed. Canadians, English-speaking and French-speaking, have certainly tried. If the tonnage of print or the cubic footage of air consumed on the subject of Quebec is any indication, Canadians and Quebeckers must understand each other. Understanding, many people assume, leads to harmony. And if these two propositions are true, then Canadians and Quebeckers have little to worry about, and very little to discuss.

At least as far as Canada is concerned, the two propositions are not true, or at least not entirely true. Canadian and Quebec history is punctuated by recurring crises, some violent but most verbal. The relations between majority English and minority French have not always been smooth, and virtually every generation has seen some kind of disputation – starting with the wars of the eighteenth century that led to the conquest of Canada by the British, and continuing through recurrent political crises in the nineteenth century and into the twentieth.

It is possible to regard Canadian history as one long confrontation, and many people, especially in Quebec, do just that. The facts are there, and the interpretation of those facts does not have to be strained very far. The relations between English and French Canadians began in violence and in war – the wars of the eighteenth century that gave Quebec to Canada and that separated Canada from the United States. Those wars and that history, some people argue, made Quebec a nation and gave it an identity – a two- or three-hundred-year-old identity.

But there are other ways of looking at relations between English- and French-speakers in Canada and their history. While it is true that there have been confrontations, disagreements, and sometimes violence, it is also true that English and French Canadians have gotten along for almost 250 years, in the same country, in the same economy, and under the same constitution. The main ethnic groups, British and French, have intermarried: to take one obvious example, Quebec has had three premiers named Johnson, all native French-speakers, and the ranks of Quebec separatists include names like Blackburn, Burns, and Johnson again, as well as Lévesque, Laurin, and Parizeau. In Canada, for more than two hundred years, business people, politicians, and tradespeople have made it their business to get along – they have had to get along, and they usually did.

In considering the history of English- and French-speakers in Canada it is essential to bear in mind that the inhabitants of Canada, now and in the past, did not speak only English or French. There are many immigrant languages, of course, but there are also the languages of Canada's Aboriginal inhabitants. And Canada's Native peoples have always been and are still a crucial component in any analysis of the relations between English and French.

So there are at least two sides, and probably more, to any examination of Canada's two main language groups, two sides to their histories, and, in some respects, two histories. History is one of the main ways in which people define their identity. By understanding where they came from, people also seek to understand where they are and where they may be going. One of French Canada's best-known historians once wrote of what he called 'notre maître, le passé' – our master, the past.

We begin, therefore, with the past, with history, with events two or three hundred years ago, that helped to shape what Canada later became. We also begin with the interpretations of those events, with what they have signified to different historians and to different generations. There are plenty of questions or problems to consider. Did French-speaking Quebeckers, the Québécois, become a distinct people, a nation, two or three hundred years ago? What kind of history do Canadians learn that makes them view their present as they do? To paraphrase the bumper sticker, how, ultimately, does Canada understand Quebec, and how does Quebec see Canada?

The bare facts, such as we know them, are that North America was first settled by peoples traversing a land bridge between Asia and Alaska roughly 20,000 years ago. Judged by this standard, European settlement, and the quarrels between European settlers on this continent, are recent indeed. But the peoples of North America, scattered, disunited, and technologically disadvantaged, were no match for the European settlers and soldiers who arrived in North America in the seventeenth century – English to the south, in what is now the United States, and French to the north, in what is now Canada.

The Europeans, having arrived, simply assumed that they, rather than the Aboriginal inhabitants who preceded them, owned the land. This is an important point: on its definition and resolution ultimately turn such questions as 'Who is sovereign in Canada?' – or, more simply, 'Who owns Canada?' Historian Jim Miller explains what European discovery and settlement implied for that question:

MILLER: The answer depends on which European state you're looking at. If you're looking at the French regime, the theoretical view was that the French owned it because the king of France was a divine-right monarch, and a Catholic monarch to boot, that is, a Christian statesman. Theoretically, then, the French owned it just by turning up and asserting crown authority. The reality under the French, however, was that they had neither the need nor the ability to impose their rule. They were there primarily to trade, not to farm, so they didn't have to displace the forest dwellers, and in fact they needed their cooperation. The French sought commercial partnerships with the Native people in the seventeenth century most notably, and they didn't desire to control them, or to usurp their use of the land. Even had they wanted to, they didn't have the means, because for many decades the French numbered only a few thousands in the northern part of North America.

With the British, however, you have a different approach to the question of ownership. The British take the view that a British monarch has the power to take control of the land. For perfectly practical reasons, from the middle of the eighteenth century onwards, the British secure access to the land through negotiation by the Crown and its agents. This doctrine is enunciated in the Royal Proclamation of 1763, and it is followed with greater or less consistency from the 1780s onwards, in central British North America, and, later, on the western plains. Although European doctrines and practice differ, they all assume they can acquire, or have already acquired, title to the Native peoples' lands.

BOTHWELL: The Royal Proclamation of 1763 was issued by the British crown after the conquest of Canada and its transfer to British rule: it attempted to regulate the relations between Aboriginals and settlers, and between English and French; and it prescribed how Aboriginal peoples and their lands were to be dealt with. The most important requirement was that any concession of Native lands to white settlement had to be done by treaty, as between the colonial governments and the Native peoples. This is an important point to which I shall return later.

It is difficult for a secular age to weigh the importance of religion in a bygone age, but to the first European settlers of North America, French or English, Christianity was at the centre of civilized existence. Indeed, Christianity defined civilization, and with it the right to sovereign authority. Nor should it be forgotten that the French and British monarchs professed different varieties of Christianity: Catholic in the case of France, Anglican Protestantism in the case of Great Britain. Both versions of Christianity differed from the pre-existing religions of North America, those of the Aboriginal peoples. Historian Olive Dickason comments on the difference between Native spirituality and that of the arriving settlers:

DICKASON: We've got two contrasts here: the first between Indian spirituality and Christianity, and the second between the French Christian ideal and the English Christian ideal. To begin with the Indian view, it was not a world of domination, but a world of equilibrium; you had many different forces in the world, and the trick was to keep them all in balance. There was no question of one force dominating the other, or one force getting control and dictating how things were to be run. Each individual made his or her own approach to alliances with the spiritual powers, and the point was to arrive at an equilibrium.

In the European approach, the Judeo-Christian tradition has a dominant, all-powerful God controlling things, and the world is created in the image of man. Man is the dominating factor, and his mission is to dominate nature, which was not at all how the Indian viewed it. The French had a centralized state and a nationalized church; the missionaries were seen as arms of the state, out to spread Christianity. The French very quickly recognized the importance of spiritual beliefs in the Indian way of life. The Indians didn't do anything without consulting with the spirits; ceremonialism pervaded the whole society, in everything they did. Because the Catholic manifestation of Christianity is strong on ceremonialism, there was much more of a blending, or rather a tolerance, between the French missionaries and the way they approached the Indians than there was between the English missionaries and the Native people.

The English missionaries were far more imbued with the idea of the Protestant ethic, the work ethic, and the idea of bringing in their way of doing things on a day-to-day basis. The English, in practical terms, were the ones who emphasized working in Indian languages. They very quickly began to ordain converts and to place them into their missionary hierarchies. The French were much slower in that regard.

BOTHWELL: Jim Miller believes that it was the French who came to terms with Native cultures much faster, and more easily, than the English. But he also sees the British differently:

MILLER: There were a few spasmodic attempts in the seventeenth-century French regime to assimilate through education and evangelization. In New France, however, every such attempt failed and the missionaries quickly came to recognize that assimilation didn't work, and, indeed, that there was no point in trying; instead, they should concentrate on trying to Christianize, without assimilating.

BOTHWELL: The French and the English, traditional enemies in the Old World, soon came to blows in the New. The seventeenth and eighteenth centuries were a period of religious and also national wars, in which France and England – Great Britain after 1707 – usually ended up on opposite sides. The wars spread to their colonies, and involved not only the Europeans but Aboriginal allies as well. Olive Dickason describes what happened:

DICKASON: As long as the English and the French were at odds with each other, this put the Indians in a strong position, because they were a third power, as it were, and their alliances were sought and were extremely important in the conflicts that erupted. As long as you had that colonial rivalry, in whatever form, the Indians were indispensable to whoever could get them as allies. They were the forest fighters, the best available. When someone observed that the French should recruit the Indians and put them in the army on a regular basis, the French general turned thumbs down on that idea instantly and said it would simply minimize what was already a very powerful force: he said that no military discipline would make these Indians better warriors and better allies than they already were.

BOTHWELL: It is important to note that the Aboriginal peoples of North America were playing a semi-independent role in the wars of the eighteenth century, balancing the British and the French in the interest of preserving their own autonomy, their own independence. Jim Miller sums up the situation:

MILLER: It is fair to say that the Indians did try to pick the side which was less threatening to them, and they usually picked the more commercial European or colonial state over the agricultural state. They sided with the French against the British early on, for the most part, and later they sided with the British north of the St Lawrence against the American rebels or the American states south of the lakes; until the nineteenth century, the more northerly community tended to be the more commercially oriented. The Native people played one side off against the other.

BOTHWELL: The centre of French settlement was the valley of the St Lawrence River, the colony of New France, with its capital at Quebec. While a trickle of immigrants flowed to New France, immigrants came by the boatload to the English colonies to the south. Historian W.J. Eccles, an expert on the French colonies, says that the reason immigration lagged in New France can be found not in the New World, but in the Old:

ECCLES: It's the land tenure system in both England and France. In France, the peasants held tight onto title to their land and the great landowners couldn't take the land away from them. But in England the peasants were turfed off the land during the enclosure movement. The capitalist agricultural system that developed was much more efficient, much more productive, and used far less labour, so it resulted in a lot of surplus labour. In addition, in England you didn't have a large standing army, whereas in France there was a standing army of 250,000.

So in England, where were the displaced going to go? Would they go for a soldier, become a vagabond or a thief and get hanged, or would they go to the colonies, where there was a great need for labour? That's why they flooded from the British Isles, over to the Thirteen Colonies. Another 55,000 convicts, a sizeable number, were shipped to the American colonies. Canada was not used as a dumping ground in that way, although a few convicts were sent out in the eighteenth century, salt smugglers. In general, then, nothing was really pushing the French out of France.

Tales of life in Canada that went back to France in the seventeenth century didn't make it appear an attractive place, the returning sailors talking about swarms of mosquitoes and black flies that made life hell, about the terrible winters, about the Iroquois and the way they treated anybody they caught – the torture ceremony, and so on. Those stories didn't lose anything in the telling in the taverns and the seaports.

BOTHWELL: Anglo-French wars punctuated the eighteenth century until 1756, when the Seven Years' War broke out. In 1763 the war concluded with a French defeat and the concession of New France to the British. It was aptly called the French and Indian War in North America. As the name suggests, it was fought between British and French troops, and their respective Indian allies: Both Great Britain and France sent large armies to North America, and for a number of years the outcome was in doubt. In the British colonies and the French, the inhabitants looked askance at their military protectors. Some historians are inclined to see the beginning of national feeling in these years – the beginning, in fact, of a French-Canadian nation. In New France especially there was considerable resentment between the colonists, who called themselves *Canadiens* by this point, and the French from France.

ECCLES: There was certainly resentment towards the end of the regime – resentment on the part of the Canadiens towards the French soldiers. What

I see there is the beginning of Canadien nationalism, resentment of the way the French soldiers were treating them. You see, France had always fought its wars on enemy soil. The French did not fight on their own soil until Napoleonic times, and so soldiers in the French army, these *troupes de la terre*, as distinct from the colonial marines in Canada, behaved the way they behaved in Flanders or in Germany, treating the Canadiens as though they were the enemy. They lived off the land, and if they wanted provisions they took them at the point of a bayonet. The Canadiens, who had a record of military victory in all their wars and who were excellent soldiers in the type of fighting that had to be done, regarded these French soldiers and officers as incompetent, and to a large degree they were.

BOTHWELL: Some historians remain cautious about seeing the origins of a French-speaking North American nation in these colonists of the mid-eighteenth century. Historian Dale Miquelon argues that applying the term 'nation' to the eighteenth century is anachronistic:

MIQUELON: We shouldn't take this idea of nation very seriously, because it is retroactive. It's an application of a nineteenth-century concept to an earlier period to gratify the sensibilities of nineteenth- and twentieth-century people.

You have a society in Canada, in French Canada, in the eighteenth century which is in many ways a distinct society, but the most fruitful way to look at it is to say that a country like France was filled with distinct societies: Normandy, Brittany, Provence, Languedoc, l'Isle de France, these are all societies quite distinct from each other, in some cases not speaking the same language, in the case of Brittany not speaking it well into the nineteenth century. So 'distinct society' can as easily have the connotation 'provincial' as 'national.'

BOTHWELL: In September 1759 the British general James Wolfe succeeded in landing an army behind Quebec City, forcing its French defenders under their commander, the Marquis de Montcalm, to come out and fight. In a battle on the Plains of Abraham the French were defeated, and Wolfe and Montcalm were killed. Quebec surrendered. After a year's further fighting, Montreal surrendered as well, and French rule was extinguished in the valley of the St Lawrence.

The verdict of war was ratified by the conclusion of peace, at Paris in 1763. The French king, Louis XV, ceded Canada to the British king, George III. The inhabitants of Canada, all 70,000 or so of them, were free to return to

France if they chose; or they could stay. Some left, but not many; most stayed and became subjects, Catholic and French-speaking, of a Protestant and English-speaking monarch. New France was finished; the valley of the St Lawrence was now called the province of Quebec, a province of Great Britain.

That was not the end of the North American wars. A few years later, in 1775, the British colonies to the south rebelled against the British government in London. This began the war of the American Revolution, and when it was over, in 1783, all but two of Great Britain's colonies in North America had become independent and formed the United States of America. The two remaining colonies were Quebec and Nova Scotia, too distant from the other colonies, and too difficult to reach by land, for American armies to conquer. To Nova Scotia and Quebec came tens of thousands of refugees from the other colonies – Loyalists – people loyal to the crown. They brought with them their allegiance to George III, but also their English language and, generally speaking, their Protestant faith. The French-speaking colonists already in Quebec had to adjust again to radically altered circumstances; but before I deal with them, I would like to mention another group, the real losers of the eighteenth-century wars.

The American Revolution resembled the other eighteenth-century wars in that it was a war between the American colonists and their Aboriginal allies on one side, and the British and their Native allies on the other. Olive Dickason comments on the turn of events:

DICKASON: By 1763, as the eastern parts, the Atlantic regions, were already being over-hunted and over-exploited, the traditional subsistence base was becoming, not impossible, but more and more difficult and more uncertain. The peace of 1783 between the Americans and the British was the coup de grâce, the peace that finally ended the colonial wars. After that the Indians really became superfluous; they no longer had a military usefulness, and the fur trade was already beginning to decline. Economically their importance was diminishing, and militarily their importance vanished after the 1783 peace agreement.

What was the alternative? As the authorities saw it, they had to go on a major program of transforming the Indians into Europeans, into European farmers. Agriculture was seen as the base on which they could build their new way of life, as the way of the future. The nineteenth century was also a period of severe diminishment in the Indian populations, of a severe decline in their numbers. The general belief was that in fifty years they would be gone.

BOTHWELL: One of the most tragic situations occurred in the Confederacy of the Six Nations, among the Iroquois, who lived in what is now northern New York state. Many Iroquois supported the British, while others sustained the Americans. Jim Miller describes what happened:

MILLER: In the case of the Six Nations, the American War of Independence did disrupt the Confederacy very seriously and for a long time. There were some like the Mohawk of the Six Nations, who were very much inclined to support the British. There were others who had been influenced by New England missionaries, who were tilted somewhat towards the Continental Congress, the American rebels. Still others simply resisted taking a part, because they didn't want to be destroyed. It really didn't matter, tragically, which side, which choice you made during the American Revolution. If you chose the British, as the Mohawk did, you ended up defeated and having to go north for refuge, into British North America. Even those who supported or were neutral towards the American rebels ultimately fared no better, because in spite of promises made to them by the rebels, American agricultural settlers flooded into their regions after the war. The promises given to them were betrayed, and they were dispossessed too.

BOTHWELL: Some of the Iroquois, defeated allies of the British, ended up as refugees near the British garrison of Montreal, where, ironically, an earlier Iroquois immigration, allies of the defeated French, already lived. They are still there, settled on three reserves clustered around the modern city of Montreal.

MILLER: The three Mohawk reserves, Akwesasne, Kahnawake, and Kanesatake, emerged mainly as refuges for defeated or converted Native groups. Most of them were developed under the leadership of missionary groups: Kanesatake near Oka, Quebec, under the Sulpicians; Kahnawake, on the south shore opposite Montreal, under the Jesuits. Kanesatake was even more complicated than the other two in that it didn't start off as a Mohawk settlement but as a mixed settlement – in the second decade of the eighteenth century it was a combined Algonquin-Nipissing and Mohawk refugee settlement under the tutelage of the Sulpicians. Moreover, the settlers at Kanesatake were never able to make their claim to the land as effectively as the Mohawk at Kahnawake to the south were able to do. What unites all three of those reserves, however, is the fact that they began as refugee settlements.

BOTHWELL: The Sulpicians and the Jesuits are French missionary orders that persisted after the British conquest of 1760. There are many more Aboriginal inhabitants of Quebec than those immediately around Montreal, but because of their location the three Mohawk reserves have been the most prominent.

I shall return to Canada's Native inhabitants a little later. For the moment, I would like to underline two points. First, that the Native inhabitants of Quebec were not a conquered people, and thus cannot be said to have become British or French subjects by force of arms. Second, that lands belonging to the Aboriginal people were acquired for white settlement through treaty or agreement, which was the method laid down by the Royal Proclamation of 1763.

I asked Jim Miller to spell out the consequences of treaty-making. Does a treaty confer some kind of land ownership or does it simply take land away?

MILLER: There are a number of ways in which the western treaties in particular, that is the treaties of the 1870s in the Prairie region, read as though the assumption is that Native groups retain full control of what we would call reserves. For example, in Canadian legislation, in order to acquire reserve lands, you have to go through a process which is exactly like the one the Royal Proclamation calls for. To acquire Aboriginal lands, you have to have a public meeting and get the consent of the community to surrender the land. That would seem to suggest that they retain title – ownership perhaps, sovereignty perhaps not – over those lands they do not surrender, that is, the reserve lands. But these are questions which are never addressed and thrashed out, and that haven't been dealt with until fairly recently.

BOTHWELL: The issue of Native land claims, and the even more touchy questions of Native self-government or Native sovereignty, cannot be divorced from the history of French-English relations in Canada. What is clear is that Canada's Aboriginal inhabitants, and especially those in eastern Canada caught up in the English-French wars, also formed a distinct society. True, as Olive Dickason has noted, there were many in the nineteenth century who believed that the Native problem would simply disappear, through assimilation or through a population dwindling from disease. The

Native people were marginalized, placed outside the mainstream, and set aside from society on reserves. But they did not disappear, and I shall return to the subject later.

So much of today's Canadian reality is founded on events that occurred long before there was a Canada, before the idea of a Canadian nation was even dreamed of. But what about the French inhabitants of Quebec? Would they too be marginalized, or assimilated, or fated to disappear? What was the fate of a conquered people in the eighteenth century?

There was, to begin with, the experience of the Conquest. That was not gentle or mild, although by twentieth-century standards not many people were killed, and not many atrocities were committed. But Quebec society had suffered severely during the war, and the colonists had been virtually bankrupted by the fact that they held large stocks of paper money that the French freely issued during the last stages of the war. William Eccles describes Quebec after the Conquest, and in passing he refers to the work of the historian Marcel Trudel on the town of Trois-Rivières under the British military governor, General James Murray:

ECCLES: Trudel wrote a book on the military regime at Trois-Rivières, and showed that the British military governors were concerned about this paper money, who had it, and how much, and so everybody had to go and register it. It's incredible the amount of paper money that people had, even humble people, peasants, habitants, and widows, registering in the tens of thousands. All that money went down the drain. The Ursulines, for example, lost all their funds; from this point on they were completely dependent on charity. In addition, tremendous devastation was done: about a quarter of the houses in New France were destroyed by the British army during the course of the war, every farm from Quebec down to the Gaspé was razed, burned. And 80 per cent of Quebec City was destroyed. On the way up to Montreal, in the last campaign, a large number of houses were destroyed by Murray's army; he had a proclamation printed stating that any farmhouse found unoccupied would be destroyed, for he would assume that the men had joined the French forces. It took a long time, two or three generations, before those scars, psychological scars, healed over.

BOTHWELL: Despite the violence of the Conquest, in some respects the Canadiens were fortunate in their timing. The eighteenth century liked to think of itself as an Age of Enlightenment, of civilization. As Dale Miquelon observes, the eighteenth century dealt relatively mildly with conquered peoples – after they had been conquered. Was it at all odd that the British allowed the new French subjects to keep their language and their religion?

MIQUELON: It certainly would have been odd earlier. In some ways it is a reflection of the true civilization that countries like France and England had achieved by the eighteenth century. They were horrified by the wars of religion, and they seem to have put on the brakes after that. They felt that they were all civilized people, that they had rights, that they should behave towards one another in a certain way. One of the great questions which arises after the Conquest is the question of property. Do people continue to have their property, or are they despoiled of it? The eighteenth-century British governing class worshipped property. They would no more have taken people's property away than they would have done many other things that we consider much more heinous. Then comes the next question, that property inheres in the system of law. If you grant people the right to their property, doesn't that mean you grant them the right to the entire system of law in which their property is embedded? And so the tradition, or the earlier laws of Canada, slid through on that particular sled.

Religion? By the eighteenth century, as opposed to the seventeenth century, and the nineteenth century that followed, members of the English governing class often had a very advanced idea of religion, others were quite simply deists, and many of them didn't take religion seriously at all. In any case, they didn't think they should force conversions. The idea of forced conversion was something from another period, especially when they were outside England, where they were not bound by some traditional situations such as the denial of civil rights to Catholics. They were reluctant to impose what they would think of as tyrannical measures.

BOTHWELL: The Canadiens survived the Conquest. But how well did they survive? Did the English, the British, allow them to keep their language only to relegate them, like the Indians, to the margins of society or the economy? Was it fair to describe Canada as a society where only the peasants stayed, and the merchants, the natural leaders of society, packed up and left? This line of reasoning is called the decapitation theory, that Quebec was a society that lost its head after 1760. But as Dale Miquelon suggests, the question is more complicated, and the assumptions in such a question are not what they seem at first to be:

MIQUELON: When we talk about the Conquest, we generally do so in a long-term kind of way: the social and economic effects of the Conquest are obviously long term, covering a generation or two. The morning after the Conquest is a different matter: buildings are destroyed, people are unemployed, harvests are uncollected. In the long term, the question is asked whether the imposition of a British government on top of the Canadien colony had any implications. One theory is that a whole social structure, or many aspects of the social structure, was destroyed. The role that the Canadiens played in their economy and their society changed, and became a subordinate role. Other people have looked at the implications from many different angles.

For many years, since the 1950s and the 1960s, historians have put a strong focus on the commercial classes of New France after the Conquest: What happened to them? People adopted a liberal or a Marxist view, that there was a social evolution going on, that the merchant class, the bourgeoisie, were the bearers of all good things. They brought social transformation, they brought light out of darkness, they brought modernity out of the Ancien Régime. If that was the case, then the fate of the bourgeoisie after the Conquest became very important. If the bourgeoisie failed to maintain their position, then they could not fulfil their function of bringing the society into a state of modernity.

BOTHWELL: But does society proceed from feudal to monarchical to bourgeois, modernizing as it goes? Miquelon continues:

MIQUELON: You could answer the question first by asking whether the model is true. More and more people have doubts whether the evolution of the modern world is really the story of the triumph of the bourgeoisie. As long ago as 1948 the American historian J.H. Hexter said that the concept that from a distance looked like solid gold was nothing but melted butter on closer inspection.

After the Conquest, you had a bi-ethnic society, and as the years went by you had all kinds of barriers built into that society, but it never became completely compartmentalized. You had a degree of compartmentalization, however, which eventually led to the replacing of a Canadien bourgeoisie by an Anglo bourgeoisie. It began with Englishmen, Americans, Scotsmen, and so forth marrying French-Canadian bourgeois and aristocratic women, so that biologically they were a mix, but culturally they were really an Anglo-

American-Scottish group who came to dominate Quebec society. At the same time, you had a French bourgeoisie that was ethnically and culturally French as well. It never disappeared, it was always there, but it was simply pushed off the top of the pyramid by this other group. You didn't have a social pyramid which was English at the top and French at the middle and bottom; rather, you had a pyramid that was divided vertically.

At the top of the heap you had more English people than you would expect proportionately, and, as you went down towards the bottom of the social pyramid, fewer than you would expect. For the French the situation was reversed.

BOTHWELL: Fernand Ouellet has spent most of his career studying what happened, economically and socially, to French Canada following the Conquest. To Ouellet, and to most historians studying Canada in the late eighteenth century, there was really no great change in the structure of the economy before or after the French regime. One indication, mentioned by Dale Miquelon, was the propensity of English-speaking fur traders, merchants on a large scale and rich men by the end of the eighteenth century, people like Simon McTavish of the fur-trading North-West Company, to marry the daughters of Quebec's minor nobility and to settle on their estates, called seigneuries, in the countryside. Fernand Ouellet takes up this point:

OUELLET: If you look at the French regime, the economy fundamentally was based on agriculture on one side and the fur trade on the other. There was no contradiction between the fur trade and agriculture, both were in one sense complementary. This economy continued to grow after 1760 as before, but the agricultural sector around wheat became increasingly commercialized. Links also developed between the agricultural sector and the fur trade. This was why fur traders were buying seigneuries: fur traders were investing in the land. Simon McTavish, for example, a director of the North-West Company, bought the seigneury of Terrebonne, and built big bakeries in order to supply the labour force of the North-West Company going west, and so on. Progressively links were built that were more complex than simply between the labour force and the fur trade. It was an expanding economy. There were fluctuations, influenced by the effects of war, both the American and the British, but there was no change, no structural change in the economy, from the seventeenth century to the eighteenth century. This is why the Canadiens, people who were born in the country of all occupations, were able to feel a connection with the territory beyond the lowlands of the centre. It was a vision of space, going towards the West.

BOTHWELL: As the eighteenth century turned into the nineteenth, it is not as easy to divide Quebec society into English and French compartments, with the English on top. The English, Scottish, or American settlers and their French-speaking counterparts often had a great deal in common. Dale Miquelon comments:

MIQUELON: In the eighteenth century in particular, although people suddenly became aware of the ethnic divide, the dominant issue was the social division of classes, or of orders – that is, whether the French or the English at the top of the social pyramid tended to have a similar view of people further down that social pyramid. In the nineteenth century the ethnic division became stronger. It's there in the eighteenth century, but it's not as strong.

BOTHWELL: Other historians agree. Historian Allan Greer goes further. He feels that the English newcomers had little impact on the French inhabitants of Quebec.

GREER: The sort of topics and themes that I researched, the aspects of rural society, didn't change drastically. I think there probably would have been much more apparent change in the cities than in the rural districts.

BOTHWELL: There can be little doubt that the French inhabitants of Quebec saw themselves as different from the English – as distinct. But they also considered themselves distinct from the local French-speaking elite, and as distinct from those who lived in the towns and cities. It is also clear that relations between the groups did not run entirely on linguistic lines, and that the French and the English did not live in entirely separate economic dimensions.

Some historians have been tempted to read this distinctiveness as meaning that the Canadiens were already more than distinct – that they were in effect already a nation. Others, especially Dale Miquelon, see the application of the term 'nation' as an anachronism. This is more than a simple historical debate. If the Canadiens were a nation then, they are a nation now, with certain inherent natural – and national – rights. As Miquelon explains:

MIQUELON: The central thread that runs through *nationaliste* historiography is a beguiling one, but one that doesn't hold much conviction for me: the idea that people develop into nations, in what is called a 'normal' fashion. It's a teleological sort of notion: you put these people in the colony, you plant them there, they begin to grow, and it's predetermined that they'll develop into a nation. Among nationalist historians of the 1950s, 1960s, and 1970s, 'normal' was a catch-word, repeated over and over again. The second part of this nationaliste historiography is pure nineteenth-century romantic nationalism: if you have a group of people who constitute a cluster of characteristics, which makes them a nation, this means they have certain God-given rights. A connection is made between being a nation, whatever that may mean, and having a right to self-government. What it boils down to is that any group which feels itself to have this cohesion also has a right to self-determination. If you really take this to its logical extreme, there are a lot of people out there who are waiting to be liberated and to achieve self-determination. It therefore becomes very impractical to link up these ideas of ethnicity, history, nationality, and the state, as has been done.

BOTHWELL: Quite often in history, as in other forms of intellectual analysis, what seems to be a series of solid, demonstrable propositions, depending on obvious – we might call them 'normal' – definitions, turns out on closer inspection to be a mirage. Obvious definitions – *nation* is a good example – are not obvious at all. And fitting the past into a twentieth-century straitjacket, jamming the peasants and merchants of the St Lawrence Valley in 1760 or 1790 into the framework of a twentieth-century society, can be very misleading.

That said, it is also clear that the origins of Quebec's place in Canada do lie in the eighteenth century. The origins lie in the wars of that century, but also in the settlements that ended the wars – the departure of Quebec from the French empire into the British, and the arrival of English-speaking settlers in the valley of the St Lawrence. That changed a lot, but it didn't change everything; and, in fact, much of French-speaking society was left intact – including the use of the French language. Starting in 1760, French entered into a kind of coexistence with English, in language, in society, and in the economy.

If what has endured for more than two hundred years can be called 'normal,' then that coexistence, English-French, is really the norm for what Canada and Quebec were to become.

Chapter 2

Two Nations Warring?
1791-1867

THE HISTORY OF CANADA is to a large degree the history of its population. A vast, empty land: this is how explorers imagined they found the country – empty of people, except for the Aboriginals. When New France fell to the British in 1760, it was partly because there were so few New French – between 60,000 and 80,000 inhabitants.

But the balance between French and English, between the *Canadiens* and the *Anglais*, took on a new dimension at the end of the American Revolution. The British colonies in North America were reduced to Quebec and Nova Scotia, and in Quebec the number of French-speakers outnumbered the English-speakers 200,000 to 25,000 around 1800. The numbers of English-speakers were substantial, so that by 1800, out of 340,000 inhabitants in British North America, about 60 per cent spoke French. The main English influx came from shiploads of refugees, called Loyalists, from the American Revolution.

The arrival of these new people led to a new political situation and a new style of politics. Population was wealth, immigration was wealth; immigration meant both the bringing of wealth and skills, and their organization into new patterns for the creation of more wealth. The early immigration was fed by the abundance of Canadian land, mostly fertile land, with the first harvest already provided in the form of vast forests. And politics centred on the organization of land and wealth, and the establishment of laws to govern the process.

It is here, at the intersection of land and agriculture, and wealth and government, that the different cultures of English and French met and sometimes clashed. Language and culture were heavily symbolic, and so were laws and property. The laws of the province of Quebec were French laws. Property, and therefore settlement, in Quebec were governed by existing practice – a practice unfamiliar in the British Empire. And society was organized differently: in an age when religion had great importance for the vast majority of the people, the Canadiens were Catholic and the British immigrants were Protestant. The British even had an official church: the Church of England, or the Anglican Church, if you were English, and the Presbyterian Church if you were Scottish. Language, law, religion: with the mixing of populations there was plenty of opportunity for contact. And contact would bring both understanding and misunderstanding.

Many of the new British – or British-American – arrivals settled in Nova Scotia, which was eventually subdivided into three provinces: Nova Scotia itself, New Brunswick, and Prince Edward Island. Newfoundland, although it had permanent settlers, was not really organized into a government. These three Maritime provinces had their own French-speaking population, the Acadians, whose settlement dated from the seventeenth century. These settlements had been disrupted by the wars of the eighteenth century, and large numbers of Acadians had been deported to the colonies to the south. Public life in the Maritime provinces was conducted in the language of the majority, and the majority was English-speaking.

Many settlers also came to the province of Quebec, which in the 1780s stretched from the Gulf of St Lawrence up the St Lawrence River valley to Detroit. The Loyalist refugees, people loyal to King George, did not for the most part settle among the Canadiens. They moved up river to the fertile land around the Great Lakes. Having come to settle in a British land, they began to complain that its institutions were not in fact British. They lacked British laws, but in particular they lacked any kind of representative government of the kind they had been used to in the colonies to the south. That meant an elected assembly, which Nova Scotia already had, and which New Brunswick swiftly acquired.

The British government faced a dilemma, which it resolved in 1791 by a reorganization of the government of Quebec. Quebec was renamed and divided in two: Lower Canada, the territory along the St Lawrence from Valleyfield to the Gaspé, and Upper Canada, roughly from Cornwall to Detroit. Lower Canada was mostly French and Catholic: it had approximately 200,000 people and was primarily rural. Upper Canada was mostly English and Protestant: it had about 25,000 people. But there were also minorities in each of the new provinces: a few French around Detroit, and rather more Anglais in Lower Canada – in Quebec City (45 per cent English in 1831) and Montreal (53 per cent English in 1831) for the most part.

The number of Canadiens may seem surprising. In the 1750s there had been just over 60,000 by official count. How could they have tripled by 1791? The answer is twofold. Birthrates in the eighteenth century were very high compared with those of the twentieth century, and they were higher in North America than in Europe. But the birthrate in Quebec was one of the highest anywhere on Earth. There were more Canadien births recorded in the single decade of the 1780s than there were inhabitants in 1760. The population of Lower Canada soon passed 200,000, and by the 1820s passed 480,000. Most of these people were French-speaking and Catholic. They outnumbered the English-speakers in Lower Canada, of course, but they also continued to outnumber the English-speakers of Upper Canada and would continue to do so down to the 1840s.

Demography, together with politics, established a political unit on the banks of the St Lawrence that was mostly French, but was also endowed with British colonial institutions. These included an elected assembly with the power to levy taxes, combined with a British colonial governor general, whose job it was to govern the colony with the consent but, if possible, not the advice of the inhabitants. The Canadiens could not be governed without the consent of the British, but the British could not govern without the consent of the Canadiens. This illogical situation lasted forty years, until political tensions grew so great in the 1830s that the constitutional lid blew off. The result, in both Upper and Lower Canada, was armed rebellion, a royal commission under Lord Durham, a famous report signed by Durham, followed by a new constitution, new politics, and, in 1867, a new country – a country in which Lower Canada was abolished and Quebec was recreated.

The new country, Canada, was founded on two old societies and on an even older politics, one based on demography: the size of the population and the number of French-speakers in it. One basic political fact was the admission that the French language was permanently implanted in Lower Canada. With French-speakers numbering in the hundreds of thousands by the 1820s, and with a much smaller English population, that recognition was not surprising.

But there were other facts. The two societies shared geographical space and some political institutions, but to a large extent they had different institutions. One in particular, the Catholic Church, has already been mentioned. Jacques Monet, a noted historian of Quebec, explains how and why the church maintained itself after the 1760s in Lower Canada or Quebec:

MONET: At first there wasn't any bishop, and then one was consecrated by going to France at the end of the war. But the main reason is that the British authorities wanted to reconcile French Canadians to British rule. Historians who have studied the period closely, Fernand Ouellet and others, have used expressions like 'the aristocratic pact.' By the end of the eighteenth century British military officials saw that they could get along well with the leaders in French Canada, the seigneurial class and the clerical class, with ecclesiastical officials such as the bishop and the canons of the cathedral of Quebec. And there followed a period of relative tolerance in the British Empire.

In that sense, the story that happened here, the accommodation of a French and Catholic colony within a British and Protestant empire, was something that was unique, that took a lot of compromises on both sides. For the British, it meant that they had to tolerate a situation where the established church (the Anglican or the Presbyterian) was not going to enjoy the kind of privileges that it had in the rest of the empire. But for the French Canadians, for the Catholic Church generally, it also meant that Catholic people had to recognize the legitimacy of a non-Catholic king, a situation that was also unique in Western Europe at the time. So, a lot of toleration was needed on both sides, but it was worked through in Quebec.

BOTHWELL: The British accepted Catholicism, and adapted, more or less, to a situation they did not have the power to alter. The French Canadians adapted, with rather more enthusiasm, to the political institutions the British imposed through the Constitutional Act of 1791 – the elected assembly. Because the right to vote was based on property, and most French Canadians, including the peasants or habitants, were landholders, the franchise, Monet explains, was widely distributed:

MONET: Historians of that period will point to places where it took some years to adapt to the electoral process, to having elections and political meetings and so on. There are plenty of anecdotes to tell how violent the elections were and how turbulent political meetings were. This was something quite new in the political history of French Canada, so it took some time to adapt. But the Canadiens could see many advantages – because of the freehold franchise, where proprietors had the right to vote, and because of the seigneurial system. The habitants were co-owners of the seigneuries with the seigneurs, and had the right to vote, so the suffrage in Quebec (or Lower Canada after 1791) was wider than in any other part of the British Empire. It was much more democratic, in the sense of a wider suffrage, than it was even in England. In addition, women had the right to vote and the right to be candidates. In fact, there were women candidates in some of the first elections of the 1790s; they didn't get elected, but they were candidates. It was not until later, in the nineteenth century, that the vote was withdrawn from women.

Essentially, as the years went on, French Canadians participated actively in politics. French-Canadian society changed, too: there were a lot more professionals and lawyers and doctors. Lawyers, in particular, increasingly got involved in politics, and the Assembly of Lower Canada became one of the main vehicles of French-Canadian nationalism. The nineteenth century saw the beginning of the age of nationalism, of looking to political institutions to preserve nationality. The first debate on the first day of the legislature of Lower Canada in 1792 was on the preservation of the French language. So that theme of the importance of the French language to French Canadians goes right back to that period.

BOTHWELL: The early nineteenth century was a time of cultural and political romanticism. Intellectuals dredged the past looking for notions of 'the sublime,' the 'original,' or 'the authentic.' Originality and authenticity, purity of sentiment, contended with an older corruption, or with the banality of compromise, while politically new ideas and new movements sought self-expression, with freedom of speech, freedom of thought, and freedom of political institutions. In the 1820s 'liberalism' was a revolutionary word, frightening to governors and bishops alike. And with liberalism there was nationalism, which in Lower Canada meant the *nation canadienne* – the French-Canadian nation. It is important to remember that nationalism appeals to a sense of tradition, a tradition that is being threatened by something not authentic, not traditional, or not legitimate. In a nationalistic sense, liberalism is to allow the traditional or the authentic to speak, to have force, and even to gain power. And liberalism, like nationalism, draws on a sense of difference.

One way of conferring authenticity was to trace it to a distant and presumably happy past. In Lower Canada it was now suggested that there was, and had been for some considerable time, a French-Canadian nation. Historian Ramsay Cook describes what French-Canadian nationalism was:

COOK: Nationalism in Quebec, as elsewhere, is a way whereby a people defines itself against something else. They didn't define themselves particularly against other Frenchmen, but they did gradually define themselves against the English, and they saw quite clearly that they were different. The constitutional regime that was set up in 1791, which allowed for elections and for a legislature, provided the machinery into which that sense of difference developed into a kind of political competition, and out of that political competition came, at least among the elites, a growing sense of them and us. That's a simple way of saying what nationalism is.

BOTHWELL: Nationalism was firmly embedded in Lower Canadian politics by the 1820s. There was a nationalist party, perhaps inevitably called the *patriotes* or patriots, and there was a nationalist leader, the Speaker of the Lower Canadian Assembly, Louis-Joseph Papineau. But while politics took on a nationalist cast, the substance of politics was never entirely nationalist, and historians disagree among themselves as to what nationalism in politics really meant.

Historian Daniel Salée believes the nationalists (or patriotes or reformers) of the 1820s and 1830s were not exclusively French in their approach to politics or in their objectives:

SALÉE: There was a conception of Canada, of the nation, or of the state, that was not as ethnicized as it is today. Even in the French press there was a conception of the nation canadienne that included everyone who was reformist, everyone who wanted to implement the notions of democracy, of liberty, of freedom, of parliamentary responsibility and accountability.

I do not want to dismiss ethnic conflicts entirely, because to a certain extent they were real. There was some kind of chauvinism on either side.

BOTHWELL: But not enough, in Salée's view, to make the politics of the 1820s predominantly nationalist in a linguistic or ethnic sense. Ramsay Cook differs somewhat in his view:

COOK: Papineau defined it as essentially a Canadien nationalism, a nationalism of those people whose origins were in the old regime, who spoke French, and who belonged to that culture. Somewhere in the late 1820s he says that it was unnatural for one ethnic group to rule over another, by which he meant the British over the French. His nationalism was focused upon what he saw as the grievances of his people, and his goal was to emancipate his people – those who spoke French – to emancipate them from this English Protestant rule. So, from its beginnings, nationalism in Quebec, like nationalism most places, is ethnic in its origin.

BOTHWELL: Papineau and his party emerged at a time of profound social and economic change. In Lower Canada the inhabitants had seen their two principal cities, Quebec and Montreal, become more and more English-speaking. Immigrants were arriving by the thousands, and none, or almost none, were French-speaking. Many passed on to Upper Canada or to the United States, but some stayed, establishing themselves in new farming areas south of Montreal and especially in what came to be called the Eastern Townships – English-language counties clustered along the American border, centring on the new English-speaking town of Sherbrooke. And this was occurring just as the French-speaking population was exploding.

Historian Fernand Ouellet sees the early nineteenth century as a time of demographic, and more generally economic, crisis in Lower Canada:

OUELLET: After the Conquest, the conflicts were not between francophones or anglophones, but between classes. English merchants and French merchants were ranged against the nobility, against even the aristocrats, the English aristocrats in the St Lawrence Valley. All this changed at the end of the eighteenth century and the beginning of the nineteenth century. This change was connected not only to agricultural and economic problems, but to other sets of circumstances. The first was a structural change in the economy – the beginning of the decline of wheat – which had an impact on farmers' incomes and resulted in a different distribution of income throughout the population; the second, the decline of the fur trade, the growth of the timber trade, and demographic pressure, also had an impact.

While farmers identified themselves as francophones and French Canadians, they also became sensitive to nationalism, partly to help offset the economic and demographic problems.

In the 1830s a shortage of land combined with a surplus of population to create grave problems in the countryside: young people could not find land, they could not go to the United States, and they could not go to the cities. They could not compete with immigrants in the cities, and tension quickly developed between Irish anglophones, and even Irish Catholics, and the francophones over available jobs. In the countryside, anglophone immigrants were seen as a threat to the traditional family way of life by francophone farmers and their sons.

All these factors were important in the growth of nationalism. At the same time, the political elite like Papineau, the middle class, and small French-Canadian merchants in the countryside fostered this nationalism for good and for bad reasons: they were interested in power or in their own advancement, and they thought that nationalism might help to solve the problems faced by francophones. So nationalism is not only negative, it's both positive *and* negative.

Nationalism developed as a reaction not only against the anglophones, inside Lower Canada, but against the Americans, who were considered very dangerous. In the 1830s, with the radicalization of the Patriote party, their nationalism focused on the idea of independence. In 1835 Papineau demanded as a minimum compromise that the government accept independence.

BOTHWELL: The government was not, of course, about to accept independence. Papineau did not stop with the government. He had ideas about the church, too, which he was careful to situate well in the future. After independence, he told his followers, it would finally be possible to separate church and state, to end the compromise between the Catholic Church and the British governors that dominated French-Canadian society.

OUELLET: In this nationalism of the 1830s, even the most radical considered that the Catholic Church and religion were a national institution. This kind of nationalism was certainly leading to independence, and Papineau favoured the separation of church and state. But he said that this separation would come only when Lower Canada was independent.

BOTHWELL: Ouellet's interpretation of a demographic crisis leading to an economic crisis leading to a political crisis has come to influence most interpretations of Lower Canadian politics in the 1830s. But there still are differences. I asked Allan Greer, a historian of French Canada and the author of a recent study of the 1837 rebellions, for his impressions of Ouellet's argument:

GREER: I'm convinced by a lot of things he says about important economic changes appearing in the early nineteenth century. He has also noticed a kind of souring of relations between a portion of the English-speaking population of Lower Canada and the French-speaking majority. I'm not so convinced that the political and cultural conflicts stem directly and mechanically from the economic difficulties. There are economic changes, certainly, and in indirect ways they impinge on relations between English and French and politics generally, but I think there are a lot of other factors at work that are at least as important.

BOTHWELL: Greer brings us back to the general culture of the age, the romanticism, liberalism, and nationalism of the early nineteenth century, in which nationalists of one persuasion took an interest in the activities and successes of nationalists elsewhere. In the 1820s, for example, nationalists and liberals everywhere took a strong interest in the liberation of the Spanish and Portuguese colonies of Latin America from European control, or revolutionary struggles in Poland, or a civil war between liberals and traditionalists in Spain, or the reform of the British constitution in the 1830s through the extension of the franchise – the Great Reform Act of 1832.

GREER: Historians of the French Revolution have been interested in the language of political discourse, and, clearly, the people of Lower Canada, and the people of Upper Canada as well, partook of not just a set of formal political philosophies, but a kind of language when they uttered certain phrases. They had things in mind that may not be what we think of immediately when we hear these words. It is important to be attuned to that larger world that the people of the time were attuned to. Newspapers read by the literate minority in Lower Canada were filled with news not just from Britain and France, but from Poland, Venezuela, and the United States. These people were part of an international community who read not only news, but serious works of politics and law, and they did their best to keep abreast.

BOTHWELL: The question is whether these people saw themselves as a nation, similar to the Venezuelans or the Poles. Greer looks at their assimilation of these experiences:

GREER: There seems to be agreement that there was, at least potentially, and probably actually, a Canadian nation, but exactly what that nation was is, of course, problematic. Was it just French Canadians? Did it include the notion of a body of citizens? Did it include Native people and women? Did it include poor people as well? These are issues for debate. There is no single view on the subject, but these are the terms in which people are discussing these important matters.

BOTHWELL: The revolutionary movement came to a head in the summer of 1837, by which point political cleavages were well established. On one side there were Papineau and his patriotes, mostly French, and on the other there were the so-called constitutionalists, mostly English. And behind the constitutionalists there were the British governor general and the British army. Greer comments on whether it is appropriate to see the rebellion as a racial or a language division:

GREER: You can't limit the rebellion like that. An influential school of thought in Canadian historiography that dates back to Lord Durham and others says that all the fine phrases about political rights and freedom spouted by the patriotes were a cover for an essentially xenophobic movement, and that what is fundamental in Lower Canada is the conflict of English and French. Everything else is secondary. I would argue that that argument is almost exactly the reverse of reality. Obviously there were some kinds of tensions, in some circumstances, between French-speakers and English-speakers, but you miss a lot if you fail to see areas of cooperation as well.

The conflict that came to an acute stage in 1837 and 1838 had everything to do with the breakdown of politics as usual and a crisis of the state, which called forth a mobilization of the majority of the population. It was anti-imperial, certainly, and it was nationalistic in all kinds of important ways. The really acute strife and conflict between English and French came after that; it followed from that fundamentally political conflict.

I spent a lot of time doing research in various parts of the District of Montreal, and I found, time and again, English-speakers who were lining up on the government side, saying, 'I always got along with my neighbours, nobody gave me any trouble over the fact that my religion and language were different until 1837, and then they told me come on, get on side, and join our movement. And when I refused, I was ostracized, I was persecuted in various ways.' So, far from people saying, 'You're English and deserve a terrible fate,' they're saying, on the contrary, 'Get on our side, you are or should be part of our movement, you're a resident and a citizen of Lower Canada, and that's what we represent – the aspirations of the Canadian citizenry, and you should be part of this movement.' It was when they refused that things became ugly, and they became increasingly ugly over the course of this crisis in 1837 and 1838.

What seems to have resulted is something that happens in a lot of revolutionary crises in other parts of the world and other eras of history. Ethnic and linguistic minorities became quite uncomfortable, as a reaction to the revolutionary process itself.

BOTHWELL: What happened, in effect, was the use of terror, although for the most part it was threat rather than direct physical violence, and damage to property rather than injury to persons.

The rebellion, when it broke out, was met by force. Papineau fled across the border. The British army defeated the rebels in a few skirmishes, and set about insuring that there would not be another rebellion. There were scores of arrests, followed by trials, deportations, and even hangings. That, too, was terror, and it was successful, as Greer observes:

GREER: There was another version of terror, the counter-revolutionary terror, that occurred after the patriotes were defeated, and that took very harmful forms. Houses really were burned down, by the dozens, possibly by the hundreds, in the wake of the fighting in 1837-8. People were killed, people by the hundreds were thrown into jail. Many were taken into custody, probably thousands, for shorter periods, although it was not well recorded. So the population in the District of Montreal, in the rural areas, was well and thoroughly frightened into submission by these tactics. Huge amounts of private property were confiscated, both officially and unofficially.

BOTHWELL: The Lower Canadian constitution was suspended, and for a time military government took its place. In 1838 a new governor general, Lord Durham, was sent out with the mission to report on what had caused the rebellion and to recommend how further disturbances might be avoided. Durham's report became deservedly famous as a state paper, but two of its observations became especially well known. According to Durham, he had found 'two nations warring in the bosom of a single state,' a phrase that has been quoted ever since, at least by pessimists, to describe and define English-French relations in Canada. Durham's second well-known phrase is not particularly remembered in English-speaking Canada, but it has not been forgotten by French-speakers. 'A people with neither history nor literature,' Durham sniffed.

Durham recommended the union of the two colonies of Upper Canada and Lower Canada into one Province of Canada, with an assembly in which half the seats would go to the less populous but English-speaking Upper Canada. Those seats, combined with the representatives of Lower Canada's substantial English-speaking population, would create an automatic and probably perpetual English majority in the Canadian legislature. It was a sign that the defeat of Papineau's rebellion was a defeat for the French language and the Canadien nation. The result was to undermine French Canadians' sense of security. Perhaps there was now no future for French-speakers in the British Empire or in North America.

Certainly some Canadiens interpreted it that way. William Johnson, a historian and journalist specializing in the history of English-French relations in Quebec, especially anti-English sentiment or ideology, explains how this sentiment emerged in Quebec:

JOHNSON: It emerged as a very real and well-founded reaction to Durham's report and the Union government. There had been some intellectual production in Quebec – two or three novels before 1840 and a couple of books of poetry – but these were erratic incidents. What really launched intellectual life in Quebec and what remained as its most central preoccupation was the question of national survival. That was raised after the revolt of 1837 and 1838, and was put down with great efficacy.

There was a sense of despair. Durham had published his report, saying, two nations warring in the bosom of one state, a people without a culture, without a history, without a literature; the only solution for their sake as well as everyone else's is to assimilate them and give them the benefits of the English language and English institutions. The Union was enacted for that purpose, to assimilate French Canadians and to eliminate them as a separate political force. Étienne Parent, the great editor of patriote newspaper *Le Canadien* and a leader of the nationalist movement, wrote at that time: We urge our compatriots not to try to fight against an ineluctable fate, but to accept with as good grace as possible the inevitable. It would have been so sweet to have kept the language of our forefathers here on the banks of the St Lawrence, but there's no question of it.

But then, very quickly, there was a strong counter-reaction to this despair. It's not true that we don't have a literature, the nationalists urged; it's not true we don't have a culture, it's not true that we're going to disappear as a distinguishable nation and as a political force.

BOTHWELL: The political reaction to the Durham report in French Canada was led by Louis-Hippolyte LaFontaine. LaFontaine had once been associated with Papineau, but largely by chance he was absent when the rebellion occurred. LaFontaine realized that whatever its aims, and whatever its deficiencies, the union with English-speaking Upper Canada still offered an assembly and elections; there were enough French-Canadian representatives to need the backing of only a few English-Canadian associates. While the equality of representation between Upper and Lower Canada in the Assembly of united Canada favoured the English in the 1840s, by the 1850s, with massive immigration from the British Isles, it would favour the French, who after about 1850 would have more representation in the legislature than they were strictly entitled to.

Out of this demographic situation, and this political calculation, an authentically Canadian tradition of French-English cooperation was born. Ramsay Cook describes what happened in the politics of the 1840s:

COOK: The inter-ethnic cooperation that came in the 1840s, at least on the French-Canadian side, but also on the English-Canadian side, was based on a calculation of self-interest. Louis-Hippolyte LaFontaine was himself a patriote. He happened to have had the good fortune to be out of the country when the rebellion of 1837 took place, so he wasn't one of those who was punished and he didn't have to make the choice whether he would fight or not. But LaFontaine was probably as much a Canadien nationalist as Papineau. The lesson that LaFontaine drew from the rebellion was that rebellion was not the route to follow. It had failed.

French Canadians were increasingly a minority in the united Canadas. Moreover, they were a minority in terms of power. LaFontaine held that, to defend the rights of French Canadians, you had to make use of the parliamentary institutions; you had to find in English-speaking Canada people who were, if not necessarily sympathetic to the French Canadians, at least not hostile to them or anxious to see them assimilated. You had to find people who had certain interests which they saw could be served by forming a majority party. That majority could only be achieved if French Canadians and English Canadians worked together.

LaFontaine did not invent bloc politics, but he benefited from the idea. He argued that if French Canadians worked together, if they all voted for the same party and the same leader, and didn't divide the way English Canadians did, they could exercise greater power in the new political-constitutional arrangements than their numbers alone would have allowed them to. His was a form of elite accommodation, an assessment of self-interest. Even the great nationalist historian Canon Groulx saw that LaFontaine was principally a nationalist, that his goal was no different from Papineau's. It was just that the means he chose were different.

BOTHWELL: Those mid-nineteenth century politicians had coped with a variety of phenomena, but there was a dichotomy between the development of the commercial, industrial society – the society of railways, the society of public works – of mid-nineteenth century politics and the ideology in French Canada that looked to the land, to survival, to traditional values, and to the established church. Cook comments on the way these people had to reconcile living in two worlds:

COOK: There was a three-way division in Lower Canadian society in the 1840s, 1850s, 1860s, and even later. First there was a political system in which French-Canadian political leaders operated, usually in cooperation with people who thought in similar ways to their peers in English-speaking Canada, except that the English Canadians were for the most part anxious to see Canadian society move into a more commercial and industrial mode. Second, there was a French-Canadian population which was, by and large, agricultural, and which had no particular stake in the development of a commercial-industrial society. And third, there was another elite in Lower Canada – the leaders of the church. LaFontaine not only made a compromise with the English in the 1840s, he made a compromise with the church. While Papineau was unhappy about the role played by church leaders, LaFontaine was prepared to accept it; he was not going to alter the relations between church and state on such matters as education, for example.

People like LaFontaine, particularly in the next generation, such as George-Étienne Cartier, became increasingly willing to participate in the economic and social transformation of this society. Cartier was, after all, the solicitor for the Grand Trunk Railway. While they still tended to see their society as an agricultural society, they were sufficiently realistic to know that in North America a transformation of an economic and social kind was taking place that would probably make an impact on that society.

BOTHWELL: The industrial and commercial revolution that transformed Canada in the later nineteenth century naturally affected Lower Canada and its largest city, Montreal. The industrial development of Canada brought wealth and jobs in its train, an encouraging sign for French-Canadian leaders who saw that young French-Canadian families would no longer have to leave the valley of the St Lawrence. They would no longer have to move away to New England. Thus, while church leaders and others mouthed the nostrum that French-Canadian society was and must remain rural, safe from impiety and the sins of the modern world, many of these same leaders accepted the fact that Canada was becoming industrialized, and that French as well as English Canadians must accept this change.

They had simultaneously to accept another fact. The bloc politics of the 1840s persisted for almost two decades. French-Canadian political leaders, especially George-Étienne Cartier, proved exceptionally adept at manipulating parliamentary coalitions in such a way as to leave the French Canadians as part of the majority, and hence of the government. But by the 1860s politics in united Canada had become so finely balanced as to be unstable and uncertain. Irreconcilable groups of English-Canadian Reformers or Liberals with a few French-Canadian allies faced a conglomeration of French- and English-speaking Conservatives under the joint leadership of Cartier and John A. Macdonald.

In 1864 political leaders on both sides of the Canadian Assembly came to accept that the existing situation could not and would not long endure. Something was needed to break the political impasse, and that something turned out to be a federation of united Canada with Britain's Atlantic colonies, at first Newfoundland, Prince Edward Island, New Brunswick, and Nova Scotia, but eventually only New Brunswick and Nova Scotia. An agreement was struck at conferences in Charlottetown and Quebec City in the fall of 1864 that provided for a new colonial federation: New Brunswick and Nova Scotia plus the two new provinces of Ontario and Quebec. This new union came into effect on 1 July 1867, and it created the Dominion of Canada.

The new province of Quebec occupied the boundaries of the former colony of Lower Canada. It had a French-speaking majority and an English-speaking minority, which lived mostly in and around Montreal, Quebec City, and in the Eastern Townships. The Confederation agreement provided for the use of the English and French languages in the parliament and courts of Canada, and in the legislature and courts of Quebec. It also entrenched a number of English-speaking parliamentary seats in the Eastern Townships, but by name rather than by language. Eventually, they all became majority French, a testament to the futility of certain kinds of constitutional prophylactics.

The notion of 'majority French' was crucial to the French-Canadian understanding and acceptance of the new Dominion of Canada. It was not so much that Canada was a new nation as that French Canadians were henceforth entrenched in their own province, Quebec. Historian Arthur Silver explains how French Canadians came to accept the Confederation bargain:

SILVER: When you say French Canadians in this context you mean the general public, because French-Canadian politicians who participated in the making of the deal undoubtedly knew well enough what their English-Canadian partners thought of it. It was sold to the general public, at least the public that read the press and discussed these sorts of questions, as a kind of sovereignty-association. Before Confederation, Quebec and Ontario formed one single province with one government, one legislature. What Confederation did was to break up that united province, and to create a separate province of Quebec and a separate province of Ontario. The pro-Confederation editorialists, speech-makers, and pamphleteers pushed that aspect of the arrangement – that Quebec was going to be separated, that French Canadians were going to have a state of their own which would have complete control over all matters of provincial jurisdiction, and that it was a move towards greater separation. That was the selling point in Quebec.

At the time of Confederation itself, the English minority in Quebec didn't get, or didn't seem to get, all that great a deal. An attempt just months before Confederation to put through a bill in the legislature with special guarantees for Lower Canadian or Quebec Protestants failed, precisely because the back-benchers in the majority party had all been sold on Confederation. They thought that Quebec would have complete control of its own school system, and that the Catholic majority would have the school system it wanted. When the government tried to put through special guarantees for the Protestants in Quebec, there was a revolt of the back-benchers and the bill was withdrawn. It was only a couple of years later, in 1869, after long negotiations between the Protestants and the provincial government, that the government, because of the political and economic clout of the Protestants, was forced to agree to give guarantees to the minority in Quebec.

BOTHWELL: The Confederation bargain should be remembered for two things. First, as Ramsay Cook noted, it was the product of a political system that political scientists call elite accommodation. Confederation was a bargain among politicians who more or less represented their voters' feelings on the issue. Some more, and some definitely less. Confederation was not submitted to the electorate for ratification, and in some cases the sponsoring politicians were intensely grateful to have avoided an election in which they knew that they, and Confederation, would be roundly defeated. But Confederation happened anyway, and when it did it was widely – and within five or six years universally – accepted.

Second, Confederation created a new majority French-Canadian province of Quebec. It was justified to nationalist-minded French Canadians as a kind of liberation: at least on provincial issues they would be able to follow their own inclinations and not have to seek cooperation or ratification from the English. Granted, other issues did not fall under French-Canadian control or provincial jurisdiction, and these included very important powers. For the Confederation bargain also created a very powerful government in the federal capital of Ottawa, and in that government French Canadians would be an even smaller minority than they had been in the old legislature of united Canada.

Undoubtedly, Confederation solved one set of political and ethnic dilemmas. But in doing so, had it created a whole new set?

Chapter 3

Living with Compromise: Quebec in Canada, 1867-1919

In 1867, according to most history books, 'a new nation' was created in northern North America. But was it? Was it a nation at all? Was it not just a bigger colony within the British Empire, the same after 1867 as before? Or was it a ratification of the existence of two new nations, English-Canadian and French-Canadian? Some historians, political scientists, politicians, and other opinion-makers argue that it was really the union of four colonies, provinces, or regions, that the provinces or regions came first and the new federal government in Ottawa came later. To cap it off, the term we usually apply to the process, 'confederation,' is not quite right as to the result. What was created was a federation, with a true central government capable of acting on its own, and not a confederation, where central institutions operate more or less by permission of the provinces.

Some facts are certain. An act of the British Parliament, the British North America Act, established a new entity, the Dominion of Canada, with four provinces – Nova Scotia, New Brunswick, Quebec, and Ontario. In 1869-70 the Dominion of Canada acquired the lands of the Hudson's Bay Company – roughly speaking, the Hudson Bay area, plus the prairies and the Mackenzie River basin. In 1871 the dominion expanded again, to British

Columbia and the Pacific. In 1873 Prince Edward Island, effectively bank-rupt, joined the Canadian federation. Newfoundland stayed out, an autonomous British colony with a history of its own; it would finally join in 1949.

How did French Canadians function inside the new Dominion of Canada, and how did Canada respond to their problems and concerns? The best place to begin is with an analysis of society, and with the fundamental question of numbers. The late nineteenth century was a time of growth in virtually all respects. How that growth was managed was a fundamental political question. While the politics of the late nineteenth century may look remote and abstract today, they were founded on the fact that there were many more French-speaking, Catholic French Canadians fifty years after Confederation than there were in 1867. There were more English Canadians as well, and they all had to be fitted into a country that was growing, too. But there were growing pains and many uncomfortable moments, as English and French Canadians adjusted to the politics of sharing a country with another linguistic and religious group.

In one sense, Canada obviously worked for French Canadians. The French language not only survived but it positively flourished, if numbers of French-speakers are any indication. Still, the great majority of French-speakers dwelt in Quebec, although pockets of French Canadians spread out across the dominion, even to British Columbia and the new provinces of Alberta and Saskatchewan. In the fifty years after Confederation, Canada as a whole increased rapidly in population and in national wealth. Canadians were much better off in 1919 than they were in 1867, and French Canadians shared in the prosperity. Montreal was the financial and industrial hub of the new dominion, growing substantially between 1867 and 1919, and in the process acquiring a French-speaking majority sometime around 1875. The growth of Montreal and the changes in its economy and population affected all of Canada, but they also affected Quebec. Historian Ramsay Cook dis-cusses the growth of Montreal and the redistribution of population:

COOK: There was considerable growth in the city of Montreal at the same time that there was outmigration to New England. The main effect was gradually to transform Montreal into a French-speaking city, which it had not always been. At the time of Confederation, the linguistic division in Montreal was about equal, but subsequently the balance gradually shifted to an increasingly French-speaking city. The principal role these people played as they moved from rural areas into the city of Montreal, particularly to the east end, around the turn of the century was to become the industrial proletariat of the new industrial system. At the same time, there always was a significant French-Canadian elite, who lived then as now in Outremont.

BOTHWELL: Montreal and its northern suburb Outremont represented an alternative to rural life, but they also represented a new kind of reality in Quebec and the rest of Canada. But the reality of urbanization was not easily recognized. Indeed, Quebec in the late nineteenth century was thought of as overwhelmingly rural, both inside and outside the province. By 1911 that was not at all the case, for an urban majority appeared in the census for the first time. Traditionally, however, French Canada was regarded as an entity with an agricultural vocation, with a special religious – that is, Catholic – mission, and as a place where the government did not play a large role. Cook describes the mental landscape of French Canada's leaders and intellectuals in the late nineteenth century:

COOK: French-Canadian nationalism was promoted by its elite as having three dominant ideas: that of Quebec as an agricultural society, that of Quebec as a society with a special mission, and that of a society where the government did not play a significant role, thereby leaving the leadership of the society to the church. That concept continues to stand up, but only partly.

This ideology was accepted by most of the nationalist leaders of French Canada and of Quebec from about the middle of the nineteenth century down to the Second World War. But it does not necessarily represent what was going on in the society, nor does it represent what all French-Canadian elites were thinking. For example, it is now perfectly plain that in the 1870s the government in Quebec was as active as the government in Ontario; neither was particularly active. Still, the Quebec government was engaged in the promotion and subsidization of railways and the encouragement of various other kinds of small economic activities in the same way as the Ontario government.

BOTHWELL: The distinctiveness of Quebec and its society begins to seem spotty the longer we look at its history. In terms of industrialization, urbanization, and even emigration – for many English Canadians left for the United States at about the same time – Quebec was not unique. Even its idealization of rural life was not unique. The uniqueness may lie more in ideology, but where ideology appears, with force and a degree of permanence, is in its political institutions, as expressed in the Canadian Constitution.

Quebec was established as a province with a French-speaking majority and with certain institutions that made it unique among the provinces. It retained its own code of civil law, different from the common law of the English-speaking provinces. Quebec was bilingual, with French and English recognized as legal in the provincial legislature and the courts. And Quebec, in this case like Ontario, had constitutionally protected Protestant and Catholic school systems. The assumption was made that almost all Protestants would be English-speaking, although within the Catholic Church there was also a substantial English-speaking group, which in the nineteenth century was mostly Irish.

Quebec in 1867 was about 80 per cent French-speaking, a proportion that remained relatively constant over the next hundred years. French-speakers did not cover all of Quebec, nor were they entirely confined to Quebec. There were French-speaking minorities, Acadians in New Brunswick and Nova Scotia, tiny in the case of the latter province, and when Prince Edward Island joined it brought an Acadian group as well. By 1860 there were also many thousands of French Canadians next door in New England – 37,000 – and by 1870 the French-Canadian population in the six New England states surpassed 103,000. At times in the late nineteenth century it seemed that French Canadians might overwhelm whole areas of New England, so great was the migration and so high was the birthrate at home in Quebec and among the immigrants in the United States. By 1900 the number of French Canadians in New England totalled 573,000: since Confederation, more than 250,000 French Canadians had crossed the border to settle in New England.

Some may have thought that Confederation would redirect French-speakers away from the United States to the Canadian West, but that did not happen. Significant numbers of French Canadians did go west, but only to the eastern counties of Ontario, to Hawkesbury or Alexandria, to the federal capital of Ottawa, or to the mining and forest regions of northeastern Ontario.

In a curious way the existence of a Canadian alternative to emigration to New England was not reassuring, at least to French-Canadian elites. Historian Ken Munro argues this point of view:

MUNRO: French-speaking people didn't go to the West in great numbers, and there was hesitancy on the part of the church. The church wanted Catholicism to be spread throughout the West, but Quebec was losing population rapidly and there was concern that the province would be depopulated too much if it encouraged individuals to go to the West. Colonization missionaries were allowed to work throughout Quebec, to try to encourage French Canadians to move to the West, but there was a great deal of scepticism, because it would weaken Quebec.

BOTHWELL: In any case, French Canadians simply felt much more attraction for the familiar, if foreign, factories of New England than they did for the West. Jim Miller reflects on this preference:

MILLER: About the time that Manitoba became part of Confederation, the archbishop of St Boniface said 'numbers will defeat us.' It was an accurate prophecy, because, in general, Ontarians migrated west to Manitoba and other regions, and Québécois did not. Québécois tended to move south, into factory towns in New England that were close enough to be congenial and affordable, but they didn't want to make the long leap over the Precambrian Shield into the Prairie West. Ontarian farmers, in contrast, did go west. That was one of the major reasons why large segments of Ontario sentiment favoured Confederation – to acquire the West as a region for agricultural settlement for the younger sons who couldn't inherit land in Ontario. These Ontarians diluted what was a bicultural or tricultural society in Manitoba, and, by 1890, made it an overwhelmingly Ontarian-derived society.

BOTHWELL: The federal authorities did try to encourage a sense of French-Canadian interest in the west by making appointments for judges, lieutenant governors, or other officials, but it did little good. The result was that for those French Canadians who did go west, there was a sense of being lost in an English-speaking sea.

MUNRO: Individuals began to join the English-speaking community, and even those who were French-speaking did not use the tools that were given them by the federal authorities. For example, the use of the court system in French, or even the school system that was allowed at the time, although the school system took longer to die out within the Catholic structure than the court system.

BOTHWELL: As for the prairies, there was already a French-speaking population when Canada acquired the Hudson's Bay Company lands in 1870. In fact, the new province of Manitoba, established that year, started off with a French-speaking majority. This French majority consisted partly of white settlers from the East, but much of it was of mixed race, Indian and white, descendants of the fur traders: the Métis. Among the Métis, some spoke French and some spoke English.

When Canada purchased Manitoba, the Métis insisted on their rights as original settlers and raised a brief rebellion under a talented and charismatic local figure. Louis Riel was, as his name indicates, of French descent and French-speaking. He proved to be a successful advocate for his people, but in the process, almost accidentally, he authorized the execution of a disruptive anglophone, Thomas Scott, who had moved to Manitoba from Ontario. Riel had no legal authority to have anyone killed, and his action was, legally speaking, tantamount to murder. So, when Canadian troops occupied Manitoba in the summer of 1870, Riel fled.

Fifteen years later, in 1885, Riel raised a new rebellion, this time in what is now Saskatchewan. Riel had come to believe that he was a religious prophet as well as a political leader, something that caused people at the time and since to question his sanity. This rebellion was a much bloodier affair than the one in 1870 and it ended with Riel's capture, subsequent trial, conviction, and execution in Regina in November 1885. Riel himself did not believe he was insane, and by the standards of the time he probably was not. The prime minister, Sir John A. Macdonald, let the law take its course, despite appeals from Quebec and from French Canadians generally. Riel's life was over, but his career as a symbol for Franco-Manitobans, and for French Canadians generally, had just begun.

Tom Flanagan has written extensively about Riel's importance as a political symbol:

FLANAGAN: Riel is a symbol for all seasons. People use symbols, they appropriate them. If you were to compare the symbolic uses of Riel to the facts of Riel's life as we know them, the most accurate symbolic use of Riel would be as leader of the French-Canadian Métis nation. Riel was not an advocate for Native peoples in general; he had no special concern for Indians. His plan for Indians, in fact, was to turn them all into Métis through miscegenation on a large scale. He was originally an advocate of the French language and the Catholic religion in the West. That would probably be an accurate description of much of his political activity in the first rebellion in Manitoba in 1869-70, but he went beyond that. He broke with the Catholic Church. Originally he had thought of the Métis as a kind of extension of the French fact in the West, but then he reversed his view and he came to think of the Métis as an error of the French evangelical missionary tradition. It is really a distortion of Riel's overall career to think of him as merely a spokesman of the French language. He did not think of himself at all as a specifically western figure. By the end of his life he thought he was the divinely inspired leader of the French-Canadian Métis nation who had a divine mission, given by the Holy Spirit, to renovate religion in the New World.

BOTHWELL: Riel's life, and especially his death, have become key events in Canadian history. In Quebec many came to believe that Riel's execution was a specifically English-Protestant response to an assertion of rights by a French-speaking Catholic, and that an English Protestant in the same position would never have been hanged. Here, again, the facts are less important than their interpretation, than Riel's legend, and the legend is probably more important in Quebec than it is in the West or even in Manitoba.

Riel's failure and death closely preceded another outbreak of ill-feeling between English Canadians and French Canadians. French-Canadian rights in western Canada, Manitoba, and the North-West Territories (the modern Alberta and Saskatchewan) came increasingly under threat and, given the lack of a large French-speaking minority, the French Canadians were politically powerless to stop it. Ken Munro has examined how French Canadians in the West came to lose their rights.

MUNRO: In 1880, Manitoba was already established as a bilingual, bicultural province. By then, less than ten years after Manitoba joined Confederation, French rights were undermined. This decline began immediately after 1870; immigration was largely English-speaking and, for the population in Manitoba, there appeared to be no need for French. This situation was magnified even more in the North-West Territories. There were major controversial debates over the loss of French rights in the West, not so much in western Canada as between politicians from Ontario and Quebec.

BOTHWELL: In eastern Canada a great quarrel arose over legislation in Quebec designed to return, after many years, certain properties to the Jesuit order. This was taken to be proof of a Catholic conspiracy to establish the Catholic religion officially in Quebec and to oppress and exclude Protestants. Jim Miller has written a book on French-English controversies in the late nineteenth century, and he examines how French rights in western Canada affected Ontario-Quebec relations:

MILLER: According to one point of view, there is a direct personal link between Jesuit Estates and Manitoba schools: that link is a maverick Tory politician by the name of D'Alton McCarthy, who was prominent in the Jesuit Estates' controversy and, some historians allege, a major spark for the Manitoba Schools' Question in 1889 and 1890. Other historical interpretations emphasize the indigenous roots of the Manitoba controversy, and say simply that discussions over religious and language questions such as Jesuit Estates merely sensitized Manitobans to look at their own institutions and their own way of doing things. In any event, for whatever reason, in 1889-90 there was an attack on both the official use of French in the Manitoba legislature and on denominational, mainly Catholic, education in the province of Manitoba.

BOTHWELL: Religion played a large role in late nineteenth-century society, English and French. The tendency for most, although not all, French Canadians to be Catholic, and vice versa, meant that racial or linguistic quarrels were often complicated by strong religious feelings. Miller examines what religion brought to relations between English and French at that time:

MILLER: Religion mattered a lot more in the late nineteenth century, in all parts of Canada, than it does today. People took these things very seriously and, within Canadian and Ontario Protestantism, there was a strong tradition of suspicion of what used to be called Catholic aggression, or French domination. There was a hypersensitivity in Ontario in the late nineteenth century towards Catholicism, a sensitivity not found in other parts of the country. Nova Scotia and New Brunswick, for example, had a much more civilized tradition. Part of the reason Ontario was much more sensitive and aggressive in reacting to a militant Catholicism in Quebec was their tradition of battles from the 1850s and 1860s, when the two regions were linked together in one political state, the Province of Canada. In Ontario, there was a well-developed militant Protestantism, as well as a strong record of conflict over church-state questions and economic questions that date from the

1850s, and the two tended to make Ontario very suspicious of Quebec in the late nineteenth century.

BOTHWELL: In 1890 French-language schools in Manitoba were abolished. The Fathers of Confederation in 1867 had not been entirely naive. They had anticipated a situation in which a majority might oppress a minority, and they had provided for the federal government to intervene, legally and constitutionally, in such circumstances. The federal government in the early 1890s, which was Conservative in stripe, was faced with an uncomfortable dilemma. Whom should it offend? Quebec and French-speakers generally, or an aroused Ontario? To complicate matters, a precedent already existed from the restriction by the English majority of French schools in New Brunswick twenty years earlier.

MILLER: By the time the question of federal intervention or remedial action arose in the 1890s, there had been about two decades of experience with the issue. The question had first arisen with the New Brunswick Schools' Question in the early 1870s. On that occasion it was decided that there would not be federal intervention, in large part because the Quebec Conservative caucus did not support remedial action to reimpose Catholic schools on New Brunswick. The reason that Quebec Conservatives, such as George-Étienne Cartier, did not want to intervene was because they did not want to create a precedent that could be used to interfere with Quebec's affairs on sensitive matters of religion and education.

By the 1890s, there was a constitutional power to take remedial action to protect a religious minority that had lost an important educational right, but the political will, and the political ability, to exercise it successfully had been seriously weakened. Compounding the problem was the fact that the leadership of the Conservative Party was in a serious decline. The party was divided and demoralized, and it simply did not have the political muscle to carry through something as courageous and controversial as interference in Manitoba educational affairs.

BOTHWELL: The lessons of the 1890s have not been forgotten, especially in Quebec. If Quebec had an ambiguous attitude to the French Canadians in the West in the nineteenth century, it has it still today. There are parallels between the 1890s and the 1990s, as Miller points out:

MILLER: It's fair to say that Quebec has always been much more interested in provincial autonomy within the federation than in using the federal power to intervene in the provinces to protect minorities. Historian Arthur Silver has written a book called *The French Canadian Idea of Confederation* that shows that this approach to federalism was present from the early decades after 1867. It has been a tradition and a cultural imperative that has informed all Quebec governments through the decades since.

BOTHWELL: The Manitoba Schools' Question brought down the Conservative Party in the federal election of 1896. The Liberal Party was returned under a veteran Quebec politician, Wilfrid Laurier. Laurier had the support of five out of seven of Canada's provincial premiers, and it is not too much to say that he rode to power by mobilizing provincial grievances against Ottawa. Once in power, Laurier would have to run a national government, but he never entirely forgot that the basis of his power was provincial. Laurier was not, therefore, one to emphasize federal powers at the expense of the provinces. He did help negotiate a compromise with Manitoba, but it was a compromise almost of convenience rather than rights. Réal Bélanger of Laval University suggests that much more was at stake than merely local autonomy:

BÉLANGER: The Manitoba Schools' Question was an important issue for French Canada at this time and for relations between anglophones and francophones. French Canada thought that English Canada could not understand the spirit of Confederation, because French Canada, French Catholic Canada, saw no place for itself in this new Canada – and, to me, French Canada was right in thinking like that. English Canada did not understand the spirit of Canada. Canada is a bicultural country, yet with the Manitoba Schools' Question, English Canada abolished the kind of school that allowed French Catholic Canadians to be part of Canada.

BOTHWELL: The experience was repeated nine years later. When Saskatchewan and Alberta were created in 1905, through Laurier's Autonomy Bills, they followed the precedent set in Manitoba and avoided protection for French rights. Tom Flanagan discusses how this neglect affected the minority question in western Canada:

FLANAGAN: When he became prime minister, Wilfrid Laurier decided – it is going too far to say that he cut the French Canadians of the West loose –

that he wouldn't use the power of the federal government to advance their cause. From that point on they had to make do with local political conditions in the provinces and to extract whatever concessions they could, particularly regarding education, which was the main issue.

BOTHWELL: Réal Bélanger argues that Laurier's abandonment of the West in the Autonomy Bills of 1905 was pragmatic, but nevertheless a mistake:

BÉLANGER: Laurier didn't think that the language was so important in the West, where there were so few French people. In 1905 French-Canadian nationalists made an effort to show Laurier that it was an important moment for the Confederation. But Laurier sincerely thought that even if the minority was right, compromise would protect them in the long term. I don't agree with him, and we still live with the result of his decision. In Quebec today, an important group of separatists have found their reason to be separatist in Canadian history. Laurier gave grist to the separatist mill in doing what he did at this time.

BOTHWELL: John English, who has written extensively on Canadian political history and is currently a federal member of parliament, characterizes Laurier's political performance and, in particular, his approach to French-English relations in Canada, as one based on practicality:

ENGLISH: Laurier, like all politicians, came to an understanding of the way the system worked, and after 1896 the system he brought with him was one that depended heavily on the provincial premiers. He established a provincial base through these premiers, who would then manage the party in specific areas. In the case of someone like Clifford Sifton, from the West, he brought in someone who was a skilled political operator. In terms of the larger question of how he handled the relationship between French and English Canadians, he felt his way in terms of a compromise: what could be done on one side, what could be done on the other. The essential point was made by André Siegfried when he wrote about it, after having watched the events of 1903 and 1904. What Laurier did was try to stifle differences, avoid confrontations, avoid issues that were difficult, do as much as possible through his ministers, and have his ministers handle particularly difficult questions. But in the overall sense, he recognized that what was dangerous were sentiments, and that these sentiments should as much as possible be contained within a political system that operated effectively and efficiently.

BOTHWELL: 'Stifle differences,' 'avoid confrontations,' 'try to avoid issues that were difficult.' To Laurier, the sectarian debates and language quarrels of the 1880s and 1890s showed that these were questions on which Canadians not only did not agree, but would never agree. Lacking consensus on a variety of topics ranging from foreign affairs to the language of education, Canadians would do best not to talk about them. But among politicians practical understandings were possible, and certainly desirable. The Laurier age is remembered for an eloquent leader (Laurier had a silver tongue), for elegance (Laurier had a sense of style, of panache), for economic progress (Laurier believed that prosperity cured many evils and distracted attention from fruitless quarrels). Where avoidance would not work, Laurier preferred compromise – and for him, compromise worked in a particular way.

Canadian political scientists and historians have drawn attention to the idea that large differences are best settled quickly, behind closed doors, and by as few people as possible, although such people should be broadly representative and politically capable. They should be like Laurier, in fact. Laurier was among the most notable Canadian practitioners of what has been labelled elite accommodation. Jim Miller comments on how elite accommodation solved political problems:

MILLER: In the late nineteenth and first part of the twentieth century, these kinds of conflicts between ethnic groups and between regions and provinces, Ontario and Quebec especially, tended to get resolved by what our political scientists refer to as elite accommodation. There was a tendency on the part of political elites to discourage populist organization, and there was generally a settlement of disputes at the federal level in parliament and in cabinet: some of the clearest examples are the language and schools issues in the Canadian West in the 1890s, where many of the disputes were resolved within the federal cabinet. It is only in the last forty or fifty years that this system has begun to break down.

BOTHWELL: Laurier had a cornucopia of problems with which to deal. Sometimes they were merely financial or economic, an aspect of life that the prime minister did not pretend to understand. There were problems of growth, such as managing the inflow of more than 2 million immigrants between 1896 and 1911 in a country of just over 5 million in 1896. This immigration went to the cities of central Canada, such as Montreal or Toronto, but also and more importantly to the Canadian West, populating the prairies and permanently altering the demographic, economic, and political balance of Canada. Canada was different when Laurier left office in 1911 than it had been in 1896 when he arrived, and the problems he had to deal with, from railways to citizenship, were staggering. Many problems were pragmatic, with quantifiable solutions, but many were not. The worst ones were issues of principle that divided English from French. These Laurier understood to be very important, because a failure to reach an accommodation on English-French matters threatened the political viability of Canada – a consideration that has led some historians to argue that Laurier believed that Canada was founded on an agreement between two founding races, English and French. This point of view is more usually associated with a younger French-Canadian Liberal, Henri Bourassa, whose insistence on it from time to time caused Laurier some political headaches. Laurier knew that in its pure form, this view was incomprehensible, if not entirely unacceptable, to English-Canadian opinion.

Réal Bélanger argues this point very strongly. In his comments he refers to the events of 1905, the Autonomy Bills:

BÉLANGER: In 1905 Laurier believed that Confederation was an agreement between the two races in Canada. Bourassa believed that, too. Laurier's entire life was based on harmony between the two races, the two peoples of Canada. He never wrote explicitly about it, but some of his letters show that he believed in this harmony.

BOTHWELL: Never explicitly – as Bélanger says. Laurier's caution, which events show was well founded, sometimes makes it difficult to follow his reasoning and, on occasion, impossible to discern his principles, apart from accommodation and pragmatism. Inside his Liberal Party, Laurier ruled uneasily over some strong-minded subordinates, especially Clifford Sifton from Manitoba and Henri Bourassa from Quebec.

Sifton was Laurier's minister of the interior, and the leading Liberal politician in western Canada. He was instrumental in pushing Laurier away from entrenching French minority rights in the West. Certainly, Sifton's vision of Canada was very different from Bourassa's and Laurier's. David Hall, Sifton's biographer, analyzes his protagonist's approach:

HALL: Sifton's view of Canada was one that would be typical of western Canadians: that there should be no sort of hyphenated Canadianism (as a later expression would have it), and that all citizens should be treated equally, with special privileges for none – the old notion of 'equal rights for all, special privileges for none.' That meant no special rights for French Canadians, as French Canadians or as Catholics, or for particular immigrant groups; there should be equivalent treatment for everybody. In his view, French Canadians had a very special status, which was not justified, certainly not in western Canada.

Sifton believed that there should be a common language, values, and culture. He had the normal prejudices of somebody who had grown up in western Ontario, in the Grit tradition, and he carried those with him to western Canada. But western Canadians in general seemed to have a prejudice against what they saw as special privileges for particular groups. There was a larger proportion of non-English-speaking immigrants in the West, and westerners were very conscious of the problems this might create for society down the road. They believed you had to have a common set of values inculcated through the schools, through a common language, so ultimately these values would generate a common citizenship. French-Catholic privileges stood apart, but they also became a kind of symbol for other groups to try to emulate, and it was precisely that problem people like Sifton wanted to avoid.

BOTHWELL: In fact, Sifton and Laurier had many things in common and, until 1911, Sifton counted himself a loyal supporter of the Liberal leader. The same was not true of Henri Bourassa, also a Liberal MP, who quite early on deserted Laurier and charted an independent and on the whole nationaliste course in Quebec. Bourassa had only scorn for Sifton and other pragmatic politicians in general.

HALL: In a debate around 1906 about corruption, Bourassa said that people like Sifton should be eliminated from the party in the same way that barnacles are scraped off a ship. That comment simply reflected the difference between Sifton's pragmatic, patronage-oriented views and Bourassa's devotion to high principles. They were worlds apart in some respects, particularly in their view of what a political party was and ought to be.

BOTHWELL: Under Henri Bourassa's inspiration, if not his leadership – Bourassa was not qualified to be either a leader or a follower, and was effectively a party of one – French-Canadian nationalistes moved away from Laurier after 1900 or 1905. John English explains why:

ENGLISH: Laurier was a man of compromise, and after a while a man who compromises becomes a bitter enemy of those who demand clear and accurate answers. As nationalism developed in Quebec, at the university, within the church, and elsewhere, Laurier's kind of bargaining seemed offensive, and the turn against him personally became very marked.

The impact of nationalism was at first not large: it linked itself with various movements that were opposed to Laurier, including some in English Canada. By 1909, 1910, 1911, Laurier had managed to offend enough people from one place or another to make nationalism a much more effective force.

BOTHWELL: Nationalism is a two-edged sword. It can sometimes focus attention and mobilize political strength in a way that omnibus political parties, scattered across the landscape geographically and politically, cannot do. But having mobilized around the issue of race, or religion, or territory, nationalism sometimes has problems deciding what to do next. Laurier was cursed by true believers from both sides of Canada's linguistic divide, and, eventually, in 1911, his political system gave way. He was succeeded in power by a curious alliance of English-Canadian imperialists and French-Canadian nationalistes, all grouped uneasily under the leadership of the Conservative prime minister, Sir Robert Borden.

It had been Laurier's misfortune to be buffeted mostly by internal issues and quarrels in Canada, although towards the end he was having foreign policy problems, too. It was Borden's fate that his term in office, which lasted until 1920, was dominated by the First World War, of 1914-18.

By 1914 Great Britain interfered very little with Canada, but Canada and especially English Canadians remained strongly attached to Great Britain and the worldwide British Empire. The empire, so big and so powerful, was, most people believed, a necessary factor in Canadians' sense of identity. It allowed English Canadians to hold up their heads beside the Americans and boast that Canada, too, was part of a great power, the British Empire. It had occurred to only a few Canadians, and some Britons, that the empire might be less impressive if it could not draw on the resources and peoples of the colonies, and that Great Britain by itself might not have the strength necessary to maintain itself against its rivals and enemies, including a rapidly growing and aggressive Germany.

For French Canadians the empire was a different matter. For one thing, the language of the empire was English. For another, the most fervent imperialists tended to define themselves in racial terms, Anglo-Saxon, and attempts to include the French Canadians as really Normans and hence honorary Englishmen were never accepted. There was another factor at work. Henri Bourassa and those who thought like him – including some English Canadians as well as Laurier – tended to believe that English Canadians were the ultimate hyphenated nationality, that they were not really Canadian in spirit, no matter what their citizenship. They responded to Britain's needs and not to Canada's. What was wrong with English Canadians was that they were too British, and that their sense of self was, in Canadian terms, incomplete. In one sense, Bourassa displaced onto the British Empire what he perceived to be the inadequacies of English-speaking Canadians. Remove the empire and, perhaps, a real sense of a common Canada would finally emerge.

The outbreak of the First World War brought an outpouring of support and enthusiasm from across Canada. Hundreds of thousands of Canadians enlisted in the army and the navy, and ultimately 60,000 died and were buried on the battlefields in France and Belgium. It has been noted – and it was noticed at the time by some – that many of those who enlisted were British-born and recently arrived in Canada. Farmers were less willing to go than city people. But, when all was said and done, fewer people enlisted in Quebec, and fewer still once the enthusiastic population of English Quebec was removed from the enlistment totals.

The casualties on the battlefield were immense and, ultimately, all the allied governments – Britain's, the United States', and Canada's – had to resort to conscription, or the draft, to fill the depleted ranks of the military. But in Canada, English and French Canadians were far apart not merely on the issue of the war and enlistment, but on language too, for just at that time the province of Ontario was trying to enforce an English-only policy on French-Canadian school districts. Why go abroad to fight Germany and its aggression in Europe, some nationalistes argued, when the enemy was really at home?

Laurier, as leader of the Liberal opposition in parliament, opposed the Ontario action, made by the Conservative government of James Whitney in the form of an administrative regulation, Regulation 17. Réal Bélanger explains:

BÉLANGER: Laurier didn't think that the language was important in the West, where there were so few French people. But it's not the same in

Ontario and, when the Whitney government passed Regulation 17, Laurier didn't agree with it. When Ernest Lapointe made an opposing motion in the House of Commons in 1916, Laurier supported him strongly. Laurier made a very important speech about language, the most important of his life. He tried to show that Canada is based on understanding, on tolerance. This is the spirit of Confederation, the spirit that French Canada understood from the beginning and that English Canada refused to understand.

BOTHWELL: By this reading, English Canada had violated an understanding, or, by extension, a pact, with French Canada. This is a view often associated with Laurier's rival, Henri Bourassa, but in Bélanger's view, Laurier also believed in it. In its modern form, this is the two-nations interpretation of Canada.

BÉLANGER: Laurier believed at this moment that Confederation was an agreement between the two races in Canada. Henri Bourassa, of course, believed in that, but also Laurier. If we read Laurier's correspondence, you will find that Laurier supported this agreement. His whole life was based on the harmony of the two races, the two people of Canada. He never wrote explicitly that it was an agreement between the two founding peoples, but he wrote some letters that gave me the impression that he believed in that, too.

BOTHWELL: Curiously, Sir Robert Borden had won the election of 1911 by mobilizing the quite different sentiments of English Canada and French Canada, but the resulting government was anything but coherent. Borden's ramshackle coalition of nationalistes and imperialists fell apart under the strain of war. His ministers and members from Quebec remained loyal to their leader, for the most part, but their followers deserted them in droves. Laurier refused to enter a coalition government with Borden that would make the government one of national unity; instead, he and the Liberals opposed Borden and a coalition of Tories and dissident Liberals in the election of 1917. Borden made sure that the soldiers overseas voted, and then, using a piece of legislation known as the Wartime Elections Act, he gave the vote for the first time to women – to women, that is, who were related to soldiers – and retracted the vote from whole classes of immigrants, many of them likely Liberal voters. Borden also promised to exempt farmers from conscription, thereby neutralizing another probable group of opposition voters. The legislation encouraged dissident Liberal politicians in English

Canada, men who approved of conscription but feared the electorate, to join Borden's Union government and to run in the 1917 election. John English describes the effect of that election:

ENGLISH: The election of 1917 had a dramatic impact. Laurier, by not accepting the coalition offer that Borden made, determined the fate of politics in Canada. He managed to keep Quebec Liberal. The Quebec seats in the election that were francophone went overwhelmingly to the Liberal side. The whole episode created a deep wound that was not exactly exploited by the Liberals, but from which they benefited enormously.

As to the election itself, what gave credence to the idea that it was unfair were the Wartime Elections Act, the Military Voters Act, and the kind of rhetoric that took place in those last days of the election, in November and December 1917. In addition, there was the farmers' exemption, which seemed an attempt to buy the election at the final point, and the fact that the election was fought on the loyalty issue. These things were not forgotten, not simply among French Canadians, but among German Canadians and others, too. The Conservative Party in Quebec survived the election because there was an anglophone community and an anglophone vote that was fairly strong. Its presence meant that there was a base for the party in the province of Quebec. Among French Canadians it survived only in very weakened form. For a generation the Conservative Party in Quebec had no life.

BOTHWELL: Laurier lost the election of 1917, and in that election he saw most, although not all, of his English-Canadian associates desert him and the Liberal Party. But Laurier and the Liberals won Quebec and virtually every constituency where French Canadians were a significant group. Quebec voters stayed with one of Canada's two traditional parties, and the Liberals continued to function pretty much as they had before conscription and the war. Around this time Laurier gave way to pessimism and reflected that perhaps it had been a mistake for a French Canadian to hope to be a true leader in Canadian politics. Blair Neatby, an authority on the Canadian party system, speculates on whether Laurier was right:

NEATBY: For Laurier, his despair sprang from the particular moment; he was not a pessimistic person, and he clearly got over things. This moment was the conscription crisis and the split in the Liberal Party, which Laurier in fact managed to reunite before his death in 1919, so that many of the

English-Canadian Liberals who had betrayed him came back into the fold. But still there is a certain validity to his question: if an issue divides English and French Canada, and the majority, the English Canadians, are intransigent about it, then the minority is going to lose.

BOTHWELL: The fact that English Canada was intransigent over conscription, as well as the bitterness of the 1917 election, came as a shock to many in Quebec. In 1918, for the first time, the Quebec legislature debated a motion that suggested that, under some circumstances, Quebec might have to leave Canada. But it was a very qualified motion, as John English observes:

ENGLISH: The resolution was very interesting. It was eventually talked out, but when it came forward it was almost in the way of an apology: If the rest of the country does not want Quebec to be part of Canada, because it does not regard Quebec as having worked effectively within a federation agreement, then Quebec should leave. The debate was interesting because the tone was not, in contemporary terms, angrily separatist, but rather had a sense of sadness, a sense of trying to make things work out better than they had for the previous three or four years.

BOTHWELL: It is clear that the first fifty years of Canada's existence, from Confederation to the First World War, were not entirely happy ones as far as French-English relations in Canada were concerned. At times the two groups seemed entirely irreconcilable, and much of the time disputes between English and French were resolved by the French giving way: over minority rights in western Canada, over schools in Ontario, over conscription in the First World War. Understandably these events, taken together, encouraged a sense of solidarity among French Canadians. They gave rise, simultaneously, to Laurier's political system, in which elite accommodation and a fixation on practical and pragmatic politics took the place of the politics of principle. Principles were left to the nationalists of the Bourassa stripe, but what the nationalists preached, except on the extreme, was not disaffiliation or disassociation from Canada. Rather, at the end of the First World War, there was a determination to try harder to make Canada work.

Chapter 4

King, Quebec, and Duplessis, 1919-48

B<small>ETWEEN</small> 1919 and 1948 Canadian political life centred on the peculiar figure of William Lyon Mackenzie King. King, born in 1874, died in 1950, leader of the Canadian Liberal Party from 1919 to 1948, was prime minister of Canada longer than anyone else – more than twenty-two years. That is certainly success of a kind, but it was the kind that King measured, hour by hour, as he gazed at the hands of the clock, looking for a fortunate minute or a lucky hour at which to transact public business. For King was a man who believed, and believed devoutly, in the significance of numbers, and in the messages conveyed by the voices of the dead. When these facts became known, as they did after King's death, many people were tempted to believe that this outwardly dull little man was, in fact, a great historical joke.

But reputations fluctuate and fashions fade. Most Canadian historians believe that Mackenzie King was our most successful prime minister. This is a view that would have sat oddly with many of King's contemporaries, as it does with many Canadians today. Historians by and large do not admire King's many eccentricities or the various peculiar traits of his character. But what they do remember is that throughout his prime ministership – three separate terms – King kept his mind and his political purpose firmly fixed on the idea of 'national unity.'

This notion of national unity had not been a slogan to conjure with for previous generations. For one thing, most English Canadians felt during the nineteenth century that they were citizens of the British Empire as much as they were Canadians. That belief had led them joyfully into the First World War and to 60,000 war dead between 1914 and 1918. It had led them into national division as well, curiously enough in the name of homogeneity and uniformity, as expressed in the suppression of French-language schools in the West and Ontario in the years before the war.

The outbreak and the conduct of the First World War had made unfashionable, in English Canada, the politics of compromise that at the time were symbolized by the veteran Liberal politician and former prime minister, Sir Wilfrid Laurier. Laurier had, however, only been the latest compromising politician to head Canada, and to perch uneasily on top of Canada's contradictions and differences. But Laurier had been defeated, and the English-speaking majority in Canada had had its way. Mackenzie King had taken note of what had happened, and he was determined not to let it happen again.

Michael Bliss, author of a best-selling book on Canada's prime ministers, has discussed the function of compromise in the Canadian political tradition. He notes that the Conservatives, who had pioneered English-French political partnerships at the time of Confederation, failed to recreate the technique in the twentieth century:

BLISS: The tradition of compromise with Quebec was raised to perfection by Liberals, first Laurier and then King. The Conservatives had a tendency to flounder about, because they could never recreate that partnership, maybe because they could never find a George-Étienne Cartier. And for John A. Macdonald, too, it had all come apart on the issue of Louis Riel and what to do about him. Riel, conscription, and maybe Meech Lake are the times in our history when a compromise could not be found, and somebody got very badly hurt. The genius of King was that he was able to get through one of these zero-sum situations and to come out of it without seriously hurting national unity.

BOTHWELL: 'The genius of King' – these are not words that come easily to mind when considering Canada's tenth prime minister. Mackenzie King lived and was prime minister in interesting times, including two world wars. He was a boy during the Riel affair of 1885, a young man and a civil servant when Laurier attempted to compromise the issue of the status of the French language in the West. And he witnessed conscription in 1917 as an adult politician. King applied what he saw as the lessons of the recent past to his own leadership of Canada.

These events, Riel, conscription, and Meech Lake, had their impact in French Canada, where even the earlier ones are still remembered. To these we could add the Manitoba Schools' controversy, and the obliteration of the French language from official use in the western provinces. Jean Charest, a French-speaking member of the Mulroney government and interim leader of the Progressive Conservative Party of Canada, reflected on the lingering memory of language disputes in Manitoba in an interview late in 1994. His words are a reminder, if not a warning, of the emotions that language, even long-ago language, can evoke:

CHAREST: The irony of it, though, was that we had a reaction in the province of Manitoba. Manitoba decided after Bill 178 to withdraw its support for the Meech Lake accord, because it felt that the government of Quebec was unfairly treating its anglophone minority. You have to appreciate the irony of this stand by the province of Manitoba, whose population was 50 per cent francophone when it came into Confederation, which deliberately, through its laws, blocked the teaching of the French language, and which was forced by the Supreme Court of Canada in the 1980s finally to abide by the conditions by which it entered Confederation and to publish its laws in French. By the time it got around to some redress in the courts, 4 per cent of the population of Manitoba was francophone. Needless to say, the people in Quebec, or the francophones in Quebec, were not impressed by Manitoba's stand.

BOTHWELL: But if French Canadians were resentful and suspicious of English Canadians, especially where the legal and public use of the French language was concerned, English Canadians were suspicious of the French, too. Had not many of the English-language communities of Quebec dwindled and vanished, replacing English majorities in the Eastern Townships with French, at the same time that French-language communities in northern and eastern Ontario were rapidly growing, thanks to the high French-Canadian birthrate? 'La revanche des berceaux,' the revenge of the cradle, was the dream of a few French-Canadian nationalists, but it was a dream doomed to be thwarted, thanks in part to immigration to Canada from abroad, and in part to emigration from Quebec, not so much to the rest of Canada as to the New England states. While Canadians of French descent reached 28.2 per cent of the population in 1931, they were still greatly outnumbered by the British alone, who made up over 50 per cent of the total Canadian population. Fortunately, once the First World War was over, English Canada flew apart into regional, political, and economic factions and could no longer form an effective political majority.

French Canadians were divided among themselves as to what to make of this 'British fact' in Canada – probably as divided as English-speaking Canadians were. On the one hand, Canada's English-speaking majority had shown what it could do during the first war, insisting on prosecuting a just war to the last soldier and, more particularly, to the last recruit. To fill the ranks, the Union government of Sir Robert Borden had resorted to conscription, and much of the manpower sought had come from Quebec. French-speaking Quebec had held back during the first war and had not sent a proportionate share of its young males to enlist. In the wartime election of 1917, Quebec was almost isolated in opposing conscription. Conscription was duly enforced in Quebec at the cost of several minor riots and a considerable waste of time and money, as the government vainly sought conscripts who nevertheless stayed largely outside its reach. Conscription was a failure administratively, and it was certainly a failure politically. Quebec remembered, and, remembering, gave its votes to anybody but the Conservatives. For the generation after 1917, Quebec was the secure bastion of the Liberal Party.

The divisions of the war were painful, and the pain lasted. But the wartime disruption did not break the bounds of the Canadian political system. Some of Laurier's English-speaking followers had crossed the floor to support the Conservatives, and that split had to be healed if the Liberals were to win again. But in 1917 most Liberals had stood by Laurier, and there was no doubt that Laurier's party was still the legitimate one. The 1917 election had been fought by established parties, Conservative and Liberal, and after the war the Liberals were in a position to capitalize on their Conservative rivals' mistakes and to take power. It might not have taken a Mackenzie King to win in the postwar federal election of 1921, but it was Mackenzie King who won.

King was probably Canada's most-educated, if not its best-educated, prime minister, with degrees from the University of Toronto and Harvard, and decades of experience as a civil servant, a labour negotiator, and a junior politician behind him. King had started early to get where he was, which, in 1919, was leader of the Liberal Party. The party's veteran chieftain, Sir Wilfrid Laurier, had died, and his followers were determined not to have as leader anybody who had been unfaithful to Laurier in the bitter 1917 election. Mackenzie King, fortunately for his political future, had run and lost as a Laurier Liberal in that election. With the support of the Quebec delegation, King won the leadership, a seat in parliament, and, in 1921, the prime ministership.

The prime ministership was his because he had won 100 per cent of the parliamentary seats in Quebec, and most of those elsewhere with a significant French-Canadian electorate. This election result may be interpreted as a kind of minority reflex in the face of a threat, or a potential threat, from an aroused English-speaking or British majority. That was a lesson to be derived from the experience of the war and the language disputes in Ontario and the West. Historian Blair Neatby summarizes the minority's impression of the majority:

NEATBY: That's the essence of the nationalist thesis, that French Canada always loses. They do lose when the chips are really down, when it's an issue where English Canadians, or the non-French citizens of this country, feel strongly. Then the majority does impose, does make the decision.

BOTHWELL: Mackenzie King's task was not only to make French-Canadian opinions count in politics again, but to make them appear to count, and to do it without arousing the sleeping demons of English-Canadian political sensitivities. King would do so through his general policies, the habitual caution of his public statements, and his natural hesitation to go too far in any direction. But he recognized that even an experienced and conciliatory English Canadian like himself would need considerable help in managing and forwarding the Liberals' political fortunes in Quebec. This was what Macdonald had done, back in the 1860s, with Sir George-Étienne Cartier.

King selected as his French-Canadian lieutenant Ernest Lapointe, a veteran politician representing Laurier's old constituency in Quebec City. Neatby comments on the role of politicians of the Lapointe stripe:

NEATBY: Politicians generally avoid a discussion of principles because they don't want to divide the society; rather, they want to maintain some kind of social homogeneity and social unity. In Canada, there are strong pressures for this kind of concession and compromise just because French Canada responds differently from the other parts on some issues. For this reason, French Canadians and English Canadians have not seriously debated some of the difficult issues that this country has been associated with. That's why the Liberal Party, which had strong support from both groups, could retain power for so much of the twentieth century.

Mackenzie King had no particular understanding of French Canada; the only thing he understood about French Canada was that it was a minority group that was sensitive and that had to be handled carefully. He didn't know how French Canadians were going to respond; he didn't have an intuitive sense of what French Canadians wanted. So he had to rely on his French lieutenant. Quite often, when he discovered what French Canadians wanted, he was somewhat disturbed; he was, after all, a Presbyterian, and he didn't think that Roman Catholics had minds of their own.

BOTHWELL: But French Canadians certainly had minds of their own – many minds, in fact. In the 1920s, the 1930s, and the 1940s the mainstream followed the politics of compromise, as reinterpreted and reinforced by Mackenzie King and Ernest Lapointe. But there were other voices and other paths. Michael Bliss examines King's relationship with Quebec:

BLISS: King was always sensitive to the concerns of Quebec. Some people thought he was sensitive to a fault. There was a belief, especially on the right wing of the Conservative Party, that King held on to power simply by catering to Quebec. That's not historically the case. King was really a splendid political tightrope walker, who understood that the job of politics is to find as much commonality among interests as you can. One of the tasks of a politician is to heal. And in the 1920s King's role was very much that of a healer.

BOTHWELL: King was fortunate in his political associates. In Ernest Lapointe, who after 1924 was the most important of his Quebec ministers, he had and relied on someone whose judgment of Quebec politics was both accurate and reliable. King consulted Lapointe on every important issue, and when Lapointe showed that he was concerned about some issue – usually in the area of foreign policy – King did his best to satisfy him.

Jack Granatstein, a biographer of Mackenzie King and an expert on what we might call the 'King era,' analyzes King's relations with Lapointe and the French-Canadian Liberals:

GRANATSTEIN: Lapointe had been one of Mackenzie King's supporters when he ran for the leadership in 1919. He was critical in delivering to King the delegate votes from the province of Quebec that put King into power. That meant that Lapointe had a special place in King's heart. To Mackenzie King, the rules for a Quebec lieutenant were fairly clear: Lapointe was in charge of patronage for the province. No one would be appointed who did not please him. He was by no means co-equal with King; there was no doubt that Mackenzie King was the boss, but on anything where Quebec had strong feelings there was a virtual guarantee that Lapointe's concerns would be taken fully into account and, unless the circumstances were extraordinary, Lapointe's concerns would be met. Nothing would be done that Lapointe said would upset Quebec. It was that sort of understanding, for example, that meant that Jewish refugees from Hitler in the 1930s would not be allowed into Canada in any numbers. Mackenzie King, if he had had his own way, would have been somewhat more charitable, but because there was strong reluctance in the province of Quebec, because Lapointe made this very clear to Mackenzie King, then Jewish refugees would not be allowed in.

BOTHWELL: The Liberal Party had a remarkable record in Quebec during this time. Inside the province it won general elections in 1919, 1923, 1927, and 1931. In federal elections Liberals won all but a handful of Quebec's seats in 1921, 1925, and 1926, and forty out of sixty-five seats in 1930, an election that the Conservatives won nationally. The Liberal Party colours traditionally are red, *rouge* in French, and in Quebec at this point it was not uncommon to hear the phrase 'rouge à Québec, rouge à Ottawa.' When the Liberals were in power in both Ottawa and Quebec, the result was a patronage bonanza for their supporters in terms of jobs and contracts. When the Liberals were out of power in one place or the other, the remaining bastion would dole out the necessary jobs to supporters, whether federal or provincial. Patronage is sometimes described as the glue that held the party system together, and the description seems exact. John English comments on how the Liberal Party worked in Quebec:

ENGLISH: In Quebec, there was more separation than in other provinces between federal and provincial Liberals. Nevertheless, there was a definite identification of a person with a party. Membership at one level meant membership at another level. Because of the closeness of the society and the small size of constituencies, everyone knew virtually everyone who was involved in party life. The press was particularly important in this sense of involvement. Literacy rates were high among both anglophones and francophones, and newspapers were widely distributed. These newspapers were, on the whole, party newspapers; they were a major way of creating opinion and, probably more important, strengthening opinion.

BOTHWELL: Liberals in Quebec had plenty of choice: in Quebec City they could read *Le Soleil*, owned by a Liberal senator, and in Montreal *Le Canada* or *La Presse*. Tories, and there were plenty on the English side, could soothe their feelings by reading the Montreal *Gazette*, while nationalistes could read *Le Devoir* or *Action Catholique*. It is fair to say that most of the time you knew in advance what kind of news – if that is the word for it – you were going to be fed and, as an ideological consumer, you paid for your choice.

In the 1920s there were Liberals and Conservatives, and both parties had their federal and provincial wings. The federal wing tended to predominate, and it is probably incorrect even to consider the federal and provincial wings as two separate parties, in Canada as a whole, or in Quebec. In Quebec the Liberals dominated the political establishment.

The Liberals were predominant, but not supreme. And here it becomes necessary to consider the officially non-political sections of Quebec society – those parts that Mackenzie King, that good Presbyterian, did not understand, and that many Protestants inside and outside Quebec deeply suspected. For some observers at the time, and since, the political phenomena of Quebec – parties, government, and the like – were really a kind of camouflage, masking a Catholic alternative state that existed within. This view might seem to be appropriate to English-speaking Protestants, but there have also been those in Quebec who subscribed to it, too. Richard Jones specializes in the history and ideology of the church in Quebec:

JONES: Many of the students of this period of Quebec, in the 1960s and the 1970s, came to the conclusion that clerical values dominated the entire period, almost to the extent that the church was monolithic, that nothing could be decided without the support of the clergy, that the clerical ideology was all-powerful. But a number of more recent books have attempted to show that there was more variety ideologically within Quebec at this time than was hitherto thought to be the case.

BOTHWELL: The Catholic Church was often thought to be the handmaiden of agriculture in Quebec, attempting to keep Québécois on the farm, out of the anglicizing, corrupting cities, and away from the United States. This was supposed to be closely linked to the survival and preservation of the French language, and hence to nationalism. But that is an oversimplification. Here again it is often supposed that there was an alternative point of view that the Quebec establishment concealed from outsiders. But far from the Catholics and the nationalists having a point of view different from the Liberal politicians who ran the government, it turns out that they thought along much the same lines.

JONES: Errol Bouchette, a French-Canadian nationalist at the beginning of the century, is remembered for one slogan in particular: Let us seize hold of industry. What he meant by that was that French Canadians should obtain a larger role in the industrialization of the province. Bouchette was no voice crying in the wilderness. He defended industrialization, the need to industrialize, in his writings, but he was saying the same thing that most of the Liberal politicians in power were saying. Where he held a different point of view was on the issue of French-Canadian participation in the economy. This was a secondary problem for the government. For the government, it was important only to industrialize. Liberal politicians continually declared that industrialization was the only hope for stemming the tide of emigration, the huge number of Quebeckers leaving the province in the late nineteenth and early twentieth centuries, for the United States. The only way to keep them from leaving was to create jobs and the only way to create jobs was through industrialization.

BOTHWELL: There were large sections of Quebec society, and of the Quebec establishment, that were either apart from the state or not especially dependent upon it. This was true in particular of the Catholic clergy, who in the early twentieth century had virtually complete control over Catholic, French-language education and over a variety of social services that were regarded more as aspects of Christian charity than as state responsibilities. Churches, hospitals, schools, charities: all were intimately linked to the Catholic Church, but all were, to some extent, state-supported, by law and by taxes, or by omission. Jones describes the role of the Catholic Church in Quebec, and how this role had changed since the early nineteenth century:

JONES: We often exaggerate, especially before 1850, the importance of the church in Quebec. In the 1840s and the 1850s, however, with the arrival of many congregations from France and with the founding of seminaries and classical colleges throughout Quebec, the church became more important in terms of the number of clergy, both male and female. This trend continued, certainly into the early twentieth century, helped notably by the anti-clericalism that was present in France in the late nineteenth and the early twentieth century.

BOTHWELL: The Catholic Church was a worldwide and multilingual organization, in which competing interests, ethnic and linguistic among them, had to be carefully balanced. To Rome, the linguistic quarrels between Irish Canadians and French Canadians were not a matter of interest at the highest levels of the church. But that was not the feeling at all levels of the church, or among the clergy.

JONES: There are many distinctions to be made here. Among individual clergy, some were more attuned to nationalist themes, while others had little interest in such subjects. Among the lower-level clergy, closer perhaps to the people, there was more sympathy with nationalist currents. This sympathy was present also among some bishops, but certainly not all bishops.

BOTHWELL: The industrialization of Quebec proceeded rapidly in the early part of the twentieth century. As the Liberals intended and expected, the new industries kept French Canadians at home by pulling them into Quebec's cities, large and small. The issue was jobs, not ownership or language, and, while some of these industries were owned or managed by French Canadians, most of them were not. English was the language of business in Canada, and business was symbolized by the powerful English-language corporations, banks, railways, power companies, and textile firms with headquarters in downtown Montreal on the rue St-Jacques, which became for these purposes St James Street.

Symbolic of the situation was the fact that the Quebec minister of finance or provincial treasurer in this period was always an English-speaker. Arthur Silver is a student of French Canada, and he reflects on the symbolism of the treasurer's appointment:

SILVER: This appointment illustrates the economic power of the English business community in Quebec. In the nineteenth century there was general agreement that English was the language of business. French-Canadian businessmen spoke English, not only with English colleagues but with each other. When they were doing business, they gave English names to their French-Canadian companies. There was a sense that English was business, and business was English, and that the great capital accumulations were English-speaking. The biggest banks were English-speaking corporations, while French-speaking banks were much smaller. Consequently, the great stakes in the economy were English-speaking, and having an English-speaking treasurer reassured the large business interests.

BOTHWELL: There is a distinction to be made between the English or British – the English, Irish, and Scots – and the 'immigrants' who came to Montreal in droves at the turn of the century. In the early twentieth century the Jewish community in Montreal became both numerous and prominent, to the extent of dominating a couple of Montreal constituencies, and becoming increasingly prominent in the professions and in business.

At the time and since, commentators have remarked on anti-Semitism in Quebec, especially among French Canadians. In the 1930s, with the rise of Nazism in Europe, this was potentially a volatile problem. Since then, the question of anti-Semitism has been a matter of immense controversy in Quebec because of the light it may – or may not – throw on the nature of Quebec society.

SILVER: One source of anti-Semitism that was much more important in Quebec than elsewhere in Canada was ultramontane Catholicism. There's a significant difference in the religious attitudes of English and French Canadians by the late nineteenth century. In Protestant English Canada, there has been throughout the century a move away from doctrinal religion, a sense that religion is an individual thing, and that all religions are ways to God. That makes it possible for Protestants to tolerate Jews and other non-Protestants. Catholics continued to have a much more doctrinal religion, to believe that there was one truth, one true church, one true religion. Jews therefore remained the enemies of truth and religion, always outsiders and always evil. They were not only the killers of Christ, but they continued to reject the revealed truth and to oppose Christian society.

BOTHWELL: Canada in the 1930s was trapped in the Great Depression, which lasted, with ups and downs, from 1929 to 1939 or 1940. The effect of the

Depression did not make Canadians in general, not just French Canadians, any more welcoming towards immigrants or refugees. Nonetheless, the issue of Quebec anti-Semitism, and the occurrence of far right-wing groups in Quebec in the 1930s, was a matter of concern then and of historical debate now. In the 1930s there was another political departure in Quebec that proved to be of considerable significance.

Down to the 1930s Quebec's politics were dominated by the two great traditional political parties, Liberals and Conservatives. Elsewhere in Canada in the 1910s and 1920s, new political formations had appeared, but these had no special impact inside Quebec. Suddenly, in 1935 and 1936, a new political formation appeared in the province, the Union Nationale, led by a formidable Quebec politician, Maurice Duplessis, and in 1936 it defeated the provincial Liberals and took power.

Duplessis himself came from politically orthodox roots. He was elected leader of the provincial Conservatives in 1933, and on his election sent loyal greetings to the national Conservative leader of the day, Prime Minister R.B. Bennett. When Duplessis became leader, the Liberal government in Quebec City under Louis-Alexandre Taschereau and its predecessors had been in power since 1897, and they looked as if they would stay there forever. The provincial Conservatives were feeble and divided, and had the image of the party of English Montreal business. As Richard Jones explains:

JONES: Quebec was in the midst of the Depression. The federal Conservative Party was itself in a serious condition. Bennett was becoming an increasingly unpopular leader, and there was nothing to be gained by strengthening links with the federal Conservative Party. Duplessis was able to profit from a certain number of political circumstances that occurred during the period. There was considerable dissatisfaction within the provincial Liberal Party. Some younger Liberals were unhappy with the corruption of the provincial Liberal Party, with its seeming inability to change, and were ready to look at any possibility of getting rid of the regime in power, even if the solution might be a marriage of convenience. For Duplessis the same possibility appeared attractive – to join forces with the Conservatives and the many Liberals who were dissatisfied with the Taschereau regime. Moreover, a number of nationalists had more reason to see Duplessis favourably than the Liberals. The Liberals had been at war with the provincial nationalists for many years, and if some kind of coalition could be arranged with these three elements – the provincial Conservatives, dissatisfied Liberals, and some of the nationalists – there might be something to be gained.

BOTHWELL: Maurice Duplessis proved to be a brilliant political leader and a first-class parliamentarian. Using his considerable political and oratorical skills, he divided and discredited the provincial Liberal government, forcing it to call an election in August 1936. Uniting Conservatives, dissident Liberals, and nationalists in an organization called the Union Nationale – which had a clear French-Canadian connotation – he swept to power. He then digested the dissident Liberals' and the nationalists' political strength and abandoned their former leaders.

Jones describes how the election of the Union Nationale, a purely Quebec party, marked a significant break in Canada's political history:

JONES: It was the first party to constitute itself autonomously as a provincial party. It certainly wasn't the last: the next example is the Parti Québécois after 1968.

BOTHWELL: Duplessis remained in power from 1936 to 1939, a period increasingly dominated in Canada, and especially in Quebec, by fears about foreign policy. The rise of fascism in Europe and the menace of Hitler's Germany suggested to many Canadians that war might not be far off. And war, as 1917 seemed to prove, meant conscription. Conscription, in turn, symbolized the subordination of French Canadians to the English majority and the division of Canada. Mackenzie King's policy of national unity was in danger, just at a time when he could not rely on the provincial government in Quebec to keep matters calm. On the contrary: Duplessis was making constant political points by attacking Ottawa, King, and the centralizing Liberals. Jack Granatstein explains how King and Lapointe viewed the rest of the world and how they handled this potentially explosive situation:

GRANATSTEIN: There is no doubt that Lapointe, as a French Canadian, had more concern with Canada directly than he did with the affairs of the world. There is no doubt that Mackenzie King was more imperial-minded than Lapointe. But Lapointe clearly recognized that Canada was part of the British Empire, that Canada was made up of French- and English-speakers with very different attitudes and views, and that if there was to be peace at home, there had to be a recognition on the part of French Canada's responsible leaders that you could not expect English Canada to stay out of the war.

BOTHWELL: It was prudent to do something to prepare for a possible or probable war, and from 1936 on Mackenzie King slowly but steadily increased Canada's defence budget. King once again managed affairs in conjunction with Ernest Lapointe.

GRANATSTEIN: It's clear that Mackenzie King built up Canadian defences in preparation for the war that was coming. The Quebec caucus in the Liberal Party wasn't cheering for big budgets for defence, nor in truth were the English-speaking Liberals. Still, Mackenzie King built up the defences slowly and, as near as one can tell, he had the support of Lapointe. There was an understanding between the two that they would play good cop, bad cop on occasion as Canada moved closer to war. One day King would say that the idea that Canada should send troops to Europe every twenty-five years was insane. The next day Lapointe would say that should bombs fall on London, Canadians would rally to the defence of the empire. They seemed to play a carefully orchestrated game where King sounded isolationist and Lapointe sounded bellicose on one occasion, and then they would switch around on the next. The net effect was to move Canada into a position where Mackenzie King wanted it, and where Lapointe probably wanted it – where Canada would of its own accord decide to enter a war if and when Britain was involved.

BOTHWELL: When Germany invaded Poland in September 1939 and Britain and France declared war on Germany, Canada went to war, too. Within days, Canada had promised to send troops to Europe for the second time in twenty-five years. But this time, King and Lapointe promised, and the Conservatives promised, too, there would be no conscription.

Their policy was soon tested, and from an unexpected source. In October 1939 Premier Duplessis of Quebec called a snap provincial election. Duplessis's motives have frequently been discussed. At the time he said that he wanted to get a mandate to limit Quebec's participation in the war. Others, also at the time, suggested that he had so mismanaged the financial affairs of the province that he was grasping at any straw, any fiction, to save his government and get it re-elected. Attacking Ottawa was the best way to do it.

In any case, Lapointe and the other Quebec ministers in Ottawa concluded that this was a challenge they could not refuse. Very much against the wishes of Mackenzie King, Lapointe and the other Quebec ministers plunged into the Quebec election, telling Quebeckers they would resign if Duplessis won and their own role in Ottawa was, in effect, repudiated. Then let Quebec deal with English Canada without the mediating effect of a strong Quebec delegation in the federal cabinet.

Duplessis lost, and Lapointe – together with the Liberal leader in Quebec, Adélard Godbout – won. There would be no contest from Quebec's provincial government to Mackenzie King's conduct of the war. And when, in March 1940, King won a crushing victory in a federal election, demolishing his Conservative and socialist opposition, it seemed that there would be no contest from English Canada either.

That situation did not last, mostly because the war went badly for the Allies and for Canada. In April, May, and June 1940 Germany conquered most of Western Europe, and France fell to Hitler's armies. Suddenly Great Britain and its empire were on their own. Next to Britain, Canada was now the principal ally in the fight against Hitler. Granatstein discusses the effects of these events:

GRANATSTEIN: All of a sudden Britain was in danger of defeat. Canada was exposed to the possibility, potentially, of an invasion from overseas, and the demands in English Canada for greater commitment to the war effort rose to a crescendo. In the summer of 1940 Mackenzie King passed through parliament the National Resources Mobilization Act, which was ostensibly an attempt to mobilize Canada's resources, but was primarily a licence to authorize conscription for home defence. In Quebec the act was greeted without too much concern. There was only one major impediment, Mayor Camillien Houde of Montreal, but he was swept off to jail with amazing speed and passed over without a whimper. So Quebec succumbed fairly easily to the first bite of the cherry of conscription, and it was a long time before home-defence conscription turned into something more menacing.

BOTHWELL: The King government did what it could to encourage French-Canadian participation in the war. Recruiting was encouraged, in the face of some public sentiment in Quebec that favoured the right-wing and ultra-Catholic Pétain government in France, which collaborated with the Germans. Opinion in Quebec did not on the whole favour the Free French, the followers of General Charles de Gaulle, who carried on resistance to the Germans from Britain and from the French colonial empire. But the King government kept the lid on the home front, despite what appear to have been deep suspicions and reservations on the part of many French-speaking Quebeckers about the nature of the war, King's conduct of it, and even the justice of the Allied cause. Was it not true, some asked, that French Canadians were being asked to die first, and were deliberately being put in harm's way? When Lapointe died in November 1941, a rumour circulated in Quebec that he had in fact been murdered, and his murderer hanged secretly in the presence of Mackenzie King. But, for the most part, French Canadians with reservations about the war kept quiet, certainly in public.

Nevertheless, many French Canadians joined up. Jean Fournier, who rose to the rank of lieutenant-colonel during the war, describes his experience:

FOURNIER: I was already in the militia and had been an instructor in gunnery at Petawawa all the summer of 1939. I joined up right away in September, but my peacetime battery was not being mobilized. I accepted the position of intelligence officer of a medium artillery regiment. I was the only French-speaking Canadian officer in the regiment, out of thirty-five officers. So I went overseas.

There was this phony war for a while, and I was sent on several courses in the United Kingdom, including, at one stage, the army staff course. Then, having had this staff college experience, I returned to Canada in 1943 to become a brigade major of an infantry training brigade group, which was bilingual in that two of the infantry regiments were French-speaking from Quebec, and one, the Halifax Rifles, was the English component.

We normally worked in English, but when I went around to supervise the training of French regiments, everything was in French from beginning to end.

BOTHWELL: A home-defence army was raised and, after Japan entered the war in December 1941, with its attack on Pearl Harbor, much of this army was stationed in British Columbia to guard against a Japanese invasion. That invasion never came, and in 1942, 1943, and 1944 Canada's main military emphasis was in Europe – at Dieppe, in Sicily and Italy, and in 1944 in the Normandy invasion, in which English- and French-Canadian units both played a part.

Canada's war effort was on a very large scale for a country whose population was then about twelve million. There were 250,000 in the air force, which had not existed in the First World War, more than 100,000 in the navy, and 750,000 in the army. Those soldiers who went overseas went as volunteers, not conscripts, while the non-volunteers, the so-called zombie

army, could not be sent overseas without explicitly volunteering. Jack
Granatstein explains:

GRANATSTEIN: This level of commitment could not be sustained without
conscription. Ultimately, we had to resort to conscription.

BOTHWELL: Once Canadian infantry began to suffer high casualties in Italy
and France in 1943 and 1944, there was soon a manpower crisis. The crisis
was in the infantry, whose casualties were unexpectedly high, while casualties in the rest of the army were unexpectedly low. The only source of
trained infantry was back in Canada, in the conscript army. The minister of
national defence, J.L. Ralston, demanded that the reinforcements be sent.

GRANATSTEIN: Canadians forget that the casualties in the Second World War
were every bit as high in terms of infantry losses, and higher in some cases,
than they had been in the First World War. In the first war, Canadian troops
were in action for three and a half years, from early 1915 until November
1918; in the Second World War the Canadian Army was in action in Italy
from July 1943 to the end of the war, and for less than a year in northwestern
Europe, from D-Day until the surrender of Germany in May 1945. In that
period, we sustained some 17,000 fatal casualties, and we simply could not
provide the reinforcements for the infantry who made up the great bulk of
those casualties, given the system we had set up on the best advice of the day.

BOTHWELL: Meanwhile, in 1942, Mackenzie King staged a plebiscite in which
he asked the Canadian people to release him from his pledge not to send
conscripts overseas. The National Resources Mobilization Act of 1940 was
duly amended, but no conscripts went. 'Not necessarily conscription' King
said, 'but conscription if necessary.' What did he mean?

GRANATSTEIN: The promises that had been made to Quebec in 1939 and
1940 were seen initially to have been broken in the plebiscite of 1942 when
Mackenzie King, pressed by the Conservatives, felt obliged to ask the Canadian people as a whole to relieve him of the promises made to the province
of Quebec. The Canadian people as a whole said yes, he could be released.
The problem was in Quebec, where probably 90 per cent of the French
Canadians voting said no. Quebec thought that was the ultimate betrayal.
Mackenzie King, however, had delayed the inevitable for some time, by say-
ing in his famous phrase, 'not necessarily conscription but conscription if

necessary.' In fact, that was a precise statement of his policy. He had the right after the plebiscite to put in conscription, but he wouldn't do it, unless it was necessary. What did 'necessary' mean? In the eyes of Colonel Ralston, the minister of national defence, and most of English Canada, 'necessary' meant 'necessary to reinforce the troops at the front.' In the eyes of Mackenzie King and in the eyes of Quebec, 'necessary' meant 'necessary to win the war.' In the fall of 1944 the war was won, or so it seemed. The Nazis were basically beaten, and it was simply a matter of time. Were we now to tear the country apart yet again, as in 1917, when the war was won? In November 1944 Ralston and company said yes; Mackenzie King and company said no. Initially it looked as if King was going to win. Ralston resigned from the cabinet, or was thrown out – you can take your pick – and was replaced by General Andrew McNaughton, who had commanded the Canadian troops in England for the first four years of the war. McNaughton was against conscription, but it didn't take long – three weeks literally – before McNaughton discovered that the troops could not be found, that volunteer enlistments had effectively dried up, and that the only source of trained reinforcements was among the National Resources Mobilization Army home defence troops, among the 'zombies' as they were called in English Canada. There's a popular misconception in Canada that all those zombies were French Canadians. In fact, there were about 35 per cent: just a shade above the percentage of French Canadians in the overall population.

In the end, the reinforcement shortage overseas, which was very real in October and November after the D-Day battles, the Normandy battles, and the Scheldt battles, tended to dry up. Why? Because the Canadian Army was, through the fortunes of war, more or less out of action for a couple of months. The Canadian corps that was fighting in Italy was moved to Northwest Europe to join up with the rest of the Canadian Army and, as a result, was out of action for a few weeks. Those two respites allowed the infantry reinforcements who were in the pipeline to finish their training, to get sent overseas, and to be integrated into units. So, in fact, the conscription crisis, through chance, was not a very real one. Only about 2500 home defence conscripts made it to the front lines in northwest Europe by the end of the war.

We're also facing a moral question here, and moral questions are always hard to consider. Mackenzie King took the view that it was a sin to divide the country, as conscription could and would and did, with the war won.

Colonel Ralston and the soldiers overseas took the view that if you send men into action, you have a moral obligation to reinforce them; the simple truth is that if you have an under-strength unit going into an attack, it will take more casualties than will a full-strength unit. What you have, then, is two equal and competing moralities. Do we tear up the country when the war is already won? Can we fail to reinforce the men that we have put in harm's way by not giving them the reinforcements they need? I don't know which one is right. That's a change from where I was twenty years ago when I first wrote on conscription, when I came down flatly on the side of Mackenzie King and argued that the army had been simply foolish in pushing for conscription. I've since concluded that to send men into action, where they must risk their lives, without the reinforcements they need to do their job, is immoral, and you can't do it. And it seems to me that if the only way you can reinforce them is with conscription, then you must have conscription.

BOTHWELL: The war ended in May 1945 in Europe, and the war in the Pacific was over before Canadian troops could be engaged in the battle for Japan. And then the troops came home.

Historian William Eccles was a soldier during the war. He remembers sailing up the St Lawrence to Quebec City on a troopship that fall of 1945:

ECCLES: It was exciting to get into the gulf and to see this country again, to see the land that God gave to Cain, as Cartier put it. The ship hugged the north shore fairly closely, and, as the ship came close to Baie Comeau, the ship's hooter went woof, woof, woof, and the ship slowed down, and we saw people pouring out of the town and down onto the dock, and waving. From then on, all the way up the river, as we approached one village after another, church bells pealed and crowds continued to greet us. It was really quite moving. When the ship reached the Ile d'Orléans, it was sunset and getting dark. The ship went very slowly up to the western tip, and we could see the lights of Quebec, the outline of the Upper Town, and that was a really marvellous sight.

We wondered what was going on, why we were proceeding so slowly. There wasn't a sound, and you could just hear the faint sound of traffic from the shore. Someone near me grumbled that they could have had a band playing for us. No sooner had he said it than two bands broke out, and there were two tug boats, one on each side of the ship, each with a band playing away. As soon as the bands struck up, the cannon on the Citadel began booming out, far more than twenty-one shots, and then fireworks;

the sky just lit up. The ship moved slowly up to Wolfe's Cove and docked. The mayor of Quebec was there, and he began an emotional speech of welcome in halting English. After striving to read a few sentences of prepared text, he gave up, tossed it to one side, and began speaking in very impassioned French. As he was speaking, a soldier was marching up and down the ship on the deck, shouting, 'When does the next train leave for Canada?' I was leaning on the ship's rail. The mayor finally wound down, and someone else began making a speech and telling us about the trains. While he was talking, my attention was caught by graffiti on the cliff face, in large letters, behind the podium: Vive Pétain. That was my return to Canada, and I realized then, when I saw that sign and heard that soldier, that it was probably a troubled country I'd come back to.

BOTHWELL: Pétain was the leader of the collaborationist government in France, the man who had hoped for the defeat of Britain and the democracies in the war. In Quebec, however, he was only one side of the war. There was another side, too – the soldiers of the war, the cheering crowds, and Quebec City's own French-speaking regiment, the Vingt-deuxième or Vandoos. And, in fact, in the victorious outcome of the war, one side was remembered and the other side forgotten.

Canada emerged politically united out of the Second World War. Mackenzie King, prime minister at the beginning, was prime minister at the end. He kept the allegiance of both his English-speaking and his French-speaking followers. He had finally imposed conscription if necessary, in 1944, but French Canadians conceded that King had done everything he could to keep his promise to them, and that nobody else could have done any better.

The Second World War did not end up as divisive as the First. National unity remained alive and even showed signs of flourishing. The war was not fought without internal strain in Canada, and at times even King came close to despair as he struggled to keep together two peoples who were, on this important issue, not really united, or at least out of sync. In 1945 King won a national election, an election in which conscription was not an important issue, and in which the things that united English and French Canadians were stressed, not the things that divided.

The agenda for Canada after 1945 would be a peacetime agenda, an agenda for economic growth and social progress. These were things on which everybody could agree. Or could they?

Chapter 5

The Awakening of Quebec: The Quiet Revolution, 1945-65

'In the country of Quebec nothing changes,' wrote the novelist Louis Hémon. Quebec: old, unchanging Quebec – the stones of Quebec City, the mills and manor houses of the seigneuries, the huge churches thrusting their spires into the pure country air. In the towns and cities, there were the black or brown crocodiles of nuns and priests and seminarians out for a walk, their soutanes swishing along the pavement, marching in long files two by two. There were the nunneries, the parish schools, the hospitals and schools staffed by the religious orders, all signs to outsiders that Quebec was a distinct society – signs disturbing to some, but reassuring to others. Inside the hospitals there were busy maternity wards, as more and more young French Canadians came into the world. They were part of the baby boom, but they were born in the province with the highest birthrate in the country. Quebec may have been a different part of the Canadian family, a growing part, but it was a known commodity. It was comforting, really, that in the bustling, go-ahead country of Canada that emerged after the Second World War there was a bit of old-world charm, different but essentially unthreatening.

In the twenty years after 1945 the bases of Quebec society, as seen from the outside, shifted dramatically. By the mid-1960s Quebec was in an

uproar, as the people of the province began to question the assumptions on
which their apparently placid, unchanging society was founded. And in the
thirty years since then, the change is nothing short of astonishing. In downtown Montreal, a secular university now sits inside the picturesque ruins of
an older church – the ultimate symbolism of a secularizing society. No more
crocodiles of priests and nuns – and no more priests and nuns, or almost.
Vast, nearly empty nunneries and monasteries have only the occasional light
in a room to testify after dark to the dwindling congregations and declining religious vocations. Churches have been turned into bingo halls, religious foundations into public junior colleges. Divorce is flourishing and the
birthrate, dropping.

An earlier generation of French Quebecker, if told what the future
would bring, might have been pardoned for concluding that Quebec had
been taken over by the English, by the Protestants and their irreligious allies.
But if there are fewer Catholics in modern Quebec, there are fewer
Protestants, too, and fewer English Quebeckers, at least of the native-born
variety. In the shrinking English-language areas there is a vista of empty
nests, as children move out and move on, and real estate signs dot the landscape – signs in French, À Vendre, and not in English, For Sale. And that is
another change.

This vista of contemporary Quebec is a startling contrast with the
apparent past, the past that is remembered. Compare the crowded devo-
tional processions and church-dominated cityscapes of Jean-Paul Lemieux
paintings with the skyline of contemporary Montreal, for example. What
Lemieux painted, whether it was desolate landscapes or crowded cities,
existed, certainly; but there was even at the time a paradox. For the paintings were bought, had to be bought, by people he seldom painted – the
Quebec upper or middle class, the English-speaking inhabitants of that
French province, or English-speakers outside.

Lemieux became something to be shared, a common cultural artifact or
symbol – even though his Québécois roots and inspirations cannot be
denied. The sharing is a point worth making, and it applies to more than
fine art, or the arts in general: it applies to economics, politics, and even
demography. In the years after 1945, both French and English Canada were
transformed, changed out of recognition. They were subject to the same
influences, the same pressures, demographic, economic, and political. But
they responded to those pressures at a slightly different rate. English Canada

responded to change in its environment by developing a set of national priorities and institutions different from those in the years around 1945; but in Quebec, authorities replied to the same circumstances by patching together what already existed, even though the forces for change were all around them – were, in fact, already present among the French-speaking population of Quebec.

Quebec's characteristic institutions, such as its church-led social welfare and educational systems, were placed under tremendous pressure by an exploding birthrate after 1945. Much the same thing happened in English Canada. In English Canada, public institutions built new schools, hired new teachers, raised new taxes, and worried about whether the federal government should take the lead in responding to what was obviously a national problem. In Quebec, much energy was taken up wondering how existing institutions, the guardians of French-language survival, could be shored up, or patched up, to meet the crisis.

But this is only one example. French and English Canada shared a common problem, indeed many common problems, as they usually do; but their responses were different. English Canada concentrated its resources and hopes in the national government in Ottawa. Quebec hesitated. Through its government, Quebec society opposed Ottawa's changes, but did little more. Some Quebeckers, impatient with their provincial government, accepted the logic of their English-speaking fellow-citizens, but others did not. Some saw the English as a solution, while others saw them as the cause of the problem, a problem that dated back two hundred years to the Conquest of 1760. In any case, Quebec's response was significantly out of sync with English Canada's; just how out of sync only time would show.

The country of Quebec in fact never stopped changing. Quebec became mostly urban around 1910, though probably most French Canadians did not start living in cities until around 1940. The English started moving out in the 1870s, soon after Confederation. The church, so powerful on the surface, so prestigious, so all-encompassing, had financial feet of clay. Instead of a government and a society dependent on the church, the reality by the 1930s was of a church dependent on the government. As for secularism, Quebec and its people were not hermetically sealed away in an intellectual and social fortress. Quebeckers, like other Canadians and like other North Americans, came and went, not just geographically, but intellectually, too: they entered into many different professions, from science to sociology;

they attended American or British or English-Canadian universities, returning with their advanced degrees and a sceptical attitude towards the myths
of their society. Those myths were never more officially prevalent, or officially subscribed to, than under the conservative and nationalist government of Maurice Duplessis, premier of Quebec from 1944 to 1959. But
Duplessis's conservatism, and his espousal of traditional values, merely
masked change: it did not, and it could not, prevent it.

Jacques Hébert, now a Canadian senator, attended a Jesuit college in
Quebec in the 1930s, and subsequently attended college in Charlottetown,
Prince Edward Island. There was a contrast between his education in
Quebec in 1938 and his experience in Charlottetown a few years later. He
starts with Quebec in the 1930s, where the idea of a separate, independent
Quebec was nothing new:

HÉBERT: I was at college when I was fifteen or sixteen. Separatism was
already there. One of our Jesuit professors was promoting it very openly at
our college. It was not a policy of the whole college, Collège Ste Marie, but
certainly there were a couple of very ardent separatists, and they were trying to arouse our enthusiasm for the separation of Quebec.

Fortunately for me, at least, I was sent by my father to a college in
Prince Edward Island, St Dunstan's College, in Charlottetown, which was an
unusual thing to do, though it was not unusual for French-Canadian parents to want their children to learn English. That was an obvious necessity.
My father did as his own father had done, before 1910, when he was sent to
Charlottetown. I don't know why they chose St Dunstan's College. Possibly
because it was a Catholic college; because my father was raised near a small
village near Rivière de Loup, on the way to the Maritimes; because there was
some link between St Dunstan's and Laval University.

In any case, I was sent there for two years, from the age of sixteen to
eighteen, crucial years in anybody's life. Suddenly I realized that what had
been told me, in Quebec, by my family, by people around, by teachers and
professors, was not true. I realized that the English, as we called anybody
who was not French, who spoke English, were not all rich. We had always
been told that the French were poor and the English were rich because they
had been exploiting us for so long. Certainly, the hundred or so students in
St Dunstan's in those days were not rich people. Most of them were sons of
farmers, and they were not rich at all. Although I was just a middle-class boy

from Quebec, my father was sending me something like a dollar a week, and I was rich; I was really rich compared with the others. Moreover, I thought they were nice people.

We thought we had all the answers and that Quebec was a wonderful place, but in Charlottetown I learned about real freedom. Of course there were some rules in the college, but the students developed true confidence. That was very unusual for me. We could go out; we could go to the cinema, which was almost a sin in Quebec in those days; we could meet with girls; we could go to dances, which was a sin in certain dioceses in Quebec and certainly not encouraged by any college I knew. So I learned about freedom in Charlottetown, and I learned that a lot of things that were told me in Quebec were not true. From that moment on, nationalism of any kind, and certainly separatism, had no appeal for me whatsoever.

BOTHWELL: 'We thought we had all the answers and that Quebec was a wonderful place.' But Jacques Hébert's experience with English Canada was unusual, something only a minority could experience. What Hébert left behind, in the late 1930s, seemed both powerful and oppressive. But if it was, it did not remain so. Lise Bissonnette, editor of *Le Devoir*, grew up in Quebec in the 1950s and 1960s, and to her, the church, and perceptions of the church in society, were an artificial framework:

BISSONNETTE: I'm close to fifty years old, and I remember leaving religion behind when I was nineteen. That was the beginning, the mid-1960s, when a whole generation left religion behind – not everybody, of course – but we're quite typical of the elite of Quebec. We're the first generation to have been widely educated, to have gone to university in huge numbers, to have played a role in the student movement at the time, to have been part of the Quiet Revolution in the 1960s, and almost all of us just left religion behind. Some went back, and some never went back, as is my case. When I look back at it, I wonder why, because it played such a part in our family life. I come from a traditional Quebec family, I'm the sixth of seven children, and my oldest sister is still cloistered in a convent – she was obviously brought up in the religion and she believed in it so strongly that she devoted her life to it. I look at the rest of the family and I can see how deep the religion was, yet at the same time how fragile. People felt the power of the church – it was there and you had to submit to it. But religion was only a framework in which the society was functioning, a rather artificial framework, and it was not deep inside us; it was not very important. It was not a question of faith so much as a question of the larger society that was imposing its values on us. So it went very rapidly; in the course of a few years it was gone. I think that the influence of the church was less deep than people suspected from the outside.

BOTHWELL: Compare Jacques Hébert's first-hand experience with the analysis of the development of thought in Quebec by William Johnson, author of a recent book on Quebec nationalism:

JOHNSON: In the postwar period there was a loss of faith in the ancestral, traditional ideology of French Canadians as being the most fortunate people on Earth with the best institutions of all sorts, living in a kind of paradise. A sense developed that maybe we were wrong when we avoided industry, when we rejected the city, when we rejected liberalism, when we rejected pluralism. With the Quiet Revolution we accepted that we were wrong, we were behind, we were not foremost in the world, and we needed to catch up with North America, to reform our institutional and our educational institutions.

BOTHWELL: In 1939 or 1940 Hébert had discovered the rest of Canada and, perhaps, the rest of North America. He was not alone. It was a discovery shared by tens of thousands of young Quebeckers in the 1930s and the 1940s, as they moved away from the farm and the village, crowded into cities for war-production jobs, joined the army, or went outside French-Canadian institutions to get a different education. Arthur Tremblay, a former deputy minister of education and Canadian senator, recalls his educational experience:

TREMBLAY: I was a teacher at Laval for eighteen years before 1960; I started in 1942. I was teaching education, the sociology of education, the psychology of intelligence, things of that kind, and, at one point, it must have been quite early, before the 1950s anyway, the kind of studies I was doing, looking at the educational situation in Quebec, made me feel that there was very much work to do. And so I started doing research, descriptive research, not very complicated research, just factual research on the school system in Quebec.

BOTHWELL: There were others, too. Pierre Elliott Trudeau left the University of Montreal for Harvard, and then the London School of Economics and the Sorbonne in Paris. Jacques Parizeau attended the London School of

Economics. Paul Gérin-Lajoie left Quebec for Oxford. A prosperous French-speaking elite could easily afford to send its children abroad to finish their education, or the children could earn their way through scholarships. And this group does not count young French-speakers at English-Canadian universities, such as McGill or the University of Toronto, attended by Laurier Lapierre or Jacques Monet, who became prominent Canadian historians. Another historian, Michael Behiels, comments on how well prepared French-Canadian society was to meet modern challenges:

BEHIELS: The majority of the population of Quebec was urban by the 1920s, though the majority of the French-speaking population of the province was not urban until 1941. It is really the war that accentuated that process of urbanization among the francophone population. By the 1950s the francophone society had to come to grips, in a psychological sense, with the fact that it was now an urban society. For many of them, the move was first to the small towns and villages, and then to Montreal, as they gained the skills required to go into the larger metropolitan Montreal job market. By 1960 the francophone part of Quebec society had come to resemble the rest of the country, in terms of demography and the urban/rural split. Institutionally, Quebec was quite unprepared to meet that sudden onslaught of urbanization among the francophones. Its institutions were still very much nineteenth-century institutions, run for the most part by the Catholic Church. The church itself was totally unprepared and ill-equipped, underfinanced and understaffed, to provide the urban infrastructure required for this rapidly urbanizing francophone population. The Duplessis government did not seem to comprehend what had happened, though the church understood and was pleading throughout the 1940s and 1950s for more government help to build convents, colleges, schools, hospitals, and everything that was required to provide the social and educational services it had been providing since the days of New France.

BOTHWELL: The Catholic Church, whose institutions dotted the province and whose leadership appeared to set the moral, social, and intellectual tone of French-Canadian society, was not what it seemed. True, the church seemed to demonstrate its prominent and essential position when it received large cheques for its activities from the government. This payment was taken to be a symbol of power, when in fact it was a sign of weakness. To underline the obvious, the church needed those cheques, because it could not raise the money for itself. The church understood the situation for what it was: a sign of permanent, not temporary, decline.

BEHIELS: Duplessis obliged on occasion, handing both the male and the female religious orders cheques now and then, making a big political scene about it, and, in effect, lording it over the Catholic Church. In a sense he was saying that the bishops and the cardinals ate out of his hand, which, in effect, by 1955 they did; they were increasingly dependent on the state to finance the growth and the expansion of their operations.

BOTHWELL: The vision of the church eating out of Duplessis's hand is now the accepted version of the church's role in Quebec. But according to historian Richard Jones, the image is sometimes too vivid, too good to be true:

JONES: I remember the film on Duplessis by Denys Arcand, in which he showed what has become the commonly accepted view of the relations between Duplessis and the church. We see the bishop of Sherbrooke, who wanted an audience with Duplessis in order to ask some favour. He is seated in the antechamber, and he sits there for hours and hours. Finally, Duplessis goes out by a back door, and that is that. You have the image of the bishops eating out of Duplessis's hands. This image is to a certain extent mythical. I don't recall ever having seen Cardinal Léger eat from Duplessis's hands. He was far more independent of the provincial government than many of the more rural bishops; but in the 1940s and 1950s Quebec was changing. I don't think that the vision of the church being a hollow shell in this period is fair. What was happening was that voters, the common people, wanted more and more social services; the demand for education was becoming greater and greater. This was the era in which the baby boomers were knocking at the doors of the primary schools, and a little later of the secondary schools. There was a need for tremendous spending in the area of social services and in the field of education. And it was obvious that the church had neither the financial nor the human resources necessary to meet those new demands. In the early 1960s Quebec experienced no wave of anti-clericalism as you saw in France in the early 1920s and in the late nineteenth century. In many cases, the clergy willingly accepted state assistance because there was no other choice. There was no way around the financial problems that were increasingly present at this time.

BOTHWELL: A hermetically sealed society might have been able to fight off the challenge of modernization posed by the English-speaking North American world. But Quebec was not, and never had been, walled away from the rest of North America, as Jacques Hébert's experience indicates. And Quebec society suffered by the comparison. The Quiet Revolution is the phrase that is used to describe what occurred in Quebec after 1960. In political terms that is probably exact: down to 1959 or 1960 Quebec was governed through a deeply conservative political system that produced regular majorities for a premier, Maurice Duplessis, who proclaimed the superiority and the desirability of doing things the old way, preserving the old values of Quebec's Catholic society. On the political surface, then, little changed. But in terms of social transformations and mental transformations, the years should be backdated to the 1950s and even the 1940s, to the Second World War. The war and later the explanations and descriptions of the war that appeared in French-Canadian novels and plays gave French Canadians a very different picture of their society. It was a society in which all the traditional defences against the English, and the English language, were suddenly irrelevant or powerless. But that did not make the need for such defences any less pressing. William Johnson has written extensively on Quebec and its ideologies, and he comments on how French-speaking Quebeckers' self-image changed in the 1940s:

JOHNSON: By the Second World War there was general recognition that French Canadians in fact were not on the land, but were in the city. Novels published by Gabrielle Roy, Roger Lemelin, and others portray, instead of a glorious farm community and a kind of paradise, the horror of the city. The French Canadians in the city are poor. The Anglos live up the mountain in West-mount, where it is spacious and they're rich, and they have servants and there are trees. Below, you have St-Henri, the slum where French Canadians live and are desperately trying to struggle out. So all of a sudden you have the intellectual problem of Quebec: How is it we have the truth, we have the most perfect institutions on Earth, the best educational system, we are faithful to the perennial philosophy, and yet people are poor in the city, they are un-equipped, they have less education, and the Anglos are the wealthier ones?

BOTHWELL: As usual, there were explanations, explanations that were rooted in Quebec tradition. Johnson describes a historical explanation that was offered by the 'School of Montreal' historians:

JOHNSON: A whole school of historians based in Montreal kept saying that they knew what had happened. During the recent occupation of France, the Nazis had simply stripped the land of all its wealth and transferred it to Germany. A similar kind of occupation was happening in Quebec. The defining moment of French-Canadian history was the Conquest. Thereafter, this poor child of a nation was brutally removed from its mother and given cruel foster parents, the Anglos. Of course, the Anglos behave in their own interests. They have their capital in Ottawa, and the capital of French Canadians is in Quebec, and that's why Quebec is poor, because of the trauma of the Conquest and the perennial minority situation in which the province exists. The only solution to the poverty of French Canadians lies in this impossible dream for the foreseeable future of independence.

BOTHWELL: The Anglos – which by the way is a term imported from the United States in the 1970s or 1980s – continued to represent an ever-present threat, not merely of subjugation but of assimilation. Ron Graham, who recently wrote a book about his French-English family, tackles the subject of assimilation:

GRAHAM: What I found in my own case was that my maternal grandfather was French Canadian. He had assimilated by marrying an Irish-Canadian woman – not an uncommon situation in Quebec because of the shared Catholicism – and he had basically given up his French language. He worked in an English environment. When he died I was ten, and I can't remember ever hearing him speak French. He wanted his children, my mother and my uncle and my aunt, to grow up in English without French accents, because he saw that was their only chance in those days of getting ahead. It was a conscious decision. To a French-Canadian nationalist, my grandfather would have been a *vendu*, a sell-out, almost a traitor, in the same way that Pierre Trudeau has been called a traitor because his mother was a Scottish-Canadian. The conflicts in my family between whether you are *pure laine*, pure francophone, pure French Canadian, meant that someone like my grandfather was excluded, and certainly someone like my mother, even though she was half French, was excluded. I was so excluded, being only a quarter French, that it took me until I was forty to start paying attention to that French quarter.

BOTHWELL: On the surface, Quebec in the 1950s was placid. English and French coexisted. There was little if any violence. The political system functioned pretty much as it always had. Even nationalist politicians like Maurice Duplessis functioned inside traditional notions of cooperation between the English and the French.

But in the 1950s, as in the 1940s and 1930s, there were other currents, such as the nationalist, separatist teachers Jacques Hébert remembers from his early education, or the idea that French-Canadian society had become deformed because of the English conquest and the two hundred years of English occupation that had followed since then. Ron Graham comments on William Johnson's idea that anglophobia is a predominant part of French-Canadian nationalist idealogy:

GRAHAM: There is truth to Johnson's argument, and he documents it quite thoroughly, though the issue is more complicated than he allows. But there's no doubt that the English were seen in mythic terms as propagated by people like Abbé Groulx and even now Michel Tremblay and other artists as the bad guy, and this caused a characterization of the English that's very hard to get past. It may be easier now with the new generation, but certainly the stereotype held for my grandfather's generation, around the turn of the century, when the Catholic Church held such sway. The English were the devils not because they were English-speaking, but because they weren't Roman Catholic. And so, particularly with the control that the church held over the school system, it meant that young francophones growing up in Quebec had an image of *les anglais* as apostates, as the devil incarnate, because they weren't Roman Catholic. You add on to that the class differences that really developed only with depressions. When you add the class element to the religious and linguistic element, then you have this idea of the English as devil.

BOTHWELL: But by the 1950s the English were becoming an increasingly familiar devil. Some observers in English Canada – though not many – took note of the rising standard of education in the province, of the increasing numbers of young French Canadians with advanced education in English-language institutions, and drew the conclusion that harmony was just around the corner. The big differences were diminishing – the customary and traditional differences emphasized by aging nationalists like Duplessis or symbolized by the church. Young French Canadians were returning home clutching their graduate degrees, just like young English Canadians, and from the same American or British universities.

This is a point worth underlining. English-Canadian and French-Canadian societies were passing through much the same demographic development – the baby boom of the 1940s and 1950s. They confronted much the same economic developments – the generalized prosperity of the postwar years. They were bombarded by many of the same ideas imported from abroad, about how best to cope with economic growth while maintaining and developing a cushion of social security. If these ideas failed to percolate directly, they were brought home by young Canadian PhDs, newly minted from the London School of Economics, Stanford, Harvard, or the Sciences Politiques in Paris.

And while these postwar trends should be examined as a separate and interesting phenomenon, it is not wise to lose sight of the fact that, over time, French Canadians and English Canadians had responded to the other developments in North America in much the same way. And if they had to adapt to circumstance by moving (or not moving) themselves and changing their language, they did. Many French Canadians – and some English Canadians on the other side – had decided over the years that the differences between English and French were not worth fighting about, and had made a personal decision to abandon language and culture, if not family, as Ron Graham's grandfather did. And to many of those who crossed the cultural or linguistic line, the differences were not so great anyway.

The real difference seemed to be that, as of the 1950s, the institutions of English Quebec still worked, while those of French Quebec were coming under increasing strain. If French Canadians in Quebec were conscious of a crisis, English Canadians living in the same city of Montreal, or in its prosperous suburb of Westmount, or further west on Montreal Island, were not. Michael Behiels describes the situation of English Quebeckers after the Second World War:

BEHIELS: The English-speaking institutions that had been put in place throughout the nineteenth century had, as time went along, modernized and expanded. They had a good tax base, and they had all the educational, social, health, and other services they required. While they were still operated privately, for the most part, they had the skills and the necessary staff to provide all the services that a modern society required.

Similarly, with the Italian and Jewish immigrants in Montreal, and many of the other groups from central and eastern Europe, they established their own institutions very quickly, raised money within their own communities, and were able to provide their communities with the full range of social/economic/cultural institutions they required. So, by the 1950s, Montreal was a very cosmopolitan city made up of a whole series of solitudes working quite well within themselves and having very little to do with one another – and that's really the way the Duplessis government liked it. There was little there for the state to get involved with, little need to raise taxes, and Duplessis said that this was the best kind of society we could have. The private sector and non-profit organizations looked after many of the needs of the citizens, and Duplessis was against any demand to modernize the state and to take over many of those services in the health, social welfare, and educational fields.

BOTHWELL: Historian Daniel Salée argues that the political institutions and political cultures of English- and French-Canadian societies are so similar as to be essentially the same:

SALÉE: I know that I won't win many brownie points with my nationalist colleagues, but, in my view, there is very little difference between the two societies in terms of the 'cultural code,' the basic norms. That's probably why we have been able to live together for so long without choking each other. Today, it's a different ball game. The reason why we can't seem to see eye to eye on many things is because we're so similar that we're trying to emphasize the differences we have. We're trying to emphasize those differences so they will justify or vindicate certain demands that we have about the political system. I'm certainly speaking from the point of view of Quebec nationalists.

BOTHWELL: English and French Canadians shared the same country, shared the same economy, but in the 1950s they still did not realize that they might share the same space, whether geographically or intellectually. True, there were attempts, particularly in Montreal, to bridge the gap, attempts especially associated with André Laurendeau, editor of the nationalist newspaper *Le Devoir*. Behiels comments on the contact between French-Canadian academics and intellectuals and their English-Canadian, American, and European counterparts:

BEHIELS: Contact began in the 1930s, though the war slowed it down. André Laurendeau, for example, made contacts with people at McGill and was able to form some sort of consensus over a certain number of issues, but the fight over conscription and the development of the Canadian social welfare state during and after the Second World War really drove the English-speaking and French-speaking communities apart. The vast majority of the English-speaking community leaders supported the development of the Canadian social welfare state, whereas the French-Canadian nationalists, the traditional nationalists, and the new nationalists around *Action nationale* were critical of the development of the social welfare state in Ottawa. They saw it as being run by and for the English-speaking majority of the country, reflecting their values, concerns, and aspirations, and this put them in a Catch-22 situation as to what a Quebec society should do. The traditional nationalists wanted Quebec to be left out of that development, to continue with its existing institutions, with the church, not the state, in charge of education, social welfare, and health. Meanwhile, the English-language community of British origin, and the new immigrants, were becoming increasingly hard-pressed to provide the full range of services that their members expected in a modern society. So they were in favour of the development of the federal social welfare state. Consequently, there was a deepening of the cleavage between the two communities, the English-speaking and French-speaking communities of Quebec, over the emergence of the social welfare state after the Second World War, and that cleavage would, in fact, grow over time and would never go away.

BOTHWELL: The cleavage was in a curious way symbolized by an entity that was, in theory, shared, common property – the federal government in Ottawa.

As far as Ottawa was concerned, the term government was, in the 1940s and 1950s, coming to have a different meaning. Traditionally, government meant the government of the day, a gaggle of politicians elected for the moment to manage the affairs of the country. Such a government needed servants, and these workers were members of the party in power who would vanish after the next election.

But there were two traditions at work in Canadian government, and my description covers only one. The other tradition, just as old and possibly more respectable, argues that government belongs to all the people, and not just to the supporters of the government. It is not enough to wait for the great wheel of politics and electoral alternation to set to work. The nation deserves something better than that – well-trained civil servants, expert at their jobs, responding impartially to whoever pulls the political levers.

When Canada passed through the great crises of the two world wars and the great economic depression of the 1930s, these events created political strains. They also, and just as importantly, caused an alteration not merely in the way Canadians looked at their governments, but also in the governments themselves.

Historian Doug Owram has investigated the ways Canadians have thought about their country and its government. In his opinion, the concept changed fundamentally in the twentieth century, in part because societies, ideologies, and governments around the world changed. He begins with the First World War:

OWRAM: The years 1914-18 wrought tremendous changes in society and in the role of government. To begin with, people had seen just how important and powerful government could be, and had been, for that short period of time. But they'd also seen it put to use for ends that weren't always satisfactory. Government had extreme powers under the War Measures Act; it was authoritarian in many of its actions. The second thing that was happening was that, from the late nineteenth century through the 1920s, there had been considerable industrialization and urbanization in Canada. In 1921, 50 per cent of Canada was urban. This statistic included a lot of small towns, but there was a feeling that an urban industrial society required different types of government from a small-town rural society. A lot of this sense of change was a myth, but it reflected the notions of unemployment, business cycles, welfare, crime, and other characteristics of the urban, industrial life. The third change was nationalism. Canadians came out of the First World War with a certain ambivalence towards the empire. They entered the war, at least in English Canada, enthusiastic about the empire, believing that they were British and that the future was somehow tied to the British Empire. The war had cost them a lot in terms of money and life, and people began to rethink, or elements in Canadian society began to rethink, Canada's role in the world. The war, to use a cliché, made Canadians think of themselves as a nation. There was to be a long transition before they eventually emerged as a nation, until after the Second World War, but, in the interwar years, there was a sense that if Canada was going to be a world power, even a small one, its government had to be competent and efficient. The simple

fact was that the Canadian government, especially the provincial governments, at the time were both small and patronage-based; there were a lot of
petty corruptions and inefficiencies that came from friends appointing
friends, that sort of thing. So, over the next generation of the 1920s and
1930s, intellectuals, professionals, and certain types of managerial groups in
Canada began to look to some sort of efficient government. This was especially important when the Depression hit, because the Depression created
an economic crisis in the country, a crisis that the provinces couldn't man-
ifestly handle. Saskatchewan nearly went bankrupt. Alberta had bonds
repudiated by the international market, and had to be propped up by the
federal government. And that was true across the country, in varying
degrees. So the federal government became more and more the focus, and
yet the federal government didn't have the powers it needed to handle the
welfare situation, to handle the Depression. It simply hadn't got to the stage
where it thought it could manage the economy in a macro sense. It also
didn't have the powers, because of a series of legal decisions emanating
from the British High Court, the Judicial Committee of the Privy Council,
in which provincial rights had been enhanced and dominion rights had been
downgraded. So the federal government of the day sought in a kind of half-
hearted way to redress the balance. The Royal Commission on Dominion-
Provincial Relations (the Rowell-Sirois Commission) is perhaps the most
famous example, the idea being to gather powers for the federal government
so it would have the leverage necessary to handle business cycles like the
Depression. In the course of one generation, then, the federal government
became increasingly the focus for many social and economic initiatives.

BOTHWELL: English and French Canadians shared politics, parliaments, and
traditions. They had shared the same political issues, even if they disagreed
about some of them. But did they share the same government? Mitchell
Sharp, a westerner educated at the London School of Economics, came to
Ottawa during the Second World War to work in the Department of
Finance and eventually to become one of the group of senior civil servants
known to historians as the mandarins. He describes Ottawa in the 1940s,
and whether there was any place for French Canadians in the capital:

SHARP: When I came to Ottawa in 1942 I didn't know very much about the
place. I came from Winnipeg. I guess I could be characterized as a western
WASP. I knew very little about Canadian society and the problems between

French Canadians and English Canadians. We had a small French-Canadian population in Manitoba, and some French Canadians lived across the river in St Boniface, but I really didn't meet them. They weren't a society in the sense that one thinks of that term. When I arrived in Ottawa I didn't think it strange that there were no French Canadians in senior positions in the Department of Finance. The group of people who made the policy in this important department were all English-speaking. There was a good geographical mix; we did have one official from Montreal, but he was English-speaking. In the cabinet, French Canadians traditionally had responsibilities that related to the less important aspects of Canadian economic policy: Public Works, the Post Office, the Secretary of State who looked after cultural activities. The Minister of Justice was almost invariably a French Canadian, though not always from Quebec. From time to time we had a French Canadian prime minister, but on the economic front there were no francophone ministers of any significance. One of the great accomplishments of the Pearson and Trudeau governments was to change all that, and, within the public service, those of us in senior positions invited French-Canadian economists to join the Canadian public service. The great difficulty for them was to leave Quebec and to come to Ottawa. French-Canadian society in Quebec is very much a family-oriented society. It was difficult to persuade economists to come to Ottawa, where it might be a bilingual society at work, but where their wives and families had to accommodate themselves to an anglophone society in which to live. However, we were successful. No longer can French Canadians say that the government of Canada seems to be a government of others, not their government. It's astonishing the changes that have happened.

BOTHWELL: Jean Fournier was recruited out of the army to join the Canadian Department of External Affairs in 1944. He describes his career as a federal civil servant and diplomat:

FOURNIER: I succeeded a French-Canadian colleague in the legal division, and I had many excellent French colleagues who functioned quite well. A lot of them were veterans. In due course, the number of French Canadians in the Department of External Affairs exceeded the number of French Canadians in any government department in Ottawa at the officer level. There was no particular racial or linguistic division in the department. If you want to be in the foreign service, to represent your country abroad, one thing you've got to do is get along with other Canadians, both French and English. If you want to prove you're a diplomat, the least you can do is get along with English Canadians if you're a French Canadian, and vice versa, too.

BOTHWELL: The years after 1945 thus represented an opportunity for people like Jean Fournier to share in the development of Canada, a Canada that was significantly changed from the conservative backwater Mackenzie King had governed. Success in dealing with the divisions of the Second World War, coupled with the greatest and most sustained burst of prosperity in Canadian history between 1945 and 1957, gave English Canadians and some French Canadians the occasion to refashion Canadian institutions. They did this by placing new hopes and new functions in the government in Ottawa.

But not all French Canadians shared in the enthusiasm for a new, prosperous, and united Canada. 'New' and 'united' were dangerous words for a minority society. How new? How united? Were the English Canadians getting too close for comfort? Couldn't Quebec rely on its own resources rather than those of English Canada?

Chapter 6

The Long Division, 1960-8

IN THE EARLY 1960s, the national columnist for *Maclean's* magazine, Blair Fraser, came to Quebec for a visit. There was something happening in Quebec, he understood, but what was it?

A well-connected journalist, Fraser talked to all kinds of Quebeckers, among them the deputy minister of education for the province, Arthur Tremblay. Many years later, Tremblay remembered Fraser's visit, and what he told him:

TREMBLAY: That was in 1963. He met quite a number of people in the Quebec administration, politicians of course, but also civil servants like me. He came to my office and asked, 'What's the meaning of all that? What's the meaning of those things we see happening in Quebec?' My answer was, 'Maybe I'll surprise you – it's no more a question of the flag, it's no more a question of a bilingual dollar, it's no more a question of symbols. What's happening in Quebec now means that we are ready to talk business with you in any language. The question is, are you ready to talk business with us?' He did not publish the exact wording in his article, but he did refer to our meeting and said that he had been impressed by it. And it's still my conviction that that was the real spirit of the Quiet Revolution.

BOTHWELL: The Quiet Revolution – in French, the Révolution Tranquille. The phrase wasn't much in vogue in 1963, and its meaning wasn't exact, then or now. But broadly speaking it meant that great changes were under way in Quebec and that they had occurred without a great deal of fuss, certainly without violence, but even without much bitter confrontation.

And such changes: even Arthur Tremblay's job had not existed a couple of years before. Until 1960, education was the province of the Catholic Church, at least for French-speaking Quebeckers. A ministry of education would have been an intolerable intrusion of the state into daily life; but in a few years the state, the provincial state, was there. Before 1960 business was the domain of the English and their corporations in Montreal – the banks, trust companies, engineering firms, and power companies that defined English Quebec. Yet by 1963 the English power companies were a thing of the past, nationalized and absorbed into the provincially owned electricity utility, Hydro-Québec, where the language of work and management was French, not English. A provincial election had been fought on this issue in 1962 and won – by a different government. For in 1960 a new government had come to power, and the old Union Nationale, in power since 1944, had been rejected.

These developments are usually treated in isolation, as internal to Quebec. Yet they had a substantial impact on Quebec's external context. For as the Quebec government acquired self-confidence and savoir-faire in managing its internal affairs, it became increasingly assertive in its dealings with the outside world – and increasingly unhappy about its place in Canada. These were events that could not reasonably have been anticipated in 1960.

The new government of 1960 was erected on familiar foundations. For one thing, its leader, Jean Lesage, was a known commodity. Lesage came from an old Quebec political family: his uncle had been a Liberal senator and organizer. Jean Lesage had entered the federal House of Commons in 1945 and had become a federal cabinet minister in 1953 – minister of northern affairs in the Liberal government of Louis St-Laurent. The experience had marked Lesage, though not quite in the way many people assumed in 1960.

The 1950s were a great time to be a federal minister; they were a great time for the federal government. Under Louis St-Laurent, the government was still basking in the success of the Canadian war effort during the Second World War. The federal government seemed almost to monopolize the talent of the country, either politically or in the civil service. Canada enjoyed abounding prosperity; the standard of living soared, revenues went up, and jobs were plentiful. The federal Liberals were leading the country towards a social welfare state – cautiously but surely. The constitutional balance in Canada between the federal government and the provinces had tilted, and tilted decisively, as historian Christopher Armstrong describes:

ARMSTRONG: Little by little, we got federal old age pensions, which required a federal constitutional amendment that was eventually agreed to. We had already got unemployment insurance, which was agreed to by the provinces and which produced a constitutional amendment just before the Second World War. Then we got more pensions: contributory pensions, the Canada Pension Plan, and the Quebec Pension Plan. We got medical care and the Canada Assistance Plan. Most of these schemes came in the 1960s, though their origins date back to the 1950s. The process of spending federal money on programs that should, constitutionally, have been under provincial control become the central issue in confrontations between Ottawa and the provinces.

BOTHWELL: From the 1940s through the 1960s, there was a record of steady incursions by the federal government in provincial jurisdiction. Ottawa had the money, it had the experts, and it had the political mandate it needed from the electorate. The English-speaking provinces were unable to resist, over old age pensions in 1951, over hospital insurance in 1957, over the Canada Pension Plan or medicare in the 1960s. And, at first, neither could Quebec. True, Quebec refused federal grants to its universities as an invasion of provincial autonomy; and it refused federal handouts for the Trans-Canada Highway in the 1950s. The result, obvious to any Quebec taxpayer, was that Quebec roads were not as good and its universities were not as strong as those elsewhere in Canada.

The rest of Canada assumed that Quebec would eventually catch up. In the meantime, English Canada would define its own nationalism – admittedly under the sponsorship of a French-Canadian prime minister, Louis St-Laurent, and with a government that included talented young French Canadians, people like Jean Lesage among the politicians, or Marcel Cadieux, a rising star in the Department of External Affairs, among the civil servants.

Canadian nationalism in the 1950s and early 1960s was oriented around Ottawa. The national government, not the provincial governments, was expected to lead the country and define its priorities. In a world threatened by war, a world of international alliances, Canadians naturally looked to the federal government, their national government, for policy direction. It responded with policies for defence, foreign policy, and social and economic affairs, too.

When the federal Liberals, too long in office, were defeated in a federal election in 1957, their Conservative rivals under their new leader, Saskatchewan's John Diefenbaker, promised more of the same. They promised it mostly in English, for Diefenbaker did not speak French, and when he tried his French-speaking listeners usually had difficulty understanding what he could possibly mean. But when Diefenbaker called a snap election in 1958, Quebec rewarded him and his government with fifty House of Commons seats out of seventy-five from the province, joining with other Canadians to found the strongest federal majority government in Canadian history. Diefenbaker and the Conservatives were in for what seemed to be the duration – a very long duration.

Jean Lesage, who had been re-elected a Liberal MP in 1958, saw the direction of events. The Liberals had a new leader in Ottawa, his old friend and colleague, Lester Pearson. Pearson would be in the job for some time. There wasn't much for a simple opposition MP to do, and the provincial leadership in Quebec was vacant. Lesage made the move, and in 1958 became head of the Liberal Party in Quebec. Pearson soldiered on in Ottawa.

So far this is a very traditional story, and even Lesage's victory at the head of the provincial Liberals in Quebec would not seem to make much difference. But there was a difference, a difference both in Ottawa and in Quebec.

In the first place, Diefenbaker's government proved to be politically accident-prone, much weaker than its very strong majority would suggest. By 1960 or 1961 Diefenbaker was on the road to becoming a political casualty, his government distinctly unpopular with wide segments of Canadian society. And those segments included, very importantly, Quebec.

Lowell Murray was a young assistant to Diefenbaker's minister of justice, Davie Fulton, in the early 1960s, and he explains Diefenbaker's problem with Quebec:

MURRAY: Most of Mr Diefenbaker's caucus from Quebec had been recruited by Mr Duplessis's Union Nationale organization in 1957 and 1958. That is not necessarily a criticism of them, and, indeed, some of them were quite promising. Unfortunately, most of Diefenbaker's Quebec ministers were in relatively junior portfolios. Léon Balcer had the most important portfolio; he got to be minister of transport. I think he might have promoted people like Jacques Flynn and Paul Martineau sooner, people who had some promise. But Mr Diefenbaker was always loath to designate anybody as a Quebec lieutenant, or indeed as a regional baron from anywhere. He didn't take kindly to the idea of a deputy prime minister, or someone who is designated as number two; that was his style of leadership. I think the reasons why we lost ground so quickly in Quebec were not really related to the talent in the Quebec caucus, or to divisions in the Quebec caucus, or to problems that they created for Mr Diefenbaker. They really didn't create many problems for him until after he left office. He had the misfortune of being in office at a time when his erstwhile provincial allies, the Union Nationale, were on the way out. Duplessis died, and Paul Sauvé, who might have made a major difference to conservatism in Quebec, died soon after. All this happened at a time when the Quiet Revolution was getting under way.

I don't fault Mr Diefenbaker particularly; he didn't fully understand what was going on in Quebec, but he was not alone in English Canada in that respect. According to his lights, he did things that he thought were positive, such as bilingual cheques and simultaneous translation in the House of Commons and the Senate. It's really extraordinary for me to recall that in 1962, the Créditiste MPs from Quebec were still agitating to have menus in the parliamentary cafeteria posted in both languages. The whole federal government was wall-to-wall English. Mr Diefenbaker's introduction of simultaneous translation was important and long overdue, but he didn't fully grasp what was going on in Quebec.

BOTHWELL: Though many Canadians thought Diefenbaker had a positive knack for bringing trouble on himself, as Murray points out, some of his problems were structural – they were embedded in the institutions that Diefenbaker inherited. He was head of a federal government that, until the 1930s, issued dollar bills only in English, and until the 1960s issued cheques only in English, and where the easiest and most relaxing job in the world was to be a unilingual French-speaking politician. There was no need to speak, no need to exert yourself as long as you were in Ottawa: after all, nobody would understand you, or even pretend to. Quebec was present in Ottawa, but as for representation, that would have to be in English if it was to be felt, or even understood. It was both politicians and civil servants who symbolized Ottawa, but it was the civil servants, really, who gave Ottawa the edge over the provinces. Doug Owram has written extensively about the Ottawa government and its inhabitants, and he comments on the balance between the federal government and the provinces in the 1950s and 1960s:

OWRAM: The federal civil service, by the 1940s and 1950s, was increasingly more competent than anything the provinces could put together, and this was important later. But the federal system had enlarged, and it had available a lot of expert advice in quite technical areas like pension plans, actuarials, and futures. The provinces had nothing to match it; not even Ontario. That meant that the provinces tended to be overwhelmed. Another factor was the media; newspapers, primarily, were tremendously pro-federalist in this period. There was a strong personal link between many of the top newspapermen in the country and the federal Liberal Party and civil service. They thought in the same way about what was good for Canada.

BOTHWELL: When Lesage left Ottawa, he knew that what had been good for Canada could also be good for Quebec. Lesage understood Ottawa's good points as well as the bad. He understood that in the 1950s, under the Duplessis regime, Quebec had not really presented an alternative to Ottawa. Government flourished in Ottawa – activist, modern government. Quebec City, by contrast, was Sleepy Hollow.

But as Lesage also knew, it was not for lack of activist French Canadians. He recruited many of them to his party, and ran them as candidates in the 1960 provincial election: Paul Gérin-Lajoie, a former Rhodes scholar and constitutional expert; René Lévesque, a prominent television commentator, whose public affairs program *Point de Mire* was well known and very popular across Quebec; Georges-Emile Lapalme and George Marler, former provincial leaders who, like Lesage, had also spent time in Ottawa.

These men became ministers in Lesage's government and, before long, things began to happen. It is important not to exaggerate or misunderstand what happened. As many observers have noted, Quebec wasn't all black before and all light and music after the magic year 1960. Paul Sauvé, who died prematurely on New Year's Day, 1960, might have been just as likely a 'founder' of the Quiet Revolution, as Arthur Tremblay points out:

TREMBLAY: But when Duplessis died, Paul Sauvé succeeded. From now on it would not be the same as it had been, and he himself tabled quite an interesting set of views on education. But he died after what, a hundred days? I always ask myself what would have been the possibilities if he had not died. Was he really motivated to change?

So the change started, you see, a few years, if not a few months, before the Liberals were elected.

Lesage was bright enough to continue things which had been started, in all their dimensions. Maybe Sauvé would not have been capable of that. He had been raised in another régime, but he himself wanted to change something. Lesage did change things, and he has lots of merit for that. That was a beginning for me, and for those who worked in education.

BOTHWELL: Lesage's impact on Quebec was tremendous. Tremblay refers to his own experience, as a sociologist at Laval University, when Paul Gérin-Lajoie was appointed minister of youth in the Lesage government:

TREMBLAY: The day after he was appointed, he called me and said, 'Arthur, all those things you've been preaching all these years, if you are ready to come with me, we will realize them.' That was the beginning for me. So I went as his assistant and as a special adviser. Being a university professor, I was quite sure that, to realize all the things we had been working out and to make the necessary legislation, it would take, at the most, two years, perhaps only one year. In fact, I spent seventeen years there.

BOTHWELL: Lesage now had the team he needed: politicians like himself; and intellectuals and administrators like Arthur Tremblay, or Tremblay's counterpart in federal-provincial relations, Claude Morin, another Laval University professor. Much of their work was internal to Quebec and could be accomplished without reference outside. But some, inevitably, impinged on Ottawa, which shared the same tax revenue from the same economy. Ottawa, too, was an activist government, impelled by its own sense of priorities and by its own sense of Canadian nationalism – a sense that was, broadly speaking, shared by all federal parties and by all or almost all federal politicians. It was a world in which the federal government was foremost, and the provinces a long way behind, if at all.

Ottawa found the new attitude in Quebec initially incomprehensible; Quebec, for its part, found Ottawa uncomprehending. Tremblay comments on the gap between the two governments in the 1960s:

TREMBLAY: In the Quiet Revolution we had developed the knowledge of and the means to fight for what we wanted. We knew what we were, and what the other parts of Canada were, too. We were ready to talk business. Outside Quebec, people did not understand what had happened.

BOTHWELL: Lord Durham once defined the Canadian dilemma as two nations warring in the bosom of a single state; but as far as French Canada was concerned, the situation was two states warring in the bosom of a single nation. The Quebec state confronted the Ottawa state; the French-Canadian nation was divided and confused as to what it should do, while English Canadians wondered what, if anything, they could do to help.

Michael Behiels, a historian who has studied French Canada before and after the Quiet Revolution, explains how the vision of a Quebec state changed around 1960:

BEHIELS: There was a long debate in the province of Quebec in the 1950s as to what precisely the role of the Quebec state should be. The neo-nationalists realized by the early 1950s that the church was no longer an asset, but a liability, to the survival and the development of a modern francophone society. A modern Quebec state should, in fact, take over the development, the administration, and the funding of all that was required in a modern society, including the development of the economy, an open and democratic educational system at all levels, and, of course, social welfare and health programs. They wanted to create in Quebec the equivalent of what the mandarins and the politicians were creating in Ottawa. They wanted French Canadians to do this for French Canadians out of Quebec City. They wanted to say to the church, 'Thank you very much. You've helped our survival for 200 years, but you can no longer fulfil that role. We have to turn to the Quebec state to do that; we cannot rely on Ottawa, where we are always a minority and never have the majority control.' André Laurendeau, Gérard Filion, Jean-Marc Léger, Pierre Laporte, and Pierre Vadeboncoeur, all these new nationalists came to believe in the development of a modern social welfare state in Quebec, run by the majority of Quebeckers in the interest of that majority.

BOTHWELL: The question is whether the nationalists saw the implications of this new and separate state. Behiels considers whether they saw Quebec already as a country:

BEHIELS: Not in a clear sense. The Tremblay Commission, which had been set up by the Duplessis government in 1953, offered two scenarios on the constitutional question. Quebec could demand and eventually receive a degree of special status in what we now call an asymmetrical federal system, with exclusive control over all social welfare programs, education, health; or Quebec, along with the other provinces, could push for a considerable devolution within the Canadian federal system, whereby all the provinces would receive full control over all these areas as well as the tax and revenue to allow them to carry on. The Quebec nationalists have always been of two minds as to which option to push for at any point in time. The constitutional implications were not discussed in any detail within the francophone nationalist elite even in the 1960s. Some academics in English-speaking Canada started to think about the question, Ramsay Cook, Jack Saywell, and others, when they were addressing the role of the Bilingualism and Biculturalism Commission and what it would say on these issues. But, for the most part, they had a nebulous notion about where all this might lead in the future in terms of Quebec's position within the existing federal system.

BOTHWELL: The 1962 election in Quebec brought some of these problems to the fore. The election was fought on the issue of nationalizing the province's private hydro companies and combining them into a large state-owned corporation, Hydro-Québec. Many people, English- and French-speaking, supported the idea. But there were some who became disquieted by the tone the campaign took. Marc Lalonde was then a young lawyer and professor in Montreal. He describes his misgivings about the 1962 election:

LALONDE: I had given a hand to the provincial Liberals in the election campaign for Gérin-Lajoie, and I had also worked in the 1962 election, which was called to approve the nationalization of hydroelectricity in Quebec. In *Cité Libre*, however, I read an article by Trudeau, who raised questions about it and expressed reservations about the whole process. Still, I thought it was the right thing to do at the time. Subsequently, I heard more of the rhetoric of the Liberal Lesage government, which was using a more nationalistic rhetoric in support of its policies. I supported the nationalization not for the promotion of French-speaking Canadians, but because it made sense in economic terms, because it was the right thing to do over all. René Lévesque was minister of energy at the time and was one of the luminaries of the Lesage government: he kept pushing. Then he started making speeches in support of a steel industry in Quebec, and advanced the creation of Sidbec, which was eventually created on the theory that somehow we had to have it: as he said, 'We owe it to ourselves to have a steel industry.' That kind of rhetoric was certainly raising more questions in my mind, and was not very much to my taste, in terms of how to govern the province at that time.

BOTHWELL: All this occurred within a very few years: no wonder that Diefenbaker, sitting in Ottawa and preoccupied with many other problems, failed to notice or to adapt. In any case, adaptation was by 1962 too late. In 1962-3 John Diefenbaker's government was in its death throes over the question of Canada's acceptance – or not – of nuclear weapons for its defence forces. Diefenbaker was defeated in a vote in parliament and forced to call a general election in April 1963. The Liberals, under Lester Pearson, won. The Liberals hoped for a parliamentary majority, but the majority was denied them, largely because, in Quebec, people opted for a new party, Social Credit, or the Créditistes, under the charismatic leader Réal Caouette. 'What have you got to lose?' Caouette asked the voters, and in more than twenty Quebec constituencies the answer was, evidently, nothing, or at any rate not enough to vote for Pearson and the Liberals. Pearson's relative lack of electoral success in Quebec also had to do with the Quiet Revolution, although not quite in the way people think.

John English, biographer of Lester Pearson, comments on why the Liberals did not do well in Quebec in the 1963 election. He believes that it was a combination of the unpopularity of Lesage's government among more traditionally oriented parts of Quebec society, as well as the unpopularity of the federal Liberals' support for the acquisition of nuclear weapons, a fact that caused one stern critic of the federal Liberals, Pierre Elliott Trudeau, to call Lester Pearson 'the defrocked Pope of peace':

ENGLISH: The first reason the Liberals did not do well is that there was a reaction, especially in traditional ridings won by the Créditistes, against the changes caused by the Quiet Revolution, by the advance of secularism, and by the modern ways of doing things. Second, Pearson's shift on the nuclear weapons question was of some significance, as we can see in editorials written by Claude Ryan and in Pierre Trudeau's remarks. But the main factor would have been the traditional appeal and charismatic leader of the Créditistes.

BOTHWELL: However imperfect the Liberal victory in 1963, it was still a victory, and Pearson became prime minister of Canada. He looked forward to good relations with Quebec.

ENGLISH: The relationship between Pearson and Lesage was initially very good. Lesage had become Pearson's parliamentary assistant soon after he came to Ottawa. The earliest letters in French to Pearson, from another parliamentarian, are from Lesage, and they occur because Pearson asked Lesage to write to him in French. They got on quite well, and Lesage seems to have been a popular senior member of parliament during the 1950s in Ottawa. They kept up their relationship in the 1960s. When Lesage came to power in Quebec, the federal Liberals, and particularly Pearson, saw it as an occasion for great jubilation and hope that this was the breakthrough that was needed to restore the federal Liberal Party. Lesage gave credibility to the Liberals again, nationally; by 1962-3 he seemed to represent a new kind of Liberalism.

BOTHWELL: Pearson did not rely only on Lesage, however. He had French-Canadian advisers of his own, and French-Canadian members of parliament. Inside parliament, he relied on the debating skills of Lionel Chevrier, a Franco-Ontarian who had switched to a Montreal constituency; but Chevrier, unfortunately, was always perceived inside Quebec as not quite a Quebecker, and was in any case thought to be un-intellectual and excessively traditional, at a time when new styles, and new kinds of political thought and action, seemed to be indicated. So Pearson, still opposition leader in the fall of 1962, turned also to Maurice Lamontagne, a former professor at Laval University and a former assistant to Prime Minister St-Laurent, for counsel.

What Lamontagne had to say was not entirely reassuring. The changes taking place in Quebec were long overdue, but they were having the effect of turning Quebeckers' attention to Quebec City and to the activist Quebec provincial government. Lamontagne, who lived and worked in Ottawa, knew just how estranged French Canadians moving to the capital might feel, and he urged Pearson to say and do something that might persuade French-speaking Quebeckers that there was room for them not just in Ottawa but in Canada, too – especially a Canada as defined by Pearson and not by John Diefenbaker. Lamontagne asked Pearson to take up the ideas of the editor of the influential Montreal newspaper *Le Devoir*, André Laurendeau: Laurendeau had asked for, and Pearson promised, a great public examination of French-English relations in Canada, bilingualism and biculturalism, as it was called: B and B for short. Pearson proposed a royal commission on the subject in a speech in parliament in December 1962. At this crucial turning-point, in the winter of 1962-3, Diefenbaker missed the boat, as Lowell Murray describes:

MURRAY: He rejected the agitation, started actually by André Laurendeau for a royal commission on bilingualism and biculturalism. While Mr Pearson was no more highly regarded in Quebec than Mr Diefenbaker was at the time, he had better advice and his party had roots in Quebec. He saw what was happening and, as early as December 1962, while he was still leader of the opposition, he made a very important speech, most of which had been prepared by Maurice Lamontagne, about the shape of things to come: cooperative federalism in terms of federal-provincial relations, and the need for recognition of the linguistic and cultural duality of the country in federal institutions. It was a very important speech. Diefenbaker rejected the idea of a royal commission and took a more incremental approach to the whole problem.

BOTHWELL: In power, Pearson quickly fulfilled his promise. A Royal Commission on Bilingualism and Biculturalism was appointed, under the joint chairmanship of André Laurendeau and Davidson Dunton, of Carleton University. Blair Neatby, a professor of history at Carleton University and a specialist on French-English relations, was made director of research for the commission, and in that capacity had plenty of opportunity to observe Laurendeau. Neatby recounts what Laurendeau meant by bilingualism and biculturalism and, more broadly, what was his vision of Canada:

NEATBY: I think Laurendeau's position on the B and B commission began with his sense of being a nationalist, a national leader, and a national spokesman on *Le Devoir*. When he was asked to take part in the commission he had proposed, there was a great deal of pressure on him to agree. But he certainly didn't have any clear idea of what the solution was. He was convinced that some recognition of the distinct society was essential if Canada was to survive. He started off assuming that Canada would survive, because to be separatist at that time was to be quite radical. Canada had survived for a long time, and nobody was really revolutionary. Presumably, Canada would continue to go on with compromises. Laurendeau thought, however, that more concessions would have to be made than had been made in the past, and that this commission was a way in which they might be achieved. He had confidence, through Lamontagne, that Pearson and his government would be sensitive to the recommendations. So Laurendeau had a certain optimism that if the commission could agree on policies, the government would accept them.

He didn't have a clear idea what these policies should be, and his initial concern was not bilingualism across the country. He thought the real problems were in Quebec, and that more power should be given to the government in Quebec. It was Quebec that was unhappy, French Canadians in Quebec who were discontent, and they were upset because they didn't have enough power to ensure that federal institutions would be appropriate for their interests. It was the emphasis on adapting the federal government that was important, because the federal government would have to become bilingual if it was to provide the services that the federal government should in a federal system. But Laurendeau's focus was not on the federal system initially: he saw it to some extent as symbolic. The army should be bilingual because it was a Canadian Army, and therefore it should be both French and English. He was prepared to agree on the commission to major research studies on the development of the public service and how it could be adjusted. Nevertheless, he thought that the real focus should be on how French and English Canadians could collaborate within the province of Quebec, and how the institutions, private as well as public, should be adjusted so that the French-Canadian majority in Quebec would be able to exercise the power that was appropriate.

BOTHWELL: The power that was appropriate. In another context, Laurendeau was speaking the same language as Arthur Tremblay, about the same issues that were such a lively part of the Quebec political debate in the mid-1960s. Blair Neatby comments how he saw these issues:

NEATBY: In French Canada the real difference was that French Canadians were no longer prepared to accept their exclusion from the industrial world. As long as they thought in terms of the rural parish, they could live in French, because in the rural parish there wasn't much English. But once they decided they had to live in Montreal, to run Montreal, to be on the board of the CPR or Domtar, then they did have to come to terms with the problem that English was dominant in those places. If they were going to be there, either they had to accept the dominance of English or they had to change the milieu. That was why French Canadians became obsessed with the problem of language in the 1960s. They realized the importance of the milieu in which French was not dominant, in which there was the pressure for assimilation.

BOTHWELL: In 1965 the B and B commission issued a preliminary report on its investigations, a report whose tone was, to say the least, startling. Laurendeau and his colleagues told their readers, including Prime Minister Pearson, his cabinet, and the rest of the country's political leaders, that, without being entirely conscious of the fact, Canada was passing through the greatest crisis in its history.

That was not precisely what Pearson had bargained for when he became prime minister, or when he appointed the commission. But by 1965 there was considerable evidence to support the thesis – evidence to be found in the relations between Ottawa and Quebec City. Contrary to expectations, the two Liberal governments did not get along very well at all.

This fact, this failure to get along, harked back to the existence not merely of two languages and two cultures in Canada, but to two nationalisms. In the political discourse of the time, this duality was sometimes expressed as the existence of *deux nations*, two nations. A great deal of breath and wordage was expended on an effort to prove that the term had different meanings in French and in English. It is true that those who accepted or proposed that *nation*-nation meant two different things shrank from the logical conclusion that two nations might mean two countries; but almost everybody accepted that, for the present at least, French Canadians and English Canadians had a very different political concentration, a very different focus for their political energies.

That was partly because the Pearson government was energetically trying to expand its activities and, in the process, to complete Canada's social security system. The Canadian electorate, outside Quebec, expected no less; and Canadians, at least the English-Canadian variety, could see no reason why Quebeckers wouldn't want the same services as the rest of the country. But the Lesage government and its supporters could and did see a reason. That reason was language and, with it, culture. Quebec's language and culture, according to this reading, were defended by the ramparts of the provincial state. Integral to the provincial state were those activities of government seen in the 1960s as the most significant, the most modern, the closest to the citizen: social security.

Social security was a provincial field, but it was also a field in which the federal government's abundant revenues allowed it to entice the provinces to cooperate. The first item to be tackled was a reform of pensions – the creation of a funded Canada Pension Plan. Such a plan required provincial consent and cooperation, but the Pearson government got both. There was a price, however. For the nine English-speaking provinces it was lending the proceeds to the provincial governments, to use more or less for their own purposes; all this was inside a single Canada Pension Plan. But the price for Quebec was different.

Quebec wanted its own pension plan, compatible with the federal plan, to be sure, but under its own separate administration. At first the federal government resisted, but eventually it gave way: there would be a Quebec Pension Plan, which would pour funds into a provincial Caisse de Dépôts, to be used as the province saw fit – for investment in the economy according to priorities set in Quebec City.

John English discusses the frantic rush to agreement on pensions between Pearson and Lesage in 1963-4:

ENGLISH: The Lesage government, which had fought the 1962 election over the nationalization question, was looking for newer things to do, and one possibility was the whole question of social security. In Canada, we didn't have a social security plan, as in the United States. Quebec wanted to work something out as a province, in the same way that medicare was being worked out in the province of Saskatchewan. The federal government did not want to let the initiative fall to the provinces by themselves, so Pearson became more determined, as events unfolded, to be aggressive in these areas. Lesage moved very quickly towards the pension plan, and, in short order, a fragment of the Quebec plan was there – in final form. In Ottawa, meanwhile, the federal plan was still being worked out. Before long, there was division in the federal bureaucracy. Tom Kent gave leadership to one faction. George Davidson thought the entire issue was horrendous: a solution was being put together too quickly, there was a rush to reach an agreement, and in the end there was both a national plan and a Quebec plan. Peace had been bought – it was impossible to look at it in any other way. The pension plans were but an example of the way that the Lesage government was pushing the agenda, nationally, and it wasn't only in this area but in many other areas as well. Pearson himself, at this point, tried to use his old relationship with Lesage, as did others – Gordon Robertson, for example – all of them thinking that they could manage the situation. By 1965, however, they realized that Lesage wasn't in control of the situation in Quebec; he was being pushed by many forces that he couldn't seem to keep in line, in the political sense.

BOTHWELL: At the time, Canadian opinion was most aware of the jurisdictional battles between Quebec and Ottawa. It was also uncomfortably aware that the solution was for Quebec to opt out of one federal shared-cost program after another, in return for financial compensation. Two of the leading officials participating in negotiations between Quebec and Ottawa during this period were Claude Morin and Jacques Parizeau, then a young economist and, at the time, a federalist. On the Ottawa end, one of the people handling negotiations with the provinces was Mitchell Sharp, Pearson's minister of finance from 1965 to 1968. Sharp recounts how he tried to reach an understanding with his Quebec counterparts:

SHARP: The two principal officials I had to deal with in the Quebec Department of Finance were Jacques Parizeau and Claude Morin. I think back to those days with some amusement, because Parizeau didn't look to me like a potential politician. He was very much a technocrat. My recollection of those events is that they worked under direction. They were not making the policy, but were carrying out the policy of the Lesage government. I knew I had to deal with Lesage, and that was very difficult. He was determined to change the direction of policy. During the whole postwar period, the federal government had gained the lead in economic policy generally, and it worked. The country just changed. We helped the provinces with equalization payments and with shared-cost programs. And Lesage just said, 'These shared-cost programs have to end. We have to assume our full responsibilities for provincial affairs.'

It seemed to me then that our whole approach of trying to coordinate activities throughout the country would have to be abandoned. In fact, that's what happened, although Quebec was the only province that took advantage of the offer we made to all the provinces to get out of the shared-cost programs. Only Quebec accepted. I had not been consulted about this proposal. The decision was made by Prime Minister Pearson when we took office that any province that wanted to get out of the shared-cost programs would be compensated. He made this offer to keep Lesage on side. I was uncomfortable about it because I thought that one of the marks of a true federal government was that federal taxes were the same in all parts of the country. When I took office, I discovered that the federal income tax in Quebec was lower than it was in Ontario, simply because that was the form in which Quebec wanted the compensation.

So, as I say, I was disappointed. It seemed to me that somehow we had withdrawn from the role that I thought we ought to be able to pursue. I thought that if any province wanted to get out, that was fine, but for them to be compensated in the form of tax reductions only made Canadian federalism look like a strange creature. And I think it did.

BOTHWELL: Pearson's response to the provinces, but particularly to Quebec, travelled under the politically saleable name of 'cooperative federalism.' Its spirit certainly was cooperative, but its practice frequently enough was muddle, inspired by the hope that somehow something would turn up, and, in the meantime, confrontations were to be avoided. It was an approach, a policy, that made many Liberals – even senior Liberals like Mitchell Sharp – deeply uneasy.

As long as Lesage remained at the helm, the federal Liberals were confident that nothing too extreme would be done: Lesage intended to keep Quebec in Canada, within the present Constitution, even if he also intended to stretch that Constitution to its furthest limits. That policy might be difficult, but, to Mitchell Sharp, it held no special terrors. Sharp comments on how flexible the Canadian Constitution could be, and whether there were any differences that could not be negotiated:

SHARP: I think any differences are manageable within the Constitution and within the present division of powers. We have demonstrated our ingenuity from time to time, and a lot of it isn't a matter of law. In a way, it's a matter of attitude. In other words, if you decide policy and it makes sense, you can usually find within the Constitution a means to carry it out. It may not be particularly tidy, but it works, and when you look at the country you realize what enormous changes you've made in the nature of Canada without any serious constitutional amendments.

BOTHWELL: By the mid-1960s, however, further enormous changes were being demanded, and some of them could not be reconciled with the existing

Constitution or, in fact, with the existence of a united Canada.

Negotiations with Quebec were, down to the mid-1960s, conducted as between federalists, even aggressive federalists like Jean Lesage. As frustration mounted on both sides – Quebec's frustration that its demands could not be achieved quickly enough or completely enough, and Ottawa's frustration that Quebec's drive for autonomy made nonsense of Ottawa's desire or ability to work as a national government – it was clear that something had to give, or at any rate to change.

But the instruments of change were not to be Pearson or Lesage. Lesage left office in 1966, defeated much to his surprise in a provincial election. Pearson left in 1968, worn out by the demands of office and unsatisfied by his inability to strike a new balance within Canada between Canada and Quebec. Pearson left a country intact, but worried and cranky. To lead it he left a very unusual Canadian. That Canadian, Pierre Elliott Trudeau, would place his imprint on his country in a manner that still shapes and may even delineate what Canadians are.

Chapter 7

The Constitution
and the Crisis,
1965-71

Until the mid-1960s, Canada's Con-
stitution was regarded as a pretty dull subject. It was the domain of a handful of constitutional lawyers, a couple of judges, and a platoon of political
scientists. In 1967 Canada would celebrate its hundredth anniversary, its
centennial year, but in the celebration it was the fact of Canadian unity,
more than the Constitution, that gave it form, that attracted attention.

True, the Constitution sometimes rose to the surface. When it did, it
received minor adjustments in the form of amendments – granting the federal government power over old age pensions in 1951 or unemployment
insurance in 1940, for example – and was sent back down to the bottom
again. The Constitution was thus little more than a road map to relations
between Ottawa and the provinces, relations in which it was Ottawa that
was the dominant partner. The fact that the Canadian Constitution was still
known as the British North America Act, and was still a British statute,
sometimes caused comment. On federal-provincial issues it could be
amended only by the British parliament, as if Canada was still a British
colony, even though the British were always obliging about it. But even finding a way of amending the Constitution in Canada – bringing it home,
'patriating' it, or giving it a home – was never a top priority. Mackenzie King

had tried it in the 1920s, St-Laurent in 1950, and Diefenbaker in the early 1960s. Lester Pearson's government tried in 1964, and failed again. The provinces would never agree. Usually one province or another wanted more than Ottawa or its fellow-provinces would give. In 1964 it was Premier Jean Lesage in Quebec who hung back and refused to agree, but in Ottawa former Prime Minister Diefenbaker was also vigorous in condemning the arrangement that had been made and had failed. Nobody was really surprised: it was just the latest tedious episode in a very long and boring series. Or was it?

The ultimate constitutional adjustment, after all, is to terminate a Constitution or a country. One part may secede from a country, or all parts may agree to wind up the country. The effect is dramatic, and, it must be admitted, anything but boring.

In the early 1960s voices began to be heard in Quebec calling not for political reform or for constitutional change, but for the secession of Quebec from Canada. Then, in 1963, the voices were supplemented by bombs – bombs in the privileged English-speaking Montreal suburb of Westmount, bombs in the symbols of federal power, of Canadian unity, in Quebec. The effect was deeply disturbing. David Bercuson was a student at Montreal's Sir George Williams University in 1963, and he remembers how the atmosphere in Quebec changed for him:

BERCUSON: It changed not so much with the rise of separatism, but with the FLQ. I remember being in the Stanley tavern the night that Wilfrid O'Neill was killed at the Armoury, and somebody came running in saying that a bomb had just gone off about two blocks away. We all ran over and we got there before the police and fire department arrived, and it was all quite eerie.

I remember going home that night, saying I would probably not be in Quebec as an adult, that something would happen that would push me out, or that I would leave; and that would be the case with most of my friends. I remember this as distinctly as I have any recollection of my life, driving home that night and having this conversation with a friend, who also subsequently left Quebec. We did not equate what the FLQ was doing with the majority of the population, but we said to ourselves that here was a group of people who clearly believed that we must be disenfranchised, that we had no rights here. The nationalism of that movement was an ethnocentric nationalism. The rest of the country thinks it has created a post-nationalist nation or a pre-nationalist nation, but the FLQ was interested in creating a nationalist nation based on a certain ethnic identity. Even if I learned to be as fluently French as the premier of Quebec, I'd still be a Montreal Jew and I'd never be accepted as one of them. That was what the big change was.

BOTHWELL: Language and ethnicity were dangerous subjects. Canadian history taught politicians to shy away from them, because of the possibility they would open up an unbridgeable abyss between English- and French-speakers. But in Quebec a separatist movement was equating the existence of Canada with ethnic oppression, and compromise with English Canada with selling out the French heritage. Only a separate Quebec state could preserve the French language and culture.

Horrified, Canadian politicians responded by trying to recast the foundations of the country, both to satisfy deep grievances in the long term and to postpone conflict until a better day in the short term. Something dramatic was needed, something that would once again link the common interests of English and French Canadians. Not surprisingly, the Constitution was the method of choice.

For the next thirty years, the Canadian Constitution was a kind of national growth industry. Federal-provincial conferences succeeded one another in a dizzying spiral, though whether upwards or downwards no two experts could agree. Ottawa and the provinces snarled and fought over the distribution of powers, and clashed over the patriation of the Constitution and – something new – a Canadian Charter of Rights and Freedoms. That most uncommon event, a national referendum, eventually took place in 1992 over a highly complicated set of constitutional amendments. Not surprisingly, it failed, in large part because nobody really knew what an amended Constitution would really do. And even today, the Constitution remains a preoccupying topic – rather like a sore tooth.

The motive force in these thirty years of constitutional wrangling was Quebec. Finding a constitutional solution to the Quebec problem became the central preoccupation of at least three Canadian governments: Lester Pearson's, in 1967-8, Pierre Trudeau's, from 1968 to 1984, and Brian Mulroney's, from 1984 to 1993. (Three others, Joe Clark, John Turner, and Kim Campbell did not last long enough for a clear pattern to emerge, while it is probably too soon to tell what Jean Chrétien will do.) The issue transcended party and personality.

'What does Quebec want?' English Canadians asked themselves, meaning, 'What will Quebec settle for?' And what would English Canadians settle for? What do they want? This would be a negotiation that involved at
least two, but often nine or ten or fifteen different camps, each of them with
its own constituency. Two main events in the 1960s set the constitutional
dance in motion. Gordon Robertson, clerk of the Privy Council and
Canada's senior civil servant under Prime Minister Lester Pearson, describes
what happened:

ROBERTSON: I suppose one has to go back to two episodes: one is the election of the Lesage government in Quebec in 1960, and the other is the ini-
tiation of the Quiet Revolution. To achieve the Quiet Revolution, the Lesage
government believed that it had to have all the instruments that the
Constitution gave to Quebec, undiluted and total. Lesage at no time sought
constitutional reform or change. What he wanted was to be sure that
Quebec could do everything possible under the Constitution as it stood.
That view led to a good deal of conflict with the Pearson government after
it came to power in 1963, because the Lesage government believed that some
of the shared-cost programs and other social security programs in which
the Liberal government in Ottawa was interested constituted invasions of
Quebec jurisdiction. Lesage wanted out of the shared-cost arrangements,
and, in negotiations with Quebec, we devised what was called opting out
and other devices. Pearson hoped that constitutional reform would be
avoided, and there was no pressure from Quebec for it directly.

In 1965 the Royal Commission on Bilingualism and Biculturalism brought
in its interim report and said that Canada, without recognizing it, was passing
through the greatest crisis in its history. That memorable phrase captured
the dissatisfaction of French Canada in general, and Quebec in particular,
with the Constitution as it stood. By 1967 Pearson had come to the conclusion that our efforts to effect changes without constitutional reform were
not going to succeed, and that there had to be constitutional change.

BOTHWELL: Shared-cost programs were programs that fell under provincial
jurisdiction, within provincial powers, but where Ottawa for its own reasons
contributed a large part of the cost. Ottawa had far greater financial resources
than the provinces, and a far more sophisticated civil service, and it used its
advantages, especially its money, to pressure the provinces to accept a series
of social reforms designed in Ottawa. The provinces, knowing that Ottawa

had both money and public opinion on its side, generally capitulated.

Until Jean Lesage and the Quiet Revolution, that is. Under Lesage, Quebec opted out, taking the money it would otherwise have received for a shared-cost program and using it for its own purposes – purposes that often enough were broadly similar to the programs Ottawa designed and legislated for the rest of the country. In an area like pensions, for example, that produced one pension regime for Quebec, the Quebec Pension Plan, and another for the rest of Canada, the Canada Pension Plan. This produced an asymmetry as between Quebec and the rest of Canada, conceding to the government of Quebec in effect, if not in theory, what came to be called special status – all this within the context of the existing Canadian Constitution.

Pearson believed, and enough people agreed with him, that these arrangements did not require any formal adjustment of the Canadian Constitution. But in 1965 Lesage's government became more adventurous. Paul Gérin-Lajoie, one of Lesage's senior ministers and himself a constitutional expert, advanced the position that in matters under provincial jurisdiction, such as education or culture, Quebec could represent itself abroad in negotiations with foreign governments. Quebec, in other words, was equal to Ottawa, not subordinate as a mere province would usually expect to be.

This position sent shock waves through Ottawa, and in particular the Department of External Affairs, Canada's foreign office. Its inhabitants, especially Marcel Cadieux, the undersecretary, strongly believed that Canada – or any country for that matter – had only one sovereign government, one government that could properly deal with foreign countries. I asked Allan Gotlieb, who was then legal adviser in the Department of External Affairs, what he made of Gérin-Lajoie's contention. He refers in passing to section 92 of the British North America Act, which defined provincial powers within the Constitution:

GOTLIEB: Gérin-Lajoie, when he was minister of education in 1965, articulated the view that the province should have treaty-making powers within the entire scope of section 92 of the Constitution. This extension of power was very strongly resisted by External Affairs, on the grounds that it would be inappropriate for a component part of a federal system to have such jurisdiction.

BOTHWELL: The key issue here is whether it is even possible for a federation to have a divided sovereignty along the lines that Gérin-Lajoie projected back in 1965.

GOTLIEB: In the nineteenth century there were forms of half states in the colonial era – states that were protected and had no domestic jurisdiction, but had some foreign jurisdiction. There were protectorates and mandates, metropolitan states and colonies. International law did come up with various types of dependencies and dependent states. These were all swept away in the twentieth century as the tide of sovereignty and independence grew, and they were all seen as relics of colonialism. International law does not recognize half states, partial states, or associate states. That's not to say that one couldn't be created, but, in the international order we know today, there is no concept of a state that has treaty-making powers only in certain areas. I don't see it myself. I don't see how you could have a state that has the right to enter into and implement agreements in the domestic field, but not in defence. All foreign policy is domestic today: economic, environmental, investment, regulation. The essence of foreign policy is merely the right international regulation of issues that are of a domestic content. The one exception is war. You could say that the state would have to be able to make agreements right across the line – human rights, civil jurisdiction, the economy, the environment, water, fish, territory – but not peace and war. I think that any attempt to give a unit of the state or a part of the state independent treaty-making powers would be highly unstable. It wouldn't cause a war, but it wouldn't last for more than a few years.

BOTHWELL: This matter of treaty-making powers bothered some of Pearson's ministers, but it was something that the prime minister believed he could live with. If Canada's jurisdiction could somehow be respected, as a formality, then Quebec could surely go ahead and enjoy relations with France. Canada signed an umbrella agreement that gave Quebec the power to do just that, trusting in the common sense of the Quebec government not to tread on any sensitive areas of federal jurisdiction.

Then two more events occurred. In 1966 Jean Lesage and the Liberals were defeated in a Quebec provincial election. Replacing them was the Union Nationale under its leader Daniel Johnson, and Johnson had just written and published a book called *Égalité ou Indépendance* – Equality or Independence. What did he, what could he, mean? Was independence truly a viable option, something that Quebeckers might choose?

Apparently it was. The next year, 1967, witnessed Canada's centennial, and a parade of state visits from official well-wishers from around the globe.

Montreal was the site of a world-class exhibition, Expo 67, and it was to Montreal that every state visitor was directed – after passing through Ottawa, the national capital. But in 1967 one visitor, French president Charles de Gaulle, decided otherwise. Instead, de Gaulle landed at Quebec City, barely acknowledged the federal presence, accepted the hospitality of the provincial government, drove to Montreal, and, in a memorable speech at Montreal's City Hall, uttered a phrase that gladdened the hearts of all those who supported Quebec independence: 'Vive le Québec libre!' [Long live free Quebec!] The crowd cheered, leaving no doubt in the rest of Canada that there were plenty of Quebeckers who did not find the idea of independence strange or repulsive.

The government of Canada did, and said so, and de Gaulle departed in a hurry. Was it possible that de Gaulle did not mean what he said, or that he was misinterpreted? External Affairs minister Paul Martin was one who thought so; Lester Pearson definitely did not, and he issued a strong statement saying so. John English comments on this dramatic episode:

ENGLISH: Pearson's reaction was a strong one. There were others who wanted to be more careful because of internal Canadian reactions and because of the possible external reaction as well, Paul Martin being one of them. I don't think Pearson could have done anything but what he did, issuing that particular statement, saying that what de Gaulle had done was intolerable, and, of course, once he did that, it was inevitable that de Gaulle would leave. In fact, de Gaulle seems to have revelled in it, and he apparently insulted Chevrier the next day at the Expo site, making particularly pointed and uncomplimentary remarks about the Canadian prime minister, and indeed about Canada itself. So de Gaulle afterwards was unrepentant, and Pearson had no alternative but to do what he did.

BOTHWELL: Lionel Chevrier, one of Pearson's former ministers, was the official host for Canada at Expo; as a French-speaker, he could of course understand perfectly what de Gaulle was saying to him, and what he meant. De Gaulle remained unrepentant. He later explained that the very idea of a bi-ethnic federal state was a logical contradiction, one that he hoped would soon be abandoned everywhere, not just in Canada. And he went further, as Allan Gotlieb explains:

GOTLIEB: The Gaullist vision was of the French as a global power radiating across the world. It was a high priority for de Gaulle. When he was in

Quebec, and after, when he went back to Paris, he always referred to Quebeckers as *les Français du Canada*. *Les Français du Canada* is not a phrase that's used in Quebec. As a matter of fact they don't even speak of French Canadian, Canadien français – they speak of Québécois more. But *les Français du Canada* was part of de Gaulle's vision. He had an extremely broad global vision of France as a world power, and there were those years when he tried to keep Britain out of the Common Market, when he took France out of NATO, the military part of NATO, and recognized China. This was a heady intellectual era and, in that time, there were groups within the Elysée (the French presidential palace) and within the intelligence services of France who were actively promoting and scheming for the independence of Quebec. They were stimulating the revival and the activities of French-speaking groups outside Quebec, but the focus was Quebec. After de Gaulle's era was over, the view was accepted in France that if Quebec became independent, that would be a fine thing, but it wouldn't be decided in Paris.

BOTHWELL: De Gaulle's remaining time in office was in fact extraordinarily short – only until the beginning of 1969, and the opportunity for active French mischief was accordingly brief. It must be admitted, however, that he touched a nerve inside Canada, and, equally, that he pleased an important segment of Quebec opinion.

The public reaction to de Gaulle's intervention divided English-Canadian from French-Canadian opinion – though not everybody was on the same side either in Quebec or in the rest of Canada. Jean Lesage, still leader of the Liberal Party, denounced de Gaulle, and one of his supporters, François Aquin, promptly quit. Jean Drapeau, mayor of Montreal, made a speech explaining why he disagreed with de Gaulle. A year or so later, René Lévesque, who had been one of Lesage's principal ministers, also quit. Raymond Garneau, who in 1967 was Lesage's executive assistant, explains what happened:

GARNEAU: What was going on in the inner circle of the Liberals was that Lévesque, Aquin, and a few others had met separately and wanted to do something about the nationalist movement. Lévesque wanted to take control of the Liberal Party in Quebec because he knew that to create a new party was a difficult job. If he had been able to use the Liberal structure and control, probably his objective would have been achieved rather more rapidly. René Lévesque at that time was not prepared to propose the separation of Quebec from the rest of Canada. After de Gaulle made his statement and the Liberals adopted a position against his remarks, François Aquin quit the party. The rumours going around at that time were that the others would follow suit, but they didn't, particularly René Lévesque, who didn't leave the party on that issue. But it certainly split the Liberals for a time.

After the 1966 general election the provincial Liberals had created a committee to try to develop a position paper on the Constitution, and it was adopted at the end of the convention in late 1967. It was at that convention that Lévesque left the party. He had been a member of the constitutional committee chaired by Paul Gérin-Lajoie and they had worked hard on a proposal. But at some point Lévesque decided not to attend any more meetings, and separately he worked out a proposal of his own. The two proposals came on the floor of the convention, Jean Lesage supported that of Gérin-Lajoie, and Lévesque's proposal was defeated. Then Lévesque quit, along with a number of people. Their departure certainly affected the Quebec Liberals for a while, but it also cleared the atmosphere and pulled the rest of the party together. We fought the 1970 Quebec election on the federalist option, and we won. Lévesque fought on his Sovereignty-Association Movement platform, and he lost. It took seven years before he was elected, and it was mainly because of the economic situation and the cost of the Olympic games. It was a very active time.

BOTHWELL: Certainly, 1967 turned out to be a momentous year. In English Canada it was a time of pride and hope, Canada's past and present joined together. But in Quebec it was a time of growing crisis that culminated in the establishment of a separatist party, the Mouvement Souveraineté-association, the Sovereignty-Association Movement, led by a credible politician of the first rank, René Lévesque. This was a sign of serious crisis, bearing out the prediction of the Bilingualism and Biculturalism Commission back in 1965. In Ottawa, Pearson took notice, and so did John Robarts, the premier of Ontario. Robarts decided to convene a conference of his own, the Confederation of Tomorrow Conference. Pearson did not attend, but all the provincial premiers did, including Daniel Johnson. Pearson again took note, and then made up his mind.

Canada was plainly in a political crisis. If there was a choice between a stable Constitution and a united country, then it was the Constitution that must give way, and he so informed his cabinet, including his new justice minister, Pierre Elliott Trudeau. Trudeau, with Pearson, would represent

Canada at a constitutional conference to be convened in Ottawa in February 1968. Gordon Robertson describes what happened:

ROBERTSON: The Confederation of Tomorrow Conference was launched by John Robarts as a response to the Quiet Revolution in Quebec and the B and B Commission report. Pearson was still hoping that constitutional change could be avoided, but there is no doubt that Robarts's conference did heighten and strengthen the point. Trudeau was minister of justice in the Pearson government, and a lot of people in English-speaking Canada in particular think that it was he who got us involved in constitutional conferences and constitutional wrangling. That is not the case. Trudeau was very much opposed to getting into any constitutional reform or conference; he said it was a *panier de crabes*, a can of worms, and should be avoided. It was Pearson who came to the conclusion that it could not be avoided, and it was he who launched the first constitutional conference in February 1968.

BOTHWELL: As for Premier Daniel Johnson's slogan 'Equality or Independence,' Robertson continues:

ROBERTSON: I never saw anything that convinced me that Johnson was a separatist. I thought that his slogan, equality or independence, was a beautifully devised slogan to appeal to both the federalists and the much smaller group of separatists. I firmly believe that Daniel Johnson was what his son, the present leader of the Liberal Party in Quebec, now is – that he was a federalist and that he preferred equality.

BOTHWELL: The constitutional conference of February 1968 was the making of Pierre Elliott Trudeau, who until then had been an unknown commodity as far as English Canada was concerned. What Liberals knew was that Pearson had brought him into the Liberal fold as a candidate in the 1965 federal election, not because he especially wanted to, but because the Liberals' new star in Quebec, Jean Marchand, a prominent labour leader, had made it a condition of running himself. And so Trudeau ran in an English-speaking riding in Montreal, Mount Royal, and was elected. Pearson promptly made him his parliamentary secretary and, in 1967, minister of justice.

Within Quebec, however, Trudeau was very well known. Independently wealthy, he could afford to defy Premier Duplessis during the 1950s. He founded and ran the magazine *Cité Libre*, where he espoused rationality, condemned nationalism, and sustained the existing Canadian Constitution.

In 1965 he and a group of friends published a manifesto, 'Pour une politique fonctionelle,' which means, crudely translated, 'For a functional politics.' One of the authors, Marc Lalonde, later federal minister of finance in the Trudeau government, explains what the manifesto meant:

LALONDE: One morning I was walking in Outremont, where I had rented an apartment, and I came across an old university friend of mine. His name was Albert Breton, and he later became well known as a professor of economics at the University of Toronto. I told him my concerns and asked, 'Am I the only one to have that kind of worry, or am I wrong? How do you feel?' I found he shared my views. We decided we would get a group of friends together who had been at university at roughly the same time and who we felt would share the same concerns. We decided to invite Pierre Trudeau, who was older but certainly one of the intellectual lights of Quebec in those days, to attend our meetings. It really started as a weekly meeting of eight or nine people on Wednesday night from 8 to 10:30, after which we would go and eat pastry at the Laurier Barbécue on Laurier Street in Outremont.

Before long, we began keeping notes and identifying subjects we would like to cover. After a year, we found we had a shared point of view, so we decided to divide the work and see whether we could arrive at a written formulation of what we felt. Two or three of us decided to put the material together, and when this was completed we asked Trudeau to polish it. It was very much a collective effort. We wanted to see if other people shared our views, so we published our text in *Cité Libre*. We had friends at *Canadian Forum* who said they would like to publish an English version of it. Michael Pitfield, who was then a junior official working for General Vanier at Government House, agreed to make an English translation. That's how it got into print, and then it was picked up by the newspapers. There was some debate, and it had its own mileage, and somehow it became a little blip on Quebec history which is still there. It was the first signal of contestation of the overly nationalistic approach of the Lesage government. There was a kind of a premonition in that message, when we see where Lévesque ended up.

BOTHWELL: Lalonde, Breton, and Trudeau, but also other figures, Jean Marchand and the journalist Gérard Pelletier, stood for a harder line against the pretensions of the Quebec government, and against the provinces generally, than Pearson had been taking. John English describes how their election was perceived:

ENGLISH: The three supposedly non-political figures were brought into politics, were immediately celebrities, and were put forward for exactly the same reasons that they had been recruited – that they could somehow speak to the new Quebec, although they didn't represent the national side of it. They had an immediate influence. Within the federal bureaucracy, there were many who were very angry with the 'flabbiness' of the federal response to Quebec; they thought that such weakness undermined the capacity of federal government to act effectively for all Canadians. Marcel Cadieux and others feared that the country would disintegrate, and that Quebec would leave by the back door. The Liberal Party in Quebec, they thought, had become so nationalist that it had lost its sense of Quebec being a province in a Canadian federal system.

BOTHWELL: Other Canadian historians also find fault with Pearson's soft approach to Quebec. David Bercuson is especially critical:

BERCUSON: For one thing, it was Pearson's responsibility to lay out to Quebec, first, that there was not going to be any secession from Canada, or, second, that if secession was going to occur, it would do so only under these kinds of conditions and these kinds of circumstances. I can understand him not saying the second alternative. That's the sort of thing you say in the late 1980s and the 1990s, with Meech and all the other wrangles, but not what was said in the 1960s. It's easy to criticize Pearson from the perspective of 1994. But the first alternative should have been said, and it wasn't. The other reason I find fault with Pearson was that he did not, at the beginning, understand what he was dealing with. He saw this problem in the same way as the struggle for responsible government in Canada in the nineteenth century, and the way the British Empire was preserved by granting responsible government. The answer then was to be flexible, not to draw in the wagons. But the answer here was to draw in the wagons. He got it all wrong. After a while, he listened to different people and he started to learn, but by then it was too late.

BOTHWELL: Allan Gotlieb was an adviser to Trudeau in 1967-8, at the time of the first constitutional conference. To Gotlieb, Trudeau's strategy was a refreshing change from the compromises and half-measures of the earlier stages of the Pearson government. Here he characterizes Trudeau's approach to the Constitution and to Quebec, and refers to 'subsidiarity,' a term applied in the 1990s to the idea that government should always be at the lowest level appropriate to or consistent with efficiency – an idea currently in vogue in the European Union:

GOTLIEB: My understanding of his approach was that federalism should be based on symmetrical concepts; that provinces, their powers and jurisdictions, should be based on appropriate concepts as to what is appropriate to do at the level of a regional government in a federal system. I was very struck and surprised by his views because I hadn't had much exposure to this type of thinking. It seemed to be an article of faith in Ottawa in the mid-1960s that special status was appropriate and the way to satisfy Quebec's 'demands.' I did not agree with that when I was legal adviser. In any event, Trudeau's views seemed to me very welcome. This was before the European Community had invented the term 'subsidiarity,' but it wasn't all that far from the concept of what is subsidiary. Trudeau had a symmetrical concept. He believed in a division of powers that was appropriate to the subject and to the nature of what was being legislated. At this time I do not believe he was particularly convinced that constitutional reform was either necessary or desirable. Although he became associated with the constitutional reform process, in the early period he didn't feel that it was essential or desirable. He felt that the British North America Act was a good basis for constitutional Canada and that it did not need significant reform, if it needed reform at all. The one area of concern where he did agree that constitutional reform was desirable was in terms of entrenching a bill of rights.

BOTHWELL: The 1968 conference on the Constitution was overtaken by events. Pearson had already announced his retirement, and in April 1968 a Liberal Party convention elected Trudeau to be his successor. Trudeau promptly called an election for June 1968, which he won handily, with a majority in the House of Commons, including most of the seats from the province of Quebec.

Then, in November 1968, Daniel Johnson died, and was briefly succeeded by Jean-Jacques Bertrand. It was Bertrand's misfortune to govern during a time of mounting social crisis in Quebec. There was a crisis, and riots, over the issue of language, in schools and in daily life. There was a student strike and riot at Sir George Williams University in Montreal, a campaign of bombing by terrorists calling themselves the Front de Libération du Québec, or FLQ, and then a police strike in Montreal, which forced the Quebec government to call in the Canadian Army to keep order on the streets.

Against this background, politics proceeded, and so did the reform of the Constitution. In terms of politics, the Union Nationale government of Quebec reached the end of its tether. In April 1970 a provincial election returned the Liberal Party to power under a new, young leader, Robert Bourassa.

Over the next twenty-five years, Quebec politics were dominated by three men: Bourassa, who would be premier twice, from 1970 to 1976, and from 1985 to 1994; René Lévesque, premier from 1976 to 1985; and Pierre Trudeau, prime minister of Canada from 1968 to 1984, with one slight interruption. Of these three, Bourassa was the youngest, the most junior in terms of service.

Bourassa should not, however, be underestimated as a politician. In the 1970 election he promised two things to Quebeckers – two sides of the same coin, in effect. He promised economic security, meaning jobs, by avoiding the disruptions and uncertainties of separatism. And he promised to turn Canadian federalism into what he called 'fédéralisme rentable' – profitable federalism. The profits of Quebec's membership in federal Canada would also contribute to economic security, and to employment and prosperity in Quebec. 'Bob le job,' as he was sometimes called, would see to it.

Raymond Garneau was an active Quebec Liberal in the late 1960s, first as Jean Lesage's executive assistant, and then as a candidate for the Quebec legislature, which had recently been renamed the National Assembly. He describes the atmosphere of the late 1960s:

GARNEAU: Beginning in 1964, and especially from 1965 to 1970, the nationalist movement developed rapidly in Quebec. And René Lévesque had been part of it. He was a charismatic leader with long experience, and was very well known as a reporter and as a politician. All sorts of movements were flourishing at the university level, and they were also good years for the union movement. Altogether a momentum was gathering speed. One of the reasons why Premier Bertrand called an election in April 1970 was because he was on the verge of a strike by construction workers. Their union was very strong. The Quebec National Assembly had appointed a House committee to work on some piece of legislation to find a solution to a strike. Construction industry workers broke down the door and came in the committee room with baseball bats – it was pretty tough. Most of those activities were supported one way or the other by the nationalistic group, because it was a way to create animosity against the party in power. So Premier J-J.

Bertrand called an election at the end of April 1970, which is an unusual date for an election because of the poor weather during the campaign month of March. He called an election before tabling a budget, so there was all sorts of turmoil.

BOTHWELL: The election was won by Bourassa and the Liberals. Bourassa formed a majority government. René Lévesque was personally defeated, and his separatist party, which had changed its name to the Parti Québécois or PQ, managed to get only seven seats in the provincial assembly. They had managed to beat the Union Nationale in terms of popular vote, but even there the distribution of votes was against them, much to the irritation of their supporters. Meanwhile, it was the time of the Liberals: Liberals in Quebec and Liberals in Ottawa could surely get along.

As events showed, they had to get along, and they did; but not happily. On 5 October 1970 James Cross, the British trade representative in Montreal, was kidnapped by a group calling itself a cell of the Front de Libération du Québec, the FLQ. They presented various demands for his release, including a pile of gold and a free flight out of the country. The federal government was involved from the beginning, because Cross was a foreign diplomat, but the combined forces of the Montreal, Quebec, and Canadian governments could not uncover where Cross was hidden. And then, on 10 October, Pierre Laporte, minister of labour in the Bourassa government and a senior member of the Quebec cabinet, was also abducted. More demands were submitted for his release.

The result was an uproar that convulsed the whole of Quebec society and eventually involved the whole of Canada. Raymond Garneau, minister of finance in the Bourassa government from 1970 to 1976, describes what he felt, as a member of the government:

GARNEAU: When the Cross kidnapping came around, we were shocked, because we were a quiet country; and after Cross had been kidnapped, then came the kidnapping of Pierre Laporte. The police – the RCMP, the Quebec Provincial Police, and Montreal Urban Community Police – the three forces didn't know to what extent this movement was organized. I remember sitting for hours with representatives of the police, who tried to explain the possibilities to the cabinet, but they had no more information than we had. The whole population was very nervous and everybody wanted to have action, they wanted something to be done. And so, it was a big shock. There was also the fact that the premier was very young; besides being young, he looked young, and a certain nervousness had been created because of that. People like Claude Ryan, editor of *Le Devoir*, and union leaders wanted to create an alternative to the government if needed, because they were scared that Bourassa would break down, but, in fact, he didn't. He was quite strong, in the circumstances. But the major point was that we didn't know, the police didn't know, nobody knew, so it was difficult for us to make decisions. If we had known that the FLQ was so disorganized that the group that kidnapped Laporte was not even in touch before the fact with the group that kidnapped Cross, we would have felt differently. There were all sorts of rumours. There were also the crackpots. One day Bourassa received an envelope with six bullets, and a note saying 'There will be one for you.' Probably, there were all sorts of disorganized groups of people playing games; one person would do something from his home, but you didn't know how many there were, and whether they were organized or not. That was the most difficult part of the crisis.

BOTHWELL: Once again the police forces proved unable to cope. As the crisis wore on, worry in Quebec City increased. Elsewhere in the province the possibility of an alternative government was discussed, should Bourassa prove inadequate. Such discussions do not seem to have been much more than speculation, and certainly did not imply removing a constitutional government by extra-constitutional means, but it was a sign of the times. There were students who wanted to organize demonstrations and mass meetings. There was an uncomfortable sense that the FLQ might speak for more than a few malcontents, that its action might send the whole political structure of Quebec into collapse.

The Bourassa government asked Ottawa for help to support the Quebec provincial police – help in the form of the Canadian Army, and the proclamation of emergency powers using the federal emergency statute, the War Measures Act. The troops arrived on 15 October, and the War Measures Act was proclaimed the next day, 16 October.

GARNEAU: I remember when we had to make the decision about the War Measures Act. We accepted the condition imposed by Trudeau, and the army came to support the Quebec Provincial Police. The mere fact that the army came in was a tremendous relief. People forget, but if you had taken a poll the day after, we would have had the support of 90 per cent of the population. At that time I was not a leader among the Liberals, though I was respected. I was what you would call a traditional liberal. I was opposed to arresting people. The cabinet had a long discussion; at the end, I was arguing with the police. Since I was opposing the arrests, I had been asked to look at the list, and with another cabinet minister I spent an hour or so going over that list. I saw the name of Gérard Pelletier and I asked, 'Is this the minister?' and they said, 'No, no.' In fact, I did not know personally any of the people on that list. Finally, I accepted the decision of the majority. In the circumstances, I thought opposition might be more damaging for the government. Two years later the police chief took me aside and said, 'Remember the debate we had? You were right.' The major factor at the time was that we didn't know the strength of the FLQ. We would have acted differently if we had known, but we didn't.

BOTHWELL: The police arrested more than 150 individuals suspected of FLQ sympathies that night, and more over the next few days. Ironically, and despite the assurances given to the Quebec cabinet, they even tried to arrest the federal secretary of state and Trudeau's colleague, Gérard Pelletier: they had got the address wrong and the Pelletiers mixed up.

The October crisis showed that the governments in Ottawa and in Quebec City were fundamentally united in resisting terrorism. Nevertheless, viewed from the inside, the crisis had some disturbing moments. Marc Lalonde, at that time Trudeau's principal secretary and in charge of the federal government's response to the crisis, comments on Bourassa's response to the crisis:

LALONDE: Whatever his personal convictions might be, which were not always easy to assess, he would let himself be guided by events, rather than managing events or influencing events very much. This quickly became evident in the October crisis, where Bourassa showed no clear vision of the situation. He was new on the job, he was young, and he provided no strong leadership. He was very much dependent on the views of Saulnier, chair of Montreal's executive committee, and Drapeau, the mayor, in Montreal, and he appeared to be influenceable by events as they occurred. He had no political position in his own mind on how to handle that kind of crisis from the start, as Trudeau did. The crisis was managed, nonetheless, and cooperatively, too, but it certainly didn't show that Bourassa had a strong sense of leadership in such a situation.

BOTHWELL: The army and the War Measures Act stabilized opinion in Quebec. As Garneau observed, public opinion in Quebec and the rest of Canada overwhelmingly approved the government's actions at the time. And, in fact, terrorism did diminish, though not in time to save Pierre Laporte's life: he was murdered by his kidnappers and his body left in the trunk of a car. Eventually Cross was found and released, and his kidnappers got a free trip to Cuba. Most of the perpetrators were either arrested or gave themselves up, and were punished with jail sentences of varying lengths.

The symbolism of 1970, of what was called the October crisis, lasted much longer. Though Bourassa's and Trudeau's actions were popular at the time, they were strongly condemned in retrospect as an unwarranted violation of civil liberties. Of the hundreds of people arrested, none was convicted of any crime. As Garneau observes, however, it is important to understand the situation as it existed in 1970, the dearth of knowledge, the fluid political situation, the lack of confidence in a young and untried government. Had Trudeau and Bourassa not acted as they did to bolster public confidence, what might have occurred? It is not a question easily answered.

Bourassa at least would have been justified in believing that his government, and federalism in Quebec, had a narrow escape. Throughout his career he had a horror of violence and disorder, and a sense that matters might very easily slip out of control. He had confronted events in 1970, and prevailed, but he seems also to have drawn the conclusion that it was better not to provoke events – to persuade sleeping dogs to lie down and dream on. As far as Bourassa was concerned, the danger lay above all on the nationalist end of the political spectrum, and for the rest of his career he was concerned to keep the nationalists, as far as possible, quiet.

Bourassa demonstrated this tendency the very next year, in 1971, when the constitutional discussions begun in 1968 finally reached a conclusion. A federal-provincial conference was held in Victoria to seek agreement on a new form for the Canadian Constitution and, miraculously, it almost reached agreement.

But not quite. Lalonde was in charge of Ottawa's negotiations with Quebec leading to the charter. In describing what happened at the conference he refers to Claude Castonguay, Bourassa's minister of social affairs, and to Claude Morin, Quebec's very nationalist deputy minister of intergovernmental affairs:

LALONDE: Bourassa had been pressing for improvements on the constitutional front, but Trudeau was very firm that he didn't want to open this issue unless he could be sure that Quebec would come along. He would not go through the exercise of convincing other provinces, only to find that the government of Quebec said no. Therefore, a pact was made that Quebec and Ottawa would try to agree on the basic objectives that Quebec would pursue in that constitutional reform. Trudeau appointed Gordon Robertson (who was secretary of the Privy Council) and me to be his representatives. Bourassa appointed Julien Chouinard, who later became a Supreme Court judge but at that time was secretary of the cabinet in Quebec, as his representative, along with himself. We met on a number of occasions in the six months before the Victoria conference. In the spring, we finally had a text that was fully acceptable to Bourassa. 'Leave it to me,' he said; 'I'll make sure that this is agreeable to my cabinet; I'll make sure that my government approves it.' So Trudeau called the federal-provincial conference in Victoria, in June, and in the meantime Bourassa procrastinated somehow; he didn't bring the matter to cabinet on an urgent basis. From what I could find out, Claude Morin, who had been completely excluded from those discussions, discovered that they had taken place and was no doubt miffed. He went to Claude Castonguay, and the two of them agreed that Quebec should get additional concessions in the social policy field. But that was never expressed before the Victoria conference; it came out only at the time of the conference. Castonguay was present with Morin and Chouinard, and Bourassa tried to get us to go further, but we could not. We ended up being able to extract an agreement on what we had already agreed with Quebec. Castonguay was pressuring Bourassa not to give in, so Bourassa left the conference without agreeing, and saying that he would reflect on the text with his colleagues in Quebec. The rest is history. From that moment on, Trudeau became convinced that he never could trust Bourassa to deliver on his promises. He saw him as the kind of politician who preferred to govern by wheeling and dealing, rather than taking a stand and fighting for it strongly.

BOTHWELL: Gordon Robertson had managed the federal negotiating team, along with Lalonde, and he explains what happened at the end of the Victoria conference, and what the failure of the conference meant:

ROBERTSON: At Victoria, it was purely and simply the problem of Quebec that occupied the conference. One of the great tragedies – in fact, I think the greatest single tragedy – of our constitutional review was that while there was unanimous agreement at Victoria, it was subject to an eleven- or twelve-day delay while the premiers went back and checked with their provinces, and this was at the insistence of Bourassa. And before the time limit was out, he withdrew the approval he had given at Victoria. Now if that approval had stood, the Victoria charter was an excellent set of arrangements; among other things, it had a better amending procedure for the Constitution than the amending procedure we've got today. If all the provinces had stood by their agreement we would have avoided most if not all the twenty-three years of agony we've had since.

BOTHWELL: Today, most of the participants at Victoria view the outcome as a tragic mistake. Claude Forget was a senior adviser to the Quebec government in 1971, and subsequently a minister in the Bourassa government. He describes what happened to the Victoria charter when Bourassa brought it home to Quebec:

FORGET: Why Bourassa changed his mind is a matter of public record. There was a feeling within the government, and outside, that he was ready to sign the charter and be done with it, but he came home to a barrage of negative editorial comment. Just about everyone in Quebec suggested that this was a sellout, this was a disappointment. We have to set this reaction in the context of the Parti Québécois having been set up just three years before and the rhetoric on constitutional affairs. Even on the federalist side, there was a 'holier than thou' sort of attitude, of trying to outdo the Parti Québécois on its own turf, which I suppose is normal competitive behaviour on the part of political parties. It was not just a question of Quebec independence, or something close to that; there was also the question of social policy. Because of the longstanding commission of inquiry on social policy that had concluded in 1970, there was a feeling that Quebec had a somewhat more enlightened agenda than the rest of Canada, and that it was somehow legitimate or appropriate for Quebec to want to strike out on its own in this area. So, the two currents combined to produce a feeling that, unless there was provincial supremacy in social policy, the charter was not an acceptable compromise. That's the basis on which Bourassa, impressed by the degree of public outrage to the proposed agreement, decided to change his mind and not accept it. But we should have accepted the Victoria charter.

BOTHWELL: Gérald Beaudoin, who is both a constitutional expert and a Conservative senator, explains what the failure of Victoria signified:

BEAUDOIN: When they made the Victoria charter in 1971, it was very good, and Quebec made a tremendous error in refusing to sign. I have always thought that way, and now it's even clearer. Many federalists in Quebec now say Quebec should have accepted the Victoria charter with the four vetoes for the formula of amendment, and so on. In my opinion, it was the greatest error Quebec had made in many years. After that Trudeau said, 'Well, we will patriate the Constitution. We will put the Charter of Rights in the Constitution. And then we will talk about the division of powers.' The fact that the Victoria charter was set aside was a major mistake, because Quebec has never obtained since then a better deal.

BOTHWELL: At the time, the failure of the Victoria conference created few ripples. It seemed to bring constitutional consultation to an end, and the country, business, and politics all carried on. But the nagging question remained: What did Quebec really want, even under Bourassa? Was Canada stable with a sizeable nationalist-separatist movement in Quebec, with a separatist party waiting in the wings to take power? Was Trudeau, who repeatedly won at the polls with strong majorities in Quebec, truly able to manage opinion in that province and keep it balanced on the federal side? Trudeau Liberals thought so; and Quebec nationalists thought not.

Louis Balthazar analyzes Trudeau's place in Quebec history from a nationalist perspective:

BALTHAZAR: I don't want to be too critical of Trudeau. He came with a government that had many other virtues and that might have been very good if Canada had been unilingual, or if Quebeckers had agreed with his 'Let's stop being Quebeckers, let's be Canadians, in both languages.' What is tragic is that Trudeau intervened and made the rest of the country forget about Quebec's vital demands, which its representatives in the National Assembly in Quebec were expressing. He talked loud enough to put us in the background, and the noise we were making was forgotten. He was very outspoken, brilliant, with lots of fine qualities, and he acted as though he was the genuine representative of Quebec. He got a great majority in parliament, due to the Quebec vote, because Quebeckers were proud of Trudeau. They liked to be represented by him, when he went abroad. They admired him, but they did not subscribe to his philosophy. That again was tested in public opinion polls.

The tragedy of the 1970s was that you had two great politicians in Quebec whom people admired and loved to some extent, Pierre Elliott Trudeau and René Lévesque. Yet there was no majority to subscribe to either one's philosophy. Lévesque's philosophy of sovereignty didn't appeal to the majority of Quebeckers, nor did Trudeau's philosophy of one Canada. So they were polarized, against their wishes.

BOTHWELL: Lise Bissonnette, editor of *Le Devoir*, suggests that Trudeau's repudiation of traditional Quebec nationalism was not wrong; where he went wrong was in failing to understand that Quebec nationalism had evolved:

BISSONNETTE: If anybody talks about Trudeau's nationalism, I challenge it. Even as a Canadian nationalist, I think Trudeau is in the realm of theory all the time, and that's basically his problem. He analyzes everything in terms of what it means theoretically. His ideas about nationalism are those of nineteenth-century nationalism. In a way, I understand what he's saying, but I think we should not talk about nationalism any more in Quebec. Political institutions should not be built on that kind of nationalism, though I know that in Quebec some people would disagree with me on that. Trudeau went to Ottawa to fight the modern-day nationalism in Quebec, which was based in part on a sense of identity and a sense of closeness, but at the same time was changing into something larger that he never admitted. He lost touch with the culture of Quebec in the 1970s. You probably could not ask him today who are the writers, the painters, the creators in Quebec. Yet that is my way of witnessing the change in Quebec, to see what's going on in the cultural milieu, and among the people who are creative: What are they writing? What are they saying? What is their view of the world? I think that Trudeau never acknowledged that Quebec nationalism was changing even among the *indépendantistes.*

Some people in Quebec will say, 'Well, he became a Canadian nationalist,' with the flag, anti-Americanism, and all of that. I'm a fascinated observer of Canadian nationalism, which sometimes I find more appalling than nineteenth-century nationalism in Quebec. I'm upset by anti-Americanism and all its negativity. You cannot build a country, whether it's in Canada or in Quebec, on hating the other. I often see that attitude in English Canada, especially in Toronto and among the intellectual community, but I don't think Trudeau ever shared that basic anti-Americanism.

BOTHWELL: The 1970s would prove to be an uneasy decade, with Quebec always lingering in the background, and with the rest of the country uncomfortably aware that the business begun in 1968, with the constitutional conference, or in 1960, with the Quiet Revolution, was incomplete. Before the decade was out, Canadians, including Prime Minister Trudeau, had plenty to worry about. For in 1976 a separatist government was elected in Quebec, and the crisis between Canada and Quebec entered a new and much more dangerous phase.

Chapter 8

The Politics of Language, 1969-77

LANGUAGE AND QUEBEC, Quebec and language. The two terms seem almost indistinguishable. From the conquest of 1760, Quebec has been defined by the French language, the language of the majority inside the province, and the language of the minority within Canada. Seen from inside the province, the survival of the French language in an English-speaking sea has been little short of miraculous. The motto of Quebec is 'Je me souviens' – I remember – and what is remembered, above all, is the French language.

That French has survived and flourished, and is the native language of more than 6.5 million people inside Canada, including 5.5 million in Quebec, ought to be an occasion for cheer, and even self-congratulation, inside Quebec. And indeed, human nature being what is, self-congratulation is not absent. But where an English-Canadian observer sees achievement, a triumph over the demographic odds, a French Canadian is more likely to see just the odds, and to wonder how much longer French Canada's linguistic gamble can possibly last in a world where English is not merely the dominant local language in North America, but where French, as a worldwide language, is in retreat.

That fact coincides with another. The population of Quebec has changed considerably since the 1950s. David Foot, an economist specializing in demography, explains what has happened to the population of Quebec:

FOOT: Back in the 1920s we were averaging three and a half children per family in Canada, and that was made up by four and a half children in Quebec and three in the rest of the country. Quebec's population was roughly a third of Canada, and all through the 1920s, 1930s, and 1940s Quebec had a significantly higher fertility rate than the rest of Canada. Therefore, they were augmenting their population at a somewhat more rapid rate, at least from domestic sources. Then, with the advent of the Quiet Revolution and the disengagement of the family from the church, fertility started to decline in Quebec, and it started to decline in Quebec before it started to decline in the rest of the country. By about 1959 the fertility rate in Quebec and the fertility rate in the rest of Canada were the same. For the last thirty-five years, the fertility rate in Quebec has been consistently below that of the rest of Canada. Not surprisingly, population growth in Quebec is now significantly smaller than in the rest of Canada, and also not surprisingly, Quebec's population has gone from roughly a third of Canada's to a quarter of Canada's. In countries where the declining group is also a minority group, we often see all sorts of concern with continuation of that particular minority, and it often results in some dramatic reactions.

BOTHWELL: There was a time when French was widespread in North America. The French colonists occupied a large part of the continent – the St Lawrence, the Great Lakes, the Mississippi valley. There are plenty of place-names that attest to the fact – St Louis, for example, or Duluth, Detroit, Baton Rouge, or New Orleans. But the odds of finding a native French-speaker in St Louis or Duluth today are pretty slight: and the odds in New Orleans or Baton Rouge are not much greater. Yet New Orleans was once the capital of Quebec's southern twin, the French colony of Louisiana, and even today the American state of Louisiana uses the French civil code, as does Quebec, rather than the English common law that characterizes the rest of North America north of the Rio Grande.

Alfred Hero, himself the descendant of French settlers in Louisiana, but also a student of Quebec-American relations, describes the fate of French in the United States, and especially in Louisiana:

HERO: There are all sorts of studies where you can track the decline. The further you get from the Quebec border the more rapid the decline, and you can trace it by generation. If you went back one generation – even the census of 1970 as contrasted with the census of 1990, which is basically one generation jump – and compared the same two age groups, it is clear that the decline is continuous and accelerating, and the same is true in Louisiana. When I was a child, I was raised by my grandmother and I went to school in town during the Depression. If I wanted a glass of water, I had to ask for it in French, or I didn't get it. So it's a recent decline among the Acadians; it has been since the Second World War, what with the influx of the oil industry and the mass media, television and so on. Among the generation of Acadians born within the last twenty-five years, it's something in the order of 5 per cent who can understand spoken French.

BOTHWELL: Canadians are often tempted into smugness when they are confronted by bad American examples. But that would not be fair: the history and geography of Canada are thickly populated by French Canadians and English Canadians who have assimilated to the majority culture in their locality, English or French. In Saskatchewan, Alberta, and British Columbia, and even Manitoba, Nova Scotia, and Prince Edward Island, French-language communities are in a steady decline. In Quebec there are also plenty of communities where, in living memory, English was the dominant language and where today it lives on, if at all, as the language of an increasingly elderly and isolated minority.

Scott Reid, a researcher with the Reform Party, has studied the distribution of languages in Canada. His work has reached the same conclusions as an earlier study by Richard Joy, *Languages in Conflict*, published in the 1960s. As Reid argues, the intervening thirty years have only confirmed trends that many have found disquieting:

REID: In his book, Joy argued that Canada's two languages were polarizing, that polarization had been going on for a long time, that it would continue to go on in the future. And he used what, at the time, were very incomplete language statistics and manipulated them in an interesting way to demonstrate, quite irrefutably, that increasingly French would be trapped within Quebec. Francophone communities would not continue to exist outside Quebec. The English would withdraw from the various small communities within Quebec where formerly they were dominant, and would retreat to Montreal. Moreover, there was no way the government could prevent this from happening. Right after Joy wrote his book the federal government introduced the Official Languages Act, a serious attempt to freeze the linguistic picture or perhaps even to reverse it; it was also an attempt to make it possible for francophones to live outside Quebec, and for anglophones to live inside Quebec, and for both groups to do so in comfort. Basically, Joy's argument is quite straightforward: he says we spend most of our lives interacting with people in our community, and if the majority of those people are English-speaking, we tend, whatever our mother tongue might have been, to learn English so we can speak to the corner grocer, the bus driver, potential friends, romantic partners, and the people we meet in the streets. This trend has continued; the number of francophones outside Quebec has dropped, the number of anglophones within Quebec outside Montreal has dropped, and the services that the federal government has provided to prevent this from happening have been totally ineffective.

BOTHWELL: Within Canada, inside Canadian history and the Canadian political system, there are several contradictory forces at work. Canada was founded as a place where French was guaranteed recognition – legal status – though legal status only in the federal parliament, the federal courts, and in the legislature and courts of Quebec. An attempt was made in the late nineteenth century to extend the protection of French to the Canadian prairie provinces, but that failed, to a greater or lesser degree.

Ron Duhamel, Liberal member of parliament for St Boniface and a former deputy minister of education for Manitoba, describes what has happened to the Franco-Manitobans:

DUHAMEL: Initially, as Franco-Manitobans, we were the majority in this province; then, gradually over time, as more and more people came to Manitoba and western Canada, we became a minority. Not only were we overtaken by the sheer number of people coming to this area, but assimilation was eating away at the core of the people who spoke French. There were a number of reasons for this loss. The power of the majority, whether it be English-speaking or any other, is always omnipresent. It's omnipresent in the way we do business, live our lives, and the rest. And we did not have the infrastructure in place to permit a response, to retain the numbers we had, or to reinforce them. The power we once had, by virtue of being the majority, was lost over time, to the point where French was not allowed to be used as the language of instruction in our schools. Then, gradually over time, a dialogue once more began.

Now we can use French as a language of instruction, and we do so. We have a number of schools where French is the language of instruction, though English is taught as well. Most Franco-Manitobans speak English as well as other Manitobans do, but because French-speakers are a minority and a very small group, they continually work at maintaining their French language and culture. We have not had a lot of people come from Quebec or France. We've usually married other French-speaking Canadians or, increasingly, English-speaking Canadians who know French. There has also been an opening of the mind.

BOTHWELL: In Manitoba, as elsewhere, the old cultural sentinels, the parish church and the parish school, no longer insulate the minority language from excessive contact with the majority. There is therefore a greater concentration on forms of culture to preserve the language and on help from the state, whether federal or provincial.

The trend in language usage was already well established in Canada when the 1960s dawned, but the events of that decade brought language to the fore. When blended with other factors, language proved a very potent political force. In the early 1960s, there were three such factors: language and social status, language and immigration, and language and education. These subjects were in fact closely linked.

The explosion may have begun with a special study by the Royal Commission on Bilingualism and Biculturalism. It examined income, occupation, and ethnicity, and revealed that in Quebec, the province where they were in a majority, where they had for a hundred years run the government and elected the majority of the province's politicians, French Canadians were firmly at the bottom of the income and occupation heap. In federal institutions, French Canadians were simply not proportionately represented, and when they were, it was in low-status and low-paying jobs. As a remedy, the B and B Commission proposed what was called 'institutional bilingualism' rather than 'individual bilingualism' – the creation of French-speaking units within the civil service, units in which the language of work would in fact be French.

In Quebec, French Canadians came after the English, and especially the unilingual English. The English had been there a long time, and anybody gazing at the mansions of Westmount might not have had too much trouble predicting such a result. But French Canadians also came after virtually every other ethnic group. These ethnic groups had come more recently and, in some cases, very much more recently. And, to add insult to injury, the new arrivals had predictably assimilated to the prosperous English, and not the French majority.

The result was serious discontent, which found expression in attempts by a suburban Montreal school board, in St-Léonard, to restrict education in English. Italian immigrants objected; and there were even demands that English-language education in Quebec be abolished. In St-Léonard there were riots, and in Montreal there were demonstrations calling for 'McGill français' – French McGill. In Quebec City, Premier Jean-Jacques Bertrand brought in legislation, Bill 63, guaranteeing the rights of parents to choose the language of education for their children. It was a broad-minded response to the problem, but observers at the time thought Bertrand had made a serious misjudgment. And, indeed, within a year, Bertrand was out, his career at an end. The provincial government had tried and failed to legislate a solution to the language question; now it was the federal government's turn. Under the direction of Trudeau's friend, the federal secretary of state, Gérard Pelletier, an Official Languages Act was prepared and passed through parliament.

The Official Languages Act derived much of its force from the recommendations of the Royal Commission on Bilingualism and Biculturalism, but it did not actually follow the recommendations of the commission, which proposed French-language work units within the federal government. The French and English languages were to be co-equal inside the federal parliament, the courts, and the civil service. Inside the civil service, certain positions were designated 'bilingual,' and their occupants, if not already bilingual, were to be shipped off for language training to become bilingual. Where numbers of French- or English-speakers warranted, bilingual districts were created so that French- or English-speakers could obtain federal government services in their own language. This, the government explained, merely guaranteed 'equality of access' for people who were, after all, paying taxes to support federal institutions and obtain federal services.

The Official Languages Act was not well received in much of English-speaking Canada. It was a sentiment that John Diefenbaker, by then compulsorily retired as Conservative leader but still an MP with a considerable political following, chose to exploit. Senator Lowell Murray, a close observer of party affairs, watched what was happening with increasing distress:

MURRAY: Where I do fault Diefenbaker is in the influence he exerted from the time he left office in 1963, practically to the time of his death in 1979. A good part of those fifteen years were spent stirring up animosity against Quebec and French Canadians, for all kinds of reasons, and using those issues in a very partisan way while he was still leader of the opposition. By this means he hoped to consolidate his own support in the caucus and in English Canada, especially in the western part of the country. Later, after he left the leadership, he tried to use those issues to undermine his successors, Robert Stanfield and Joe Clark.

BOTHWELL: Robert Stanfield was leader of the Conservative Party from 1967 to 1976; it was his misfortune to be defeated by Trudeau in the federal elections of 1968, 1972, and 1974. Stanfield took a soft line on Quebec, and tended to believe that Trudeau's strident anti-nationalism, Quebec-style, and especially his harsh attacks on his critics in Quebec, also played to or confirmed English-Canadian prejudices.

MURRAY: Trudeau's concept of Canada, while completely rejecting what he called Quebec nationalism, had this other important aspect to it, that is, minority language rights across the country, but Canadians didn't hear that. English Canadians didn't hear that, and that is why so many of them were so shocked apparently, and angry and bitter, when he set about bringing in an Official Languages Act, and all the implications of that.

BOTHWELL: Others, though for different reasons, also believed that Trudeau's Official Languages Act was mistaken. Senator Jean-Robert Gauthier, for many years member of parliament for Ottawa East or Ottawa Vanier (a largely French-speaking riding with many French-speaking civil servants living in it), evaluates whether Trudeau's Official Languages Act was a success:

GAUTHIER: I didn't buy that. I'm still of the opinion that bilingualism per se was an irritant for a lot of Canadians, and I didn't think it was the appropriate way of doing it. I said so publicly at the time. I believed and I still believe that Canada is not a bilingual country; I believe that Canada is a country which has two official languages; it is a different concept altogether from bilingualism. Two official languages, equal status before the courts – these are the factors that should be promoted and supported across the country. In the West, people saw bilingualism as ramming French down their throats; if they weren't bilingual, they couldn't get a job in the public service. Now, all these myths were wrong, because at that time, even today, 75 per cent of the jobs in the federal government are unilingual English and 25 per cent are identified as bilingual. I make a difference between institutional bilingualism, which is something I believe in, and national bilingualism, which is something I think is worthwhile, but which we'll never reach.

BOTHWELL: Nevertheless, Trudeau's prestige was such that the government, with support from the opposition parties, or most of them, was able to carry its Official Languages Act. Robert Kaplan, who was then an MP for a Toronto riding, describes how the official languages policy played in his constituency:

KAPLAN: In my riding, the second language was definitely Italian and, even more in those days than nowadays, there was a bit of explaining to people why a language other than English should be given a status higher than Italian, or higher than some other language which was much more widely spoken. There was always some explaining to do, but the prime minister provided such a magnificent personal leadership that members of every community in Toronto gradually entered into some kind of national way of thinking, thinking like national Canadians. They came to recognize that however much Italian was spoken around here, there were ten times as many people in the country speaking French. When they came to this country, they came to the whole of it, they adopted all of Canada, so it was fairly easy to explain what we were trying to do. There were still some people who argued that this is an English-speaking country because, centuries ago, our side won, but that's just not true. This country was built on an agreement that respect would be paid to the French language and culture. I used to enjoy explaining that to people who disagreed.

BOTHWELL: The government – indeed every government since 1968 – accepted the political costs of the Official Languages Act, costs that were really not very great. But for some federal politicians there was an uneasy feeling that the law was not working quite as it should. As a minister under Trudeau, Kaplan daily confronted language qualifications and language training in the civil service. What he saw was not entirely reassuring:

KAPLAN: The more difficult question is, Did it work? It seemed to be quite wasteful in a lot of ways. A lot of people just can't acquire a second language at a certain point in their lives, and we refused to recognize that ideologically.

We encouraged them and we paid for it, and the bills are a matter of public record. But it didn't work as well as we thought it would.

But it worked well enough. Knowledgeable people still talk about it as a fundamental characteristic of Canada – that it is a country of two languages. Certainly, young francophones in Canada had a terrible and justified grievance about the limitations on their aspirations in their own province and in the federal bureaucracy and government, and that has changed. I think bilingualism has moved a long way forward.

BOTHWELL: Bilingualism, then, worked on balance – not perfectly, but as a necessary gesture from the majority to the minority. And most people, like Kaplan, agreed that it worked 'well enough.'

Trudeau and his successors as prime minister enforced and reinforced the official languages policy, which we generally know as bilingualism over the twenty-five years since its enactment in 1969. When the Constitution was reformed in the early 1980s, and a Charter of Rights and Freedoms was inserted, language rights were included in the package. Scott Reid describes where official bilingualism stands in the mid-1990s:

REID: Legally, the main institutions are the Official Languages Act, which was originally passed in 1969, and which was rescinded and replaced by another act, also called the Official Languages Act, in 1988. Even more fundamentally, there are sections of the Charter of Rights, sections 16 through 23, which provide for certain legislated rights to be guaranteed, and those include, for example, the publication of all law and regulations in Canada in both languages, the right to have a trial conducted in the official language of one's choice, and, most controversially, the right to an education in one's own official language outside of Quebec. Within Quebec there's a somewhat lesser right; if one has been educated in English in Canada, one is guaranteed an education in English in Quebec, but not otherwise. For French it's different; if one is a francophone or, more correctly, if one's parents had been educated in French, one has the right to education in French, so it's a little bit broader. In general, that has been controversial because of the fact that there are some areas of the country where there are fairly small numbers of people, but nonetheless they've argued: 'We have a right under the Constitution to have an education publicly funded out of general tax revenues, in French.'

BOTHWELL: Though attention in English Canada is naturally focused on minority rights in French, there was also dispute over minority rights in English inside the province of Quebec. Those rights were coming under fire at the end of the 1960s from Quebec nationalists; and unlike Diefenbaker and his followers in English Canada, Quebec nationalists were eventually able to force political action in support of their cause.

Premier Bertrand had not solved the language issue with his legislation in 1969. It was generally assumed that the Parti Québécois, the PQ, if it came to power, would act decisively on the language front. In 1973 Bourassa called an election, in which the PQ was reduced to a scant six seats (from seven in 1970) in the National Assembly. But the PQ won as well as lost. The other major party, the Union Nationale, was wiped out, and the PQ became the official opposition in Quebec City. In a parliamentary political system in which parties alternate in power, sooner or later the PQ would win an election and come to power.

It was evident that the PQ had a powerful issue ready to hand in the state of the French language. There was a problem of numbers, first of all: according to demographers, university experts in the field of population studies, the number of French-speakers in Quebec was in decline. Their conclusions are described by historian Michael Behiels:

BEHIELS: Since the late 1950s, demographers in Quebec have played a significant role in the debate because they started to predict that, with the declining birthrate and the ongoing process of immigration into Canada, the French-speaking proportion of the Canadian population would decline very rapidly from around 29 per cent down into perhaps the mid and even low 20s. As a result, Quebec's position within Confederation would be seriously weakened. They begin to understand the need in demographic terms to integrate immigrants into their society, something they had always shunned and, in fact, had rejected as an option for that community. That policy created a deep division within French-Canadian society in Quebec, because a lot of French-speaking Canadians, especially those outside Montreal who have little contact with immigrants, see such assimilation as the beginning of the end. They do not see how you can integrate non-francophone Quebeckers into their society and still retain their traditional culture. Other French-speaking Canadians and Quebeckers see that it is necessary to have a pluralistic francophone society all sharing the same language and similar institutions and values, but having different ethnic backgrounds and different cultures.

BOTHWELL: According to linguists, the state of the language was deplorable: the people of Quebec spoke a kind of French infiltrated with, infested by, all kinds of anglicisms. And, finally, the working world was dominated by English – a world in which it was necessary to learn and to use English to get ahead, and in which the use of French was discounted. The Bilingualism and Biculturalism Commission had pointed to this state of affairs, and the Quebec commission on the state of the French language in Quebec, chaired by Professor Jean-Denis Gendron of Laval University, said the same thing. The inferiority of French would have to be remedied by diminishing the status of English.

This analysis was received sceptically by some commentators, such as William Johnson, a historian and journalist who has studied French-English relations in Quebec:

JOHNSON: For all these people, the backwardness of French Canadians has only one solution. They accept the view of the past, that the Anglo is pretty much the enemy and the threat, the threat to the language, the threat to the culture, the threat to the religion. The only strong instrument is the state: they don't mean the state of Canada, but the state of Quebec. So, whether they eventually end up as federalists or whatever they call it, or whether they speak about two nations or special status, or sovereignty-association or independence, they all accept the same fundamental view – that we must build an ethnic state, a state of Quebec, which is for francophones and against anglophones. Given their concept of besieged Quebeckers, with the Anglos as the threat, they claim they need a very powerful instrument to protect them – and that instrument is the state of Quebec. The state of Quebec can build up its powers and pass laws to constrain languages other than French.

BOTHWELL: Premier Bourassa was determined to forestall the PQ, and the best way to do it, in his judgment, was to take the sting out of the language issue by acting first. Acting on the report of the Gendron commission on language, in 1974 the Liberal government brought in Bill 22. That law made French the only official language of Quebec, channelled immigrant children into French-language schools by removing their parents' freedom of choice, and compelled English-speaking businesses to erect bilingual signs.

Claude Forget, who was a minister in the Bourassa government at the time, comments on whether Bourassa did the right thing in bringing in his language law:

FORGET: We had no choice. Memory of this tends to be lost now, twenty or more years later, but the language issue began not under his government, but under the preceding government in Quebec, when there was a quarrel over access to English-speaking schools in Montreal, at St-Léonard. The large Italian minority there wanted to send their children to English-language schools. The school board of Greater Montreal, a Catholic board, raised an objection, saying that it was not appropriate that children of immigrants should automatically be absorbed in the anglophone group in Quebec, thereby changing the linguistic balance in the province. That quarrel had been an ongoing process in the 1950s and 1960s, but in the late 1960s it came to a head.

Studies done by the Royal Commission on Bilingualism and Biculturalism had produced a number of studies that were real eye-openers, providing a scientific basis for the widespread feeling among francophones in Quebec that the rules, as they existed at that time, were basically playing against them. Then, the St-Léonard crisis erupted, in an emotional context, too, because of the growing fortunes of the Parti Québécois. The provincial government decided to set up its own commission of inquiry on linguistic matters, the Gendron commission, and it sat for most of Bourassa's first term, eventually producing a report. Many of its recommendations pointed to the need for linguistic policy. The government could not just leave things alone. A laissez-faire attitude was not appropriate; it would lead to social disturbances. There was lots of passion involved. This thing had to be managed, and certain things had to be done, including something very much like Bill 22, the bill that incorporated the first version of the charter of the French language in Quebec. So Bourassa had no choice, because all the events were pushing in that direction. I remember debates within the provincial cabinet at the time, where that question was raised. He did not just assume that this would go forward, but we debated whether we had any alternatives. There were proponents on both sides, but the majority of opinion was that there was really no choice; we had to move in that direction. And what debates those were! We had no experience in North America of linguistic policy. There was no precedent, and our path was strewn with all manner of conceptual and practical difficulties. It was a debate that lasted for the better part of a year, with special sessions of the cabinet, and then special sessions of the caucus. And heated discussions they were.

BOTHWELL: Quebec, then, was increasingly defined in French-speaking terms. On the territory of Quebec, French would be, must be, the dominant language. Naturally, comment from outside the borders of Quebec was not welcomed: Quebec on its own territory was effectively sovereign, sovereign in defence of its own language or its own ethnicity. This was not good news for the French-speaking minorities outside Quebec.

JOHNSON: The result has been to cut French-speaking Quebeckers off from French Canadians in the rest of Canada. In theory, the ethnic state could not think of the state as Canada, so they had to have a doctrine that limited itself to Quebec. Quebec was what could be decolonized, not the rest of Canada. So they simply cut off the other French Canadians. And instead of backing French Canadians in the rest of Canada to acquire rights, to press for a full expansion of the *Francophonie canadienne*, you have the opposite, when you had René Lévesque opposing the francophones of Manitoba in the 1970s. He didn't want Franco-Manitobans to acquire rights to have an official language, because it might mean that Anglo-Quebeckers would acquire rights. You then have Bourassa opposing the francophones of Alberta when they went to court to acquire rights. You have this schism between the francophones of Canada based on this illusion that sometimes Quebec can become a quasi-independent state and, at other times, an independent state. You also have a schism between French-speaking Quebeckers and English-speaking Quebeckers, instead of viewing English-speaking Quebeckers as an asset, an economic asset as partners in building the society. And so Bourassa passed Bill 22, which had all kinds of restraints we don't talk about now because it was superseded, but it was a law which would have restricted freedom of speech, of expression, and of work in Quebec drastically.

BOTHWELL: Bill 22 had its defenders even among anglophones, including Gretta Chambers, who in the 1970s was a columnist for the Montreal *Gazette*:

CHAMBERS: Before the Liberal government of Robert Bourassa brought in Bill 22, the premier had tried really hard to get General Motors to write its labour contracts in French for the big plant in Ste-Thérèse. He never succeeded. This was not only symbolic, but a kind of a flag that if companies dealing in Quebec, and with a majority of French-speaking employees, couldn't even bend that far, there had to be legislation. Although the English were completely horrified by this legislation, there wasn't a francophone Quebecker who didn't think that, even though it was unpleasant, it was high time this happened. English Quebec suddenly found itself threatened culturally, socially, economically, and linguistically. It had to decide what to do, and it had no minority mechanism: it didn't know how to behave or to think like a minority, because it had never seen itself as a minority.

BOTHWELL: Bourassa's attempt to defuse the language issue failed. Immigrants and the English minority defied the provisions of the bill that made children five years old take language tests to determine into which side of the linguistic divide they fell. There were underground classes and phantom enrolments. But above all, there was resentment among English-speakers.

Unluckily for Bourassa, there was resentment among French-speakers too. In 1976 the federal government became embroiled in a quarrel with French-language air traffic controllers and pilots who demanded the right to speak French in the air over Quebec. That was apparently a reasonable demand. The other side argued that English was the universal language of aerial navigation and that the common language of North America would have to be English.

This was not an argument calculated to appeal to French-speaking Quebeckers. Trudeau lost his minister of transport, Jean Marchand, over the issue, although in fact the controversy was eventually resolved by permitting French in the air – where it remains, twenty years later. But that was later. Meanwhile the problem continued to simmer through the summer and fall of 1976, just as Bourassa called another provincial election. The Bourassa government had endured a nightmare of labour unrest and social disruption, and no doubt Bourassa hoped to put all that behind him. But he failed.

In 1970 and 1973 Bourassa had the advantage of running against an overtly separatist party, the PQ, which promised to implement Quebec sovereignty almost as soon as it came to power. But in 1976 the PQ did not run on the issue of separatism. It ran instead on the issue of good government, an area where Bourassa was extremely vulnerable, not only because of the public disorder of the previous few years, but because of a widespread perception that his government was corrupt. To induce people to get rid of

Bourassa first, the PQ promised to bring in separation only after a provincial referendum, some time in the next five years. And on that basis, on 15 November 1976, the PQ won.

Claude Forget, a member of the government that was defeated, explains why Bourassa lost popular favour so completely. He identifies two factors in particular: dislike between Bourassa and Trudeau, the two principal federalists in Quebec; and the public belief that the Bourassa government was corrupt:

FORGET: I had not detected in the government any major problems with honesty. There was no corruption on any extensive scale, certainly not at the level of cabinet members. But innuendoes and half-truths were used very skilfully; they played well in the media and thus created an image problem, which was compounded by Bourassa's personality. Not being confrontational, he would simply decline to answer or rebut charges of that nature, would shrug, and say, 'Well, this is not true; why should we bother about that?' This was his general attitude, not just his response to the question of honesty. He reacted the same way to personal insult. Trudeau once gave an interview in one of the popular media, and he casually dismissed Bourassa as a hot-dog eater, basically as someone who was not sophisticated, not very bright. It came through as a tremendous slight. I was incensed, and I went to see him in his office. I said, 'Robert, you cannot tolerate that. Everybody in your government feels personally insulted if you are insulted, and we want you to say something and bite back.' He simply would not be persuaded to say anything. He would not be bothered to answer criticism, if he thought that it was beneath him. That was the sort of man he was.

BOTHWELL: Bourassa was personally defeated in the 1976 election. He resigned as Liberal leader, and took time off to travel to Europe to study the institutions of the European Common Market, institutions that might prove instructive in a future Canada.

His successor as premier, PQ leader René Lévesque, promptly set about settling Quebec's language policy once and for all. He appointed Camille Laurin, a long-time nationalist, to define a policy. After a suitable period of study, in 1977 Laurin produced a Charter of the French Language, which became known as Bill 101.

The basic principle of Bill 101 was that French was the only public language of Quebec. Minority languages might enjoy exceptions, but always in the context of French predominance. The language of the workplace was to

without rupture from the status quo into a kind of linked identity with English Canada. His vision of sovereignty-association had all kinds of problems with it. One of the problems that existed for him inside the Parti Québécois was partly his charisma and elusiveness as a politician. Even though very few members of the Parti Québécois really shared his passion for this formula of sovereignty-association, he managed to keep their loyalty. And he kept their loyalty because nobody in the Parti Québécois really believed he was as fervently attached to this formula as he turned out to be. Some people in the Parti Québécois thought that because sovereignty-association seemed a pretty unworkable formula, this was a bargaining position that would result in Quebec having some kind of special status inside Confederation. Alternately, people like Jacques Parizeau felt that because sovereignty-association wouldn't work, it was simply a political stepping stone towards independence, and the fluidity and illusiveness of Lévesque's own rhetoric never really clarified that. Lévesque had a passionate attachment to Quebec and to the idea of independence, but he was also extremely reluctant to move farther and faster than he felt the people of Quebec were prepared to go. He devised this formula of sovereignty-association as a way of presenting the vision of an independent Quebec, but one, at the same time, that had the protection, the security, of an economic link with the rest of Canada. He felt, probably rightly, that he would not be able to win support for Quebec independence at that stage, without this sense of a protective process of moving to sovereignty-association.

BOTHWELL: Political scientist Louis Balthazar sees sovereignty-association as just one of a range of options that would have appealed to nationalist-leaning Quebeckers:

BALTHAZAR: Sovereignty-association, when it was tested in the referendum in 1980, had a very particular meaning. At the time it meant full political sovereignty for Quebec, and some form of economic association with the rest of Canada – it meant something like the European Community. The proponents of sovereignty-association wanted a very tight economic union with the rest of Canada, but they also wanted the symbols of sovereignty and the internal power associated with sovereignty in places like Europe. In my opinion, a great majority of Quebeckers would be satisfied with less than that.

BOTHWELL: The 1976 election was, therefore, only the first step on an uncertain path – a very uncomfortable step for the rest of the country. No one was absolutely clear how Quebeckers would make their decision. If it had taken only ten years for separatism to transform itself from a political novelty into political power, it was not unreasonable to believe that it could easily transmute its power into government.

Graham Fraser observed politics in Quebec City in the late 1970s as a *Globe and Mail* correspondent, and he explains Lévesque's attraction for the electorate:

FRASER: He was an extraordinarily charismatic figure who had a very ambiguous relationship with his own party. Lévesque had founded the Parti Québécois, but he never really thought of himself as a politician. His formative experience had been as a television journalist, and he had this quite accurate sense that he had a link with the public that went behind the structures of his own party. He was very impatient with those people in the party who kept sticking to the rule book and poring over all the resolutions that party congresses adopted. He accepted this as a necessary part of the democratic process, but he didn't like it much, and he had a journalist's distaste for people who liked to go to meetings. So you had this paradox that ran through his entire career – of somebody who was idolized by his party and had created the party, yet who had this profound distrust of people who really wanted to spend entire weekends poring over resolution books in drafty hockey arenas. Every few months, it seemed that the Parti Québécois was ruining a perfectly good weekend in some community college, as people pored over documents and workshops. And Lévesque had a phenomenally ambivalent relationship with that whole aspect of the structure and routines of a party.

BOTHWELL: Lévesque was the same generation, roughly the same age, as Pierre Trudeau, Jacques Hébert, Jean Marchand, and Gérard Pelletier. But his formation and attitudes, his likes and dislikes, were very different. Douglas Fisher, a journalist like Lévesque but also a former member of parliament, knew Lévesque and liked him:

FISHER: I had quite a few talks with him, a couple of really good long talks, one not long before he died. We shared the experience of both having been in the war, but he was with the Americans. He conceded that his war experience and his time in the American forces had given him a somewhat different outlook on the North American situation from that of most Canadians. He was very pro-American: he said when he went to Maine, or even to Florida or Washington, he felt at home. So he didn't look at Canada or the United States in the same way the Walter Gordon or the Hurtig types do. In that sense he wasn't negative about Canada. His feeling was more that the whole Canadian establishment and the British tradition, particularly in economic terms, had got in the way of French Canadians realizing their potential. It had kept them from being the captains of industry and running their economy, from having the kind of pride that comes from knowing, in a mill town in Quebec, for example, that all the big houses on the hill aren't held by Anglos. And he wanted to turn that around.

BOTHWELL: Lévesque's party was, by most criteria, very well qualified for power. Members and leaders were well educated, young or youngish, and highly committed to their cause. Men like Claude Morin, the minister of intergovernmental affairs, or Rodrigue Tremblay, a professional economist, or Jacques-Yvan Morin, a constitutional lawyer, or Jacques Parizeau, another economist, were impressive and knowledgeable – and most of them had already worked in or around government in Quebec City and, in some cases, Ottawa, too. But Lévesque was the master of the government, and at times a distant master. Graham Fraser explains:

FRASER: He was not really close to anybody in his cabinet personally. One of the things I've concluded over the years is that it is impossible for somebody who leads a government or a political party to have a relationship of genuine friendship with anybody who is in the cabinet; there are too many arbitrations that have to be struck. Lévesque was a distant, suspicious figure in many ways, in his own party and in his government. He shared with Claude Morin, however, a fundamental caution. In the tension in the Parti Québécois, between Claude Morin on the one hand and Jacques Parizeau on the other, Lévesque shared Morin's instinctive caution.

BOTHWELL: The 1970s were the period when the baby boom, the post-1945 generation, came to prominence and to power. Simply put, there were more young people, proportionately, in Canada than there had ever been. That fact gave a particular edge to the politics of the period, not just in Quebec but elsewhere in Canada – and indeed elsewhere in the Western world. The

Lévesque government, the Lévesque cabinet, the PQ caucus, and the civil service drew on the idealism and commitment of this generation – and on their sheer numbers, too, for political support.

Fraser was himself part of this generation, and had already met many of the PQ leaders via student politics in the 1960s. He comments on what it was like to meet them in government:

FRASER: I came to the conclusion that the postwar generation in Quebec had been kept in a kind of greenhouse for fifteen years after the Second World War. They were, in many cases, the first generation of Quebeckers to get a university education. They all knew each other from Laval University or the Université de Montréal, but they were basically excluded from the private sector, and from anything but low-wage intellectual work, by the power that Duplessis still had over the universities. In 1960, when the Liberals came to power, the explosion that generation represented burst forward not only to transform Quebec and create a government and a state, but to support and gather around René Lévesque and Pierre Trudeau. There was still enough energy in that generation to transform Ottawa, as the other half was in the process of transforming Quebec.

BOTHWELL: Lévesque aimed to overturn English-speaking dominance within Quebec and over Quebec. Ironically, his government confronted what was probably the strongest group of French-speaking Quebeckers ever to inhabit the federal government.

But the relationship between the federal government and Quebec really went considerably beyond the language spoken or the geographical origins of certain federal politicians and administrators. Trudeau's prominence belied the fact that for years both Quebec and Montreal had been losing ground to Ontario and, especially, Toronto. Over time, Quebec's relative position in the Canadian economy had been changing, declining, and shrinking in relative though not in absolute terms. Historian Michael Behiels describes the phenomenon, particularly the way Montreal's and Quebec's position worsened after 1945:

BEHIELS: The changes had been going on for some time. In terms of development of the private sector in the province, Quebec had always had difficulty in competing with Ontario for both domestic and foreign investments, and that competition became fierce in the 1950s. Toronto in large measure gained the upper hand over Montreal in that battle. A number of factors conspired to give Toronto the dominant position in the period from 1945 to 1970, though much of that loss in fact was offset by the growth of the federal government, or the national state, from the time of the Second World War. The federal government spent billions of dollars in the province of Quebec, funding the private sector and assisting the public sector in non-profit organizations. That help continued in the 1960s, this time with both the federal state and the provincial state picking up the slack in public investments when private investment lagged behind that of Ontario. The secular decline of the Quebec regional economy, including that of Montreal, was thereby hidden until the difficult times of the 1970s, the stagflation period, and the recession of the early 1980s. The massive public investment in the Quebec economy by both levels of government had shored up a lot of the traditional private-sector industry that had been established there since the national policy of 1879, but it did not prepare these industries for the free-market economy that was developing internationally through the GATT changes and the North American Free Trade Agreement. While this government support would only postpone the inevitable economic shakedown, it did allow the francophone population in the province of Quebec to make the transition by 1970 from a traditional society based on the primary resource industry of farming to an urban, industrial, service-sector society. Without that support from the federal and the Quebec state, the Quebec economy would have gone into the skids much sooner. So that support helped to keep Quebec within Confederation.

BOTHWELL: The structure of the Canadian federal state may indeed have favoured Quebec during the 1970s and earlier. Indirectly, Quebeckers benefited from federal transfer payments to the province in the name of equalization. They benefited, too, from federal policies that depressed domestic oil and gas prices in the face of the international oil cartel and a general, international price rise. The federal government itself controlled, and paid out, unemployment insurance and a wide variety of other subsidies to individual Quebeckers. Trudeau was determined that all this support should be known. The federal government would not leave anything to chance. Marc Lalonde, in the late 1970s Trudeau's minister of justice, describes the federal government's reaction to the approaching Quebec referendum:

LALONDE: For the first time we had a government in Quebec that was committed to the separation of Quebec from the rest of Canada. This situation was totally new; we had no precedent to go from. Although we saw that a lot of people had voted for the Péquistes, they had voted for them not because they believed in separation but because they wanted a change in government – they were fed up with the Bourassa government. In Lévesque, they had a leader who was very charismatic. This situation was obviously a cause for concern. At the same time, on the political side, we were perplexed about what this all meant and what the social forces were behind this radical change. While recognizing that a good number in the electorate had not voted for separation, and that support for separation in surveys was still low, we were very concerned that the PQ was going to be in office. We hoped that this official position would not allow that government to implement policies that would, on either an immediate or a gradual basis, achieve the goal it had given itself. We had to have a counter-revolutionary strategy, which we didn't have, and which we had not developed. In practice, this challenge required a reorganization of the federal government.

The federal administration was totally unprepared for this kind of change. We had to develop instruments that would allow us to understand what was going on and to have a response to issues as they were created by the Péquistes. Alternatively, we had to take a pro-active stance and initiate programs or actions that would run counter to the aspirations of the Péquistes or their policies and objectives. This meant, for instance, making sure that every measure adopted by the federal government was carefully examined in terms of its potential impact on Quebec, negative or positive. The federal government was doing a lot of things that people were not even aware of, such as equalization payments, and financial contributions to medicare, public assistance, and university education. That was mainly my role: to try to ensure that we would take the preventive approach, and, if necessary, the remedial approach.

BOTHWELL: The Trudeau Liberals were out of power between May 1979 and February 1980, the period of the brief Conservative government of Joe Clark. Clark announced that he saw Canada as 'a community of communities.' Trudeau described Clark's Canada as one where the federal government would be little more than the headwaiter at an endless provincial banquet.

The Clark government was weak in Quebec, and the prime minister, though bilingual, was not at ease in French. Lowell Murray, whom Clark appointed to the Senate, describes the government's difficulties:

MURRAY: Clark was very keen to develop policies and approaches to important policy areas that would demonstrate that there was a new government in office in Ottawa, with a new approach to federalism and to Quebec. We were busy with that exercise when the roof fell in, in December, nine months after we took office.

BOTHWELL: Clark risked defeat on a budget motion in the House of Commons, and he was defeated – by an opposition that stood higher in the polls than he did. In the ensuing general election of February 1980, Trudeau was rewarded with yet another majority government – his third.

It would be Trudeau versus Lévesque in the Quebec referendum. Formally, it would be Claude Ryan, the Liberal leader, who would lead opposition to the Quebec government's referendum question. It asked citizens to vote *Yes* or *No* to the proposition of handing Lévesque a mandate to discuss sovereignty-association with Ottawa.

Ryan might lead, but he led a group in which he was overshadowed by the federal Liberals. Trudeau, after all, was recognized as a distinguished citizen of the province, and his right to participate in the referendum campaign was not seriously challenged. Claude Forget, a prominent provincial Liberal at the time, recalls the events of February 1980:

FORGET: There was a meeting days after the federal election, at 24 Sussex, the residence of the prime minister. It was a private meeting between Trudeau and Ryan, but I had an almost verbatim description of what went on, the morning after from Ryan. And Trudeau played a very interesting game there; he persuaded Ryan to drop his own party's constitutional platform. Ryan, along with a group of advisers (I was one of them), had been working on a statement that was to be put forward in the referendum, as our vision of the future. It was to be some kind of contract; if people voted *No* to independence, they would explicitly underwrite this view of the future. It was a very important paper to write because, although it paid some heed to national sentiment, it had to be without doubt a federalist document, something that Canada, a united Canada, could live with comfortably, albeit with a number of substantial changes. So, this draft was done very responsibly.

BOTHWELL: The result was Ryan's Beige Paper. It was this document that Trudeau wanted to discuss.

FORGET: And lo and behold, Trudeau persuaded Ryan to drop any mention of the Beige Paper in the coming referendum campaign – not to mention it, not to discuss it, not to distribute any publication about it, to behave as if he had no plan. Trudeau said, and these were important commitments: 'This is a battle for Canada. It's not a battle for your views or my views. Let's win it, and after we've won the referendum together, we will then have this other debate. I will not make any comment, and you don't make any comment.'

BOTHWELL: Under the Quebec referendum legislation, there were two committees, one for the *Yes*, and one for the *No*. Alex Paterson, a prominent Montreal lawyer, sat on the *No* committee under Claude Ryan; he describes Ryan's qualities:

PATERSON: Ryan did one thing that was exciting at the beginning: he made us look for the first time at the merits of the case. He was a man who liked to address the arguments, and then address the strategy. I think in the end he got too interested in the strategy, but at the beginning we used to have these extraordinary meetings, where everybody, no matter what their involvement or interest or background, was brought into a room and made to go through the Beige Paper in detail. People felt that they were really being bought into a process.

Despite this process, he had a terrible time. This referendum committee was not big, there were about fifteen of us, and the question was always between what Ryan was going to do and what Trudeau was going to do. Chrétien was the representative of Trudeau on the committee. Ryan had a very difficult time dealing with that; he didn't want Ottawa to have anything to do with it at all. It wasn't just political; it was very personal. Ryan and Trudeau go back forever, and they have a very different view of the world. The organization could have been much stronger if the federal Liberals and the provincial Liberals had worked more closely together.

Then we had the distraction of thinking that Joe Clark was going to run the campaign for a short period of time, which unbalanced it, but, in the end, I think it worked amazingly well. The door-to-door involvement was absolutely down to a science. We didn't look at polls, because our polls were a whole lot better, and we had so many people. Instead of having just the members of a political party, we had all the parties out there involved – and they had armies out there, all the time, and great enthusiasm.

BOTHWELL: Curiously, what is remembered most about the referendum are the two or three interventions made by Pierre Trudeau. He had the most dramatic personality, he was the leader of the country, and he was a natural focus for news coverage. But was he really the crucial factor in the referendum?

In his climactic speech on 14 May at the Paul Sauvé arena in Montreal, Trudeau promised that after the referendum he would not stand still: there would be a renewed federalism.

What did Trudeau mean? Roger Tassé, federal deputy minister of justice in 1980, comments on the prime minister's promises:

TASSÉ: It's difficult to answer that question. I'm not sure that Trudeau had anything specific in mind. Certainly, he was talking about patriation, about the Charter, about some adjustments in the powers. But in terms of the powers, this was not something that was very specific.

BOTHWELL: Trudeau, whose views were well known, promised unspecified action. He meant to have an effect. Marc Lalonde assesses the impact Trudeau had:

LALONDE: This was in the very last few days of the campaign. Frankly, if you look carefully at the polling, and where the undecided were going to go anyway, by then the campaign for the *No* was won. Trudeau's appearance, his strong statement, and a very enthusiastic and emotional audience probably strengthened the *No* answer. Even if Trudeau had not showed up, this campaign would have been lost by the Parti Québécois. That is my conviction, first of all. Second, Trudeau said what he said. Now, the separatists since have been trying to read into this speech what they wish. Somehow they assume that when Trudeau made this statement he meant that there would be a tremendous amount of decentralization in favour of the Quebec government – the sort of thing a moderate separatist would hope for if he couldn't get separation. Separatists can say this, but it's wishful thinking; it's a lot of nonsense and it's dishonest. It bears little relationship to what Trudeau actually said.

BOTHWELL: Referendum night, 20 May 1980, was exciting for both sides. Polls right up to the end contradicted each other, some showing a majority for the *Yes*, and others a majority for the *No*. In the event, 59 per cent voted *No*, and 41 per cent voted *Yes*. Of French Canadians voting, a slight majority voted *No*; while among non-French Canadians, the *No* carried overwhelmingly.

Maurice Pinard, a practitioner of polling, reviews the reasons for *Yes* and *No* votes:

PINARD: Support for independence and support for sovereigntist issues did not vary much in the first four years the PQ were in power, between 1976 and 1980. If they had held the referendum the week after the election, they might have had worse results. The week after the election the proportion for independence dropped from 17 or 18 per cent to 12 per cent, but very soon it rebounded, and then it remained relatively stable until 1980. A referendum held in 1977, 1978, 1979, or 1980 would have given about the same results as it did in 1980. The PQ realized that the only way of winning the referendum was with the weakest, softest possible question – sovereignty-association, a mandate only to negotiate, and a promise to come back to the population before any final decision – but even that was not enough to make them win.

The 40 per cent of the electorate who voted *Yes* were people who were basically in agreement with a lot of the traditional grievances of French Canadians, the nationalist or ethnic grievance of French Canadians. They thought that French Canadians were dominated economically in Quebec by English capital; that French Canadians were dominated politically in Ottawa by the majority; that not enough power was given to the provincial government, where the French Canadians were the majority. The one thing that was crucial, but was not often mentioned, was that French Canadians felt they were considered by English Canadians to be 'second-class citizens,' inferior in status. They considered that English Canadians were not treating them as equals.

Conversely, many people who perceived a class barrier voted *No* in the referendum. They shared these grievances, but they thought that independence was too costly. The people who voted *No* were affected mainly by perceptions of cost, economic costs of one kind or another.

BOTHWELL: The loss of the referendum left the Parti Québécois becalmed. It was still the provincial government of Quebec, but without a mandate to act on the issue, sovereignty or independence, that lay at its emotional core. As a provincial government, it had a mandate to govern inside its constitutional sphere. It could of course run for re-election, and it did, in 1981. Lévesque won that election, and Ryan and the Liberals lost.

Rodrigue Tremblay, minister of industry in the Quebec government from 1976 to 1979, describes how the PQ dealt with its 'good government' mandate. In his recollection, the PQ was balanced between two different policies, almost two different theories, of how to manage the economy; thus, while some of the PQ's policies can today be seen to have looked to the future, others looked more to the recent statist past of the Quiet Revolution, which, as a result of other developments in the economy, was rapidly becoming obsolete:

TREMBLAY: There was some encouragement in direct industrial development, trying to redo what C.D. Howe did at the federal level after the war, with the government getting involved in the Sidbec steel mill, in mining industries, and in a silkworm corporation. There were whole litanies of corporations, either state-owned corporations or partly state-owned corporations. In 1976 there was also a disastrous involvement in the asbestos industry, when the government tried to nationalize an industry that was beginning to decline. In that year, a lot of the problems that had been camouflaged during the beginning of the Quiet Revolution came into fruition. There was also the management of these state-owned corporations, which had to be streamlined. When I was minister of industry, Sidbec was experiencing problems; I tried to deal with that by downsizing the corporation. Today, Sidbec has been completely privatized. Part of the illusion of the Quiet Revolution – that you could use the state as an engine for industrial development – has been disproved in a sense, as it has been everywhere else in the world. A government cannot dictate industrial development. In Quebec, it is now accepted that the private sector should be the main engine of industrial growth.

I was also minister of commerce, and we liberalized the sale of liquor in Quebec, for example, in 12,000 grocery stores. Quebec was then the only province in Canada where an important portion of the liquor trade was done through private outlets rather than state-owned outlets. The year 1976 was the beginning of the dismantling of the state-controlled industrial apparatus and the beginning of 'privatization,' with the exception of the asbestos industry. When I was minister of industry, I opposed that nationalization. That put me into conflict with other colleagues, including René

Lévesque. We had a promise of going ahead with that, but it turned out to be a mistake.

BOTHWELL: Governments win or lose elections, and oppositions hope a government will defeat itself. When Lévesque went to the polls in 1981, not enough Quebeckers had been alienated by the PQ, and they voted accordingly. The Liberals were surprised at their loss.

The PQ victory in the provincial election set the stage for the next confrontation between Quebec and Ottawa, by determining that the antagonists in the next round of constitutional battles would be the federal Liberals and the PQ, acting through their respective leaders, Pierre Trudeau and René Lévesque.

Trudeau had already opened the dance. In the summer of 1980 he dispatched his justice minister, Jean Chrétien, on a tour of the provincial capitals. Chrétien's mission was to seek agreement on a new constitutional package. Trudeau had defined, in broad terms, what should be in such a package: first, a true federal government with real powers, matched by true provincial governments with real powers; second, a Charter of Rights and Freedoms that would apply to all Canadians; and third, a formula transferring the power to amend the Canadian Constitution from the British parliament to Canada – what was called 'patriation.'

Trudeau called a constitutional conference for September 1980 and met total failure. Roger Tassé, as deputy minister of justice, was a federal representative in the discussions, and he explains why the talks failed:

TASSÉ: There was some possibility that they might succeed, but we were not very optimistic that they would. During the summer it became clear that it would be extremely difficult to get Lévesque and other premiers on side. One of the difficult issues was whether Canada should have a Charter of Rights in the Constitution. Some premiers were vehemently opposed to Canada adopting its own Charter of Rights. So there were a lot of difficulties facing the premiers as they got together in that room. The prime minister had seen that coming, as our discussions were proceeding, and he had decided that, as Chrétien had said, 'If we can't go together to London, we will go ourselves,' meaning, 'We'll do it unilaterally.' So there had been some plans, in the event that the conference failed. We came to realize that it was not possible for a separatist government in Quebec City to accept the kind of consensus that was developing.

Roy Romanow remembers that he had always suspected that Quebec's position and that of the other provinces might be incompatible:

ROMANOW: We always held the view that it was more likely than not that the day would come when there would have to be a parting of the ways with Quebec, because the choice before us was going to be very stark: either no deal or an imperfect deal without Quebec. The consequences of no deal, with the unsightly spectacle already in play at that point of Canadian governments and politicians being over at Westminster, pitching their points of view, would be very destructive not only to Canada's position in the eyes of the world but to Canadians at home.

So Saskatchewan's position, Premier Blakeney's position, was very clear. If we could get a reasonably acceptable deal, not perfect, we would buy into that; we warned Lévesque, and all the other premiers, that that's what we were going to do. I recall specifically in that week in November 1981, when we were doing the negotiations, that on the Tuesday Saskatchewan put forward a proposal – we were all advancing compromise proposals. This was an attempt to break the deadlock. Looking back at it now, I suspect that Saskatchewan was aware of the possibility that there would be this break. But I have to say this in defence of Lévesque and Morin in their discussion with us, working with the Gang of Eight, that they played by the rules of the game. They bargained hard, and perhaps they wanted too many powers for a province, more than we would want, but I did not get any explicit statements that their objective was simply to block the entire exercise. We were hoping against hope that somehow we could score a real coup and have everybody on side. That was perhaps naive, but that was at least my impression.

BOTHWELL: In the middle of the discussions, Trudeau dropped the apple of discord, the offer of a referendum. For Lévesque, who believed in popular consultation and who had just run a referendum of his own, the bait was too tempting to refuse. Romanow continues:

ROMANOW: Trudeau is right that it was the bait that split us. One of the fundamental agreements of the Group of Eight was that before any member would leave the group, it would notify the others. And it would tell them why it was doing so. What happened on that Wednesday was that, when the referendum idea was thrown out, Quebec jumped for it and, in effect, broke the constitutional position of the Gang of Eight. When the conference broke up for coffee and the liberation of that particular exchange, one had to consider again the prospect of a national referendum. How would you decide whether it was carried: Would you decide it on the basis of a Victoria formula, on a province by province basis, or on a straight simple majority across the country? The divisiveness of that question was potentially destructive, and it set the stage for yet another attempt to get a compromise accepted, and effort that involved, among others, Jean Chrétien, Roy McMurtry, the Ontario attorney general, and me.

How did I view it? We were surprised, all of us were, absolutely surprised. We didn't know whether this was just an intemperate response by Lévesque, occasioned by the surprise of the moment, or whether it reflected some thought-out strategy on his part. Clearly, however, it was a breach of the agreement of the Gang of Eight, and it freed the rest of us to see what we could do to find other compromises.

BOTHWELL: The compromises were found. On 5 November 1981 a pleased Trudeau told the conference and the country that the federal government and nine provinces had agreed on a package that included the patriation of the Constitution, an amending formula, and a Charter of Rights and Freedoms.

It was not a complete victory for the federal position. The amending formula was substantially the formula proposed by the Gang of Eight. It did, however, preclude a veto on the part of any province, including Quebec. It allowed provinces, if they wished, to pass resolutions specifically overriding the Charter of Rights and Freedoms on particular issues – what was called the 'notwithstanding' clause. This was, in effect, a last remnant of the doctrine of parliamentary supremacy.

The package was not through yet. Women and Aboriginals had been left out of the new document, and, after the mobilization of considerable protest, both were included. Citizen participation had arrived in Canada, and with a vengeance.

The loser at the table had been the PQ government of René Lévesque. Lévesque took it hard. Some time afterward he talked about the experience to Douglas Fisher:

FISHER: He told me that he put a great deal of trust in Blakeney and that's why, when he got up that morning, he was shocked to discover that he had been euchred and that all the provincial premiers were ranked against him, behind Trudeau. Of course he blamed himself; he said he shouldn't have trusted them and he shouldn't have trusted Trudeau. And he detested Trudeau. One of the reasons for his detestation – I understand it because I come from the boondocks, as Lévesque did, and I come from a working man's family – was that he had a chip on his shoulder about Trudeau as a favoured fellow who was born to a family with money, who had been spoiled, who had been given everything, and who had ducked an awful lot of responsibility. Trudeau hadn't really done a day's work until he was forty – and this really bothered him.

BOTHWELL: The new Constitution now passed through parliament with minimal opposition. One who did oppose it was Senator Lowell Murray:

MURRAY: Ultimately, I voted against the 1982 package, because I thought that it was wrong. It was historically wrong for the English-speaking majority of the country to impose a constitution against the will of the Quebec legislature, both its government and its opposition. If anyone had told the Quebeckers in 1867 that this was ever likely to happen, they would have thought you were insane. I was against it, and I voted against it. I thought the party should have voted against it, and I made my views known to the leader. I thought that if any party should stand for the concept of an English-French partnership, the essential partnership in our Confederation, it was the Conservative Party. What happened is that a number of very good people in the Conservative caucus (Flora MacDonald, David MacDonald, Ray Hnatyshyn, Jim McGrath, and so on), could not see themselves voting against the package and believed it would be fatal for the Conservative Party to be seen to vote against a charter of rights and freedoms, and to a lesser extent against patriation, which everybody agreed was a good thing. An important part of the calculation was that they could not see the federal Conservative Party voting against an agreement of which six or seven Tory provincial premiers were part. These were good people and they knew their history, but they simply didn't think it was on for us to vote against it. I think Clark, in his heart of hearts, would have liked to have voted against it. In the event, there was a small group of Tory MPs who voted against it – people who were offended by the Charter, by the loss of parliamentary supremacy and sovereignty. And there were some of us in the Senate, the Quebeckers and a few others, who voted against it.

BOTHWELL: The new Constitution was signed into law by Queen Elizabeth II in a ceremony on Parliament Hill in Ottawa in April 1982. René Lévesque was not present, but the federal team were: a beaming Trudeau, his justice minister Jean Chrétien, and a galaxy of federal officials and dignitaries.

Canada had a new Constitution. Trudeau, after fourteen years of contention and discussion, had achieved patriation, an amending formula, and a Charter of Rights. He had done so by defeating the separatist government of his home province, Quebec, and without any substantial concession of powers to that province or any other. Opinion leaders in Quebec were not pleased, and said so, but for the moment they could do nothing.

The immediate situation was therefore clear. Quebec was in Canada, with a new constitution, and quite possibly a new political balance, a new politics. What the long-term implications would be remained very unclear.

Chapter 10

Meech Lake and the 'Beau Risque,' 1987-90

Until the mid-1980s, Meech Lake was known, if at all, as a pond of water north of Ottawa, snuggled inside the Gatineau National Park. The well-informed might also know it as the site of an old-fashioned summer house that the federal government had acquired as a rustic retreat. The water, the isolation, and, not least, the RCMP guards around the property guaranteed calm and reflection for those privileged enough to use it.

In the late 1980s, however, Meech Lake came to symbolize something different – in fact many different things. And so it does today. What is certain is that, on 30 April 1987, Prime Minister Brian Mulroney and ten provincial premiers reached an agreement to reform, once again, the Canadian Constitution. This agreement was the culmination of negotiations between eleven Canadian governments over the previous year. It produced a revised amending formula for the Constitution, a redefinition of certain federal powers, an alteration in appointments to the Senate of Canada and the Canadian Supreme Court, and a few other minor changes. It also mentioned that Quebec, with a majority of French-speakers, constituted a 'distinct society' within Canada. According to Canada's constitutional rules, the Meech Lake agreement or accord had to be passed by all

Canadian governments by 23 June 1990. It did not pass, and its failure plunged Canada into a prolonged political crisis. Meech Lake may, therefore, be one of the most important events in Canadian history.

The roots of Meech Lake, and the origins of its failure, are not simply a constitutional story. Constitution-making and constitution-repairing are highly technical tasks, in which expert opinion and professional performance become extremely important. But constitutions also rest on first principles, on which public opinion may become engaged and deadlocked.

History does not provide an easy answer to the question of who was right and who was wrong on Meech Lake. It is a case where good intentions abounded and principles were prominent. David Peterson, the Liberal premier of Ontario at the time, sees Meech Lake as symbolic:

PETERSON: For thirty years we've been asking ourselves, What does Quebec want? How many times have you heard that question at various parties and places you've been to? And the answer is, what Quebec wants is dignity and self-respect, more so than a big fight over the constitutional powers – it is a sense of self-worth. So, in Quebec, the average guy on the street, if you'd asked him what was in Meech Lake, he'd have no idea, but to him if you agreed on Meech Lake it was a sign of respect for him or her individually, it was a recognition of dignity.

BOTHWELL: The analysis of Meech Lake starts with a disagreement about history. It starts with the defeat of René Lévesque's brand of separatism in the 1980 Quebec referendum, and Pierre Trudeau's subsequent reform of the Canadian Constitution, culminating in the patriation of the Canadian Constitution from Great Britain, the imposition of an amending formula, and the establishment of a Canadian Charter of Rights and Freedoms, all of this in the teeth of Lévesque's separatist government in Quebec, but also in defiance of Quebec nationalist opinion generally.

There are two questions here. Did Trudeau have the right to do what he did, and, a different question, was he right to do it? The first question is really a first-principles issue, or a constitutional problem. The second is a matter of political judgment.

As to the first question, it is clear that the government of Quebec, but also the Quebec National Assembly, did not consent to the new Constitution. On the other hand, seventy-four Quebec members of the federal parliament, out of seventy-five, did vote for Trudeau's Constitution, along with MPs from all other provinces. So did nine out of ten provincial governments, a proportion that the courts accepted as satisfactory. And Lévesque in the constitutional negotiations of the early 1980s had abandoned Quebec's claim to a veto over constitutional change.

A number of political scientists and constitutional specialists have debated whether Trudeau had the right to do what he did. First, Peter Russell:

RUSSELL: I believe it was illegitimate to go ahead and make those changes without the consent of Quebec, politically illegitimate, and against the traditions and practices of this country. I think the Supreme Court of Canada, when that issue was put to it after patriation, couldn't give an intellectually honest answer. I understand that, and I'm not a critic of the Supreme Court. There's no way it could attribute political illegitimacy to the new Constitution. But I think history has shown that the political traditions of this country require Quebec's support for major changes in the Constitution.

BOTHWELL: Guy Laforest, a Quebec political scientist, agrees:

LAFOREST: Let me turn to the essence of the matter, the issue of the legitimacy of the Canadian Constitution. It seems to me that in the end this is what will justify what will probably occur if the *Yes* side carries the day in the Quebec referendum. Quebec will base itself on that illegitimacy to make a unilateral declaration of independence.

BOTHWELL: And yet, as Laforest concedes, Trudeau's Constitution was a magnificent achievement, something only Trudeau could have managed:

LAFOREST: Trudeau was the last of our founders. He was the equivalent of Lincoln for twentieth-century Canada. He was the last political leader who was able substantially to modify the thought and the idea of the foundation of Confederation. What Trudeau almost single-handedly achieved in the early 1980s is incredible; whether you like it or not, you have to be awed by the achievements of the man. He changed the political culture of Canada from a culture enshrined in the traditions of British parliamentarianism to a political culture much closer to eighteenth-century republicanism, much closer to American influence. He entrenched a Charter of Rights, he cultivated in the souls of all Canadians a spirit of equality interpreted as uniformity, as homogeneity. Classically, what Aristotle asked is, What is justice? Well, justice is treating equals equally and treating unequals unequally. Trudeau made sure there would be only one nation, ten equal provinces.

BOTHWELL: Marc Lalonde, Trudeau's energy and then finance minister, argues that Trudeau had little choice but to do what he did:

LALONDE: Historians or political scientists may sit back and say it might have been better to wait and wait and wait. Well, the historical 'might have beens' are all very nice for political scientists, but I don't think it would have been a realistic solution. We had a limited time with Trudeau to do it. Trudeau was the man who had the prestige, the leadership, and the political base to carry it. Who knew what would have been available after, and at what cost? I think it was the right thing to do. I have no regrets.

BOTHWELL: Alan Cairns, also a constitutional authority, has argued that Trudeau's objectives in the new Constitution were clear, and ultimately were accepted by most Canadians:

CAIRNS: The really big development in this search for a new constitutional identity was the Charter in 1980, which clearly was designed with two purposes in mind by its chief architect, Trudeau. The prime one, the obvious one, is what the Charter appears to be on its face, a way of protecting citizen rights against the state. From Trudeau's perspective, however, the much more important goal was the attempt to generate a national identity, and this really meant an attack on provincialism. It was a way of trying to get Canadians to think of themselves as possessors of a common body of rights independent of geographical location, which would constitute a lens through which they would then view what all governments were doing. So it was really a de-provincializing strategy, primarily aimed at Quebec nationalism, but also at the general centrifugal pressures that were developing across the federal system. Trudeau's thought on this goes well back to before he entered politics. In one sense it's undeniable that, in the rest of Canada (and this is apparent if you look at all the parliamentary proceedings dealing with the Meech Lake episode), the attachment to the Charter that showed up with many of those groups was absolutely astounding. It really had become an icon to people who couldn't tell section 6 from section 12 from section 28. The success of the Charter seems to indicate that there was a kind of psychological void in the constitutional order it displaced.

BOTHWELL: But what of the second question, Was Trudeau right? Was the constitution politically acceptable? What about the French-Canadian public? Were French-speaking Quebeckers alienated by the Trudeau Constitution? After all, in 1984 the federal Liberals, with Pierre Trudeau no longer at the helm, went down to a crushing defeat in Quebec as elsewhere in Canada, and Brian Mulroney's Progressive Conservatives won an equally crushing victory. On the other hand, in 1985 René Lévesque resigned as premier, and his Parti Québécois successor, Pierre-Marc Johnson, was defeated by the federalist Quebec Liberal Party. So what did Quebeckers think?

Maurice Pinard, who has studied Quebec politics and public opinion for many years, explains the state of Quebec politics and public opinion in the mid-1980s:

PINARD: What happened at that point is that the Parti Québécois had tremendous internal problems in terms of where do we go next. In the short run the more moderate wing of the party won over Lévesque, and then adopted the platform of *le beau risque.*

BOTHWELL: *Le beau risque* was a term used by Lévesque in response to Mulroney's overwhelming election victory. Mulroney had promised to right wrongs, especially on the Constitution. Lévesque would meet him halfway, even if that meant risking 'smothering our fundamental option' – separatism. If Canadian federalism could be made to work, that was a risk worth taking. Jacques Parizeau and hard-liners in the Quebec cabinet promptly quit. Lévesque would not be around long in any case, for he resigned as premier in August 1985.

PINARD: He was soon succeeded in power as leader of the party by Pierre-Marc Johnson, who adopted as a platform not independence, not sovereignty-association, but 'national affirmation,' going back basically to the Union Nationale type of autonomy, a moderate nationalist platform. Then, by all the measures we have, there was demobilization in terms of members of the Parti Québécois, in terms of organizers of the Parti Québécois, in terms of money collected by the Parti Québécois, and very soon in terms of a vote. They had won the 1981 election because the party had shelved the idea of independence altogether. They had been in power only one term, and they did a second term, but soon after that they were defeated in 1985. All that period, 1981 to 1988, was one of demobilization and loss of support.

Support for independence went as low as 15 per cent, the level that had been reached already in 1970. So the movement really went into a phase of decline that lasted until 1988 or 1989.

BOTHWELL: Political scientist Stéphane Dion agrees with Maurice Pinard, up to a point:

DION: At the start it wasn't perceived to be as serious in Quebec. The first polls showed that Quebec public opinion had three reactions in 1981-2. The first was to say to René Lévesque that it would have been a good idea for him to sign the agreement. Second, since Lévesque did not sign it, Trudeau was wrong to go ahead; he had no right to sign the Constitution, if the premier of Quebec was against it. Third, although we don't understand them well, this Constitution and this Charter of Rights seem good. These were the three reactions in 1981-2, but the sense that the process was not fair, that it was not right to isolate the premier of Quebec, was there; it was latent.

BOTHWELL: In 1984-5 separatism was at a low ebb. Separatists, nationalists, people who had voted *Yes* in the 1980 referendum, were looking for a new political home. Mulroney recruited many of them to the Conservative camp for the 1984 federal election, including an old friend named Lucien Bouchard, and, in the event, many of them got into parliament. Trudeau's supporters, Quebec MPs who had voted for the 1982 Constitution, had either left politics or been decimated in the election.

Mulroney's nationalist supporters were taking a *beau risque* on federalism, but it was not a one-way deal. The Conservative Party adopted the nationalist interpretation of what Trudeau had done in the referendum of 1980 and the subsequent constitutional settlement.

The constitutional events of the later 1980s, Meech Lake, originate in this alternative interpretation of the Trudeau constitution, an interpretation that was, obviously, highly offensive to supporters of Trudeau, but potentially also to the many Canadians who had come to accept and identify with the 1982 Constitution. But there is a way of squaring the circle. Roger Tassé, Trudeau's deputy minister of justice, was still deputy minister under Mulroney. He suggests that Trudeau's reforms were both good and necessary, but that they were incomplete:

TASSÉ: I think Trudeau didn't have much of a choice and that he did the right thing. But I never considered that this was finished business. I recall coming back home and telling my family that we had resolved the issue, and my daughter asking me, 'But what about Quebec? They're not in. How can you explain that?' She was right. I had thought it was just a question of time, that someone would come back and say, 'We need to complete this negotiation that was not finished in 1982.' But you have to wait for the right time for that. You have to wait for a federalist party to be in charge in Quebec City, and, in effect, this was the chance that we missed. I have always considered that you have to look at the 1980-2 episode and the 1987 episode as one, as the same, single negotiation. You make a step in a certain direction in 1981, and you complete the business later on. I thought that's what it really was about in 1987. I worked towards it as an adviser to the federal government, at the time of Meech, until 1990; I thought that Meech really was in sync with the basic philosophy of Trudeau's constitution, despite many arguments that were raised at the time. I thought it was really the finishing touch to the 1981-2 amendments to our Constitution.

BOTHWELL: Brian Mulroney preferred to wait until after the next Quebec provincial election. Held in December 1985, after Lévesque had resigned as premier, it resulted in a Liberal victory – under Robert Bourassa, who had replaced Claude Ryan.

The Quebec provincial election of 1985 did not turn on sovereignty. Because Quebec had not signed the 1982 Constitution, that document was not 'complete.' A Liberal provincial government would sign (and 'complete') the 1982 Constitution subject to five conditions: the restoration of Quebec's veto over constitutional amendments; recognition of Quebec in the preamble to the Constitution as a 'distinct society'; more power for Quebec over immigration; participation by the Quebec government in the naming of Supreme Court justices; and limits on the federal spending power.

At the same time, Bourassa also made promises on another front. The Liberals would legislate guarantees for the English-speaking community of Quebec, protect their access to services in English, increase the minuscule number of English-speakers in the provincial civil service, and loosen somewhat the rules prohibiting signs in English. This might involve amending the Charter of the French Language, Bill 101.

These two sets of promises – the five constitutional conditions and the promises made to the English-speaking minority – were not linked. As premier, Bourassa proceeded as if they were not. On English rights he hesitated.

There were a number of court cases that involved Bill 101's prohibition of English-language commercial signs. These, Bourassa decided, would proceed. There would be time enough to act once the courts, including the Canadian Supreme Court, had ruled.

Why did Bourassa act as he did? In the opinion of Eric Maldoff, one of the leaders of the English community at the time, Bourassa thrived on uncertainty:

MALDOFF: After 1985, things started to slide away. Robert Bourassa, as premier of Quebec, had it in his hands to put the language debate and the stress between the communities substantially to bed, for a long time to come. Bourassa was a very clever strategist, and what he determined was that keeping the pot boiling was not an entirely bad thing for him politically. He's always been one to straddle a lot of different political ideologies, and to ride different tides.

BOTHWELL: Clifford Lincoln was first elected to the Quebec National Assembly in 1981, and re-elected in 1985, representing a largely English-speaking riding. From 1985 to 1988 he was a member of Bourassa's cabinet. He takes a less Machiavellian view of Bourassa's actions:

LINCOLN: Bourassa was not a guy who anticipated events and made decisions that way. He tended to be somebody who looked at a checkerboard and moved the pawns as events dictated, on almost a continuous basis, more in reaction than in anticipation in making decisions.

BOTHWELL: But in failing to act in 1985 on English-language grievances, Bourassa missed an opportunity.

LINCOLN: It would have been far better. It was clear it was our policy; everybody knew it was, and I think we could have just done it and had a fantastic mandate afterwards.

BOTHWELL: On the constitutional front, however, there was action. The first involved the 'notwithstanding clause.' The notwithstanding clause is a peculiar feature of the Canadian Constitution that Trudeau accepted as part of the compromises he felt he had to make to get his constitution. Mulroney actually gave it quite a good definition. Stanley Hartt, Mulroney's chief of staff in 1989-90, remembers what Mulroney used to say on the subject:

HARTT: I many times saw him explaining to Americans, I remember particularly Elizabeth and Bob Dole, 'Now, could you imagine if the first thirteen amendments to your Constitution, the so-called Bill of Rights, had a clause that said, "notwithstanding any of the above," the legislature of any state, or the United States Congress, can, simply by using the words "notwithstanding the Bill of Rights," overcome it? And how would you think about that?' And they were truly and legitimately shocked.

BOTHWELL: As Trudeau had anticipated, the notwithstanding clause was not much used after 1982. Lévesque did use it on each and every piece of Quebec legislation, to negate the authority of the Charter of Rights over Quebec laws; Bourassa now halted this practice. Second, Bourassa sent his minister of justice, Gil Rémillard, to sound out the federal government and the other provinces on their reaction to his five conditions for constitutional reform.

The federal reaction was extremely positive. Senator Lowell Murray describes what the Mulroney government made of Quebec's proposal:

MURRAY: The five conditions seemed to offer not just the opportunity, but the responsibility for the federal government to respond. Some people argue now that it was a mistake to have 'opened up the Constitution again.' I don't know how you could have given the back of your hand to the new federalist government of Quebec, which was proposing five conditions – all of which, as Bourassa reminded us, had been offered by federal governments before. I don't know how you could have simply rejected that out of hand.

In June 1986 Mulroney asked me to join the government as leader of the government in the Senate. He said, 'There's something else. I want you to be minister of federal-provincial relations. I think the time has come to get Quebec into the Constitution formally, and I want you to go out and see if we can get that done.'

BOTHWELL: At first, things went well – much better than anyone had anticipated. The premiers' meeting in Edmonton agreed that Quebec's concerns needed to be addressed, and needed to be addressed first. Murray remembers being surprised at the pace of the negotiations:

MURRAY: I felt that our chances of agreement were very strong when I met Rémillard in December 1986 to compare notes on the meetings each of us had had with provincial governments across the country. I said to him, 'Look, do you want to continue? Now is the time: we can close the book honourably now, and without too much political damage to either of our governments. What do you want to do?' And we discussed it all one stormy Sunday afternoon in Quebec City, and there was no doubt he wanted to continue. He felt that an agreement was possible.

BOTHWELL: It was not that the negotiations were easy, or that Quebec's conditions were quickly accepted.

MURRAY: I knew that the other provinces could never accept that Quebec by itself would be able to entrench immigration agreements, or that Quebec alone would have a say in judicial appointments. I knew that, on those matters, those provisions would have to apply to all provinces.

I wondered how hard a sell it would be to combine the distinct society provision with the recognition of linguistic duality. This was the federal government's bottom line on that, and I wondered how difficult a sell it would be, both in Quebec and in the rest of the country, but we managed that. The spending power remained a difficult one all the way through, and, of course, the amending formula. But we were almost there, when the officials met in February 1987, and we reported to the prime minister that he should call the premiers in at Meech Lake, in early April. And that was the negotiation that led to the actual accord.

BOTHWELL: The Meech Lake accord was made in two stages. On 30 April 1987 there was the successful meeting at Meech Lake. The agreement that was made followed the direction of Bourassa's five conditions. First, there would be a change in control over immigration, giving Quebec, and any other province that wanted it, a larger say in immigration matters. Second, not just Quebec but all the provinces would participate in nominating Supreme Court justices. Third, the federal spending power would be limited by allowing any province to opt out of new federal spending programs and to receive the money that would otherwise have been spent in that particular province – as long as it introduced its own program compatible with what were called 'national objectives.' On the veto, not just Quebec but all provinces were given larger powers than they had received in 1982. As a concession to Alberta, which was demanding reform of the Senate as a means of strengthening regional voices in Ottawa, the federal government agreed to name future senators from lists submitted by provincial governments.

That left the reference to a distinct society, Quebec, which Quebec had asked to be placed in the preamble of the Constitution. Placement in the preamble would have been symbolic, a beau geste in the direction of the *beau risque*. The Meech Lake meeting did two things. It expanded the distinct society to say that French- and English-speaking societies were fundamental characteristics of Canada, that French was concentrated in but not limited to Quebec, and that English was also present in that province. Then the premiers agreed to move the expanded clause from the preamble to the first substantive section of the Constitution, meaning that it would serve as a guide to judges in the interpretation of the rest of the Constitution.

Finally, there were two clauses that spoke to the concerns of two other provinces, Alberta and Newfoundland. Alberta wanted real Senate reform – what was called an equal, elected, and effective (or Triple-E) Senate. It got only a small part of that, but in return the rest of the provinces and the federal government committed themselves in the Constitution to an annual constitutional discussion of the subject. Newfoundland demanded and got the fishery as an obligatory subject at an annual first ministers' conference – in perpetuity. Endless constitutional conferences, plus fish, thus lurked in Canada's future.

Peter Russell describes his thoughts on the annual conferences:

RUSSELL: I can't think of a stupider, dumber, more laughable provision in any constitution. The idea that every year you sit down, put the Constitution on the table and say, 'What are we going to do with it?' shows a total ignorance of what constitutions are all about. It's a symptom of the Canadian disease, that the way you develop your constitution is going to a table and putting the whole thing there, all up for grabs, all in a big package. And that's nonsense. Few countries have ever developed their constitution that way. You develop your constitution incrementally, if you have any sense at all.

BOTHWELL: On Meech Lake, public reaction was very positive. The Quebec government had the topic debated in its National Assembly and carried the day over predictable separatist misgivings from the Parti Québécois. Another conference was summoned for early June, in the more formal setting of the Langevin Building in Ottawa, just across from Parliament Hill.

Two provincial delegations, Manitoba and Ontario, had serious doubts. Ontario's worry centred around the meaning of 'distinct society.' Peter Hogg, who was among those advising the Ontario government, describes Ontario's concerns at that point:

HOGG: There was one major area of difficulty in the Meech Lake accord for Ontario, the distinct society clause: Ontario felt that an explicit statement should be added that the clause did not expand the legislative powers of the province of Quebec. The Langevin draft and the draft that originally was agreed to did have a provision that nothing in the distinct society clause took away from the powers either of parliament or of any province. The Ontario delegation also took the position that it would be desirable to say that the clause did not add to the powers of the Parliament of Canada.

In response, Quebec took the position that the clause did not extend the powers of a province, that it wasn't seeking additional powers, but that it didn't want to make that point explicit in the language. In other words, the line Quebec took was, 'It is perfectly clear that this does not give new powers, and it isn't necessary to put any additional language in the clause.' Quebec was right in this interpretation, but I still thought that Ontario was taking a prudent approach in seeking an explicit reassurance in the section to that effect. As later events unfolded, it would have been highly desirable to have had a provision like that in, because it turned out to be perhaps the most controversial element of the accord.

BOTHWELL: On this point, Bourassa seems to have thought that what was politically prudent in Ontario would not be useful to him in Quebec. There was a divergence, not on the substance or meaning of the accord, but on the method of selling it – a difference in style which, when it became public, could be construed to be a difference in meaning.

When the Langevin meeting reached a triumphant conclusion early in the morning of 3 June 1987, the proponents of Meech Lake had apparently secured all they could have wished. Gordon Robertson, the former clerk of the Privy Council and a veteran of constitutional talks dating back to the 1940s, considered it a splendid achievement:

ROBERTSON: I have no doubt at all in my own judgment. I think it was a modest agreement that would not have had any of the deleterious consequences on our federalism and on the Constitution that most of the opponents, including my old friend, Pierre Trudeau, suggested. The allegation that the distinct society clause would have conferred great powers on Quebec, quite different from those of the other provinces, is totally unfounded: the relevant section makes it perfectly clear that the distinct society clause does not alter the distribution of powers. It says that it doesn't detract from the powers of the federal or provincial governments. Well, you can't add to the powers of a provincial government without detracting from the powers of the federal government. So, in my judgment, there is no question whatever but that the distinct society clause would have had only one significant constitutional effect, and that would have been to have made it imperative for the courts, particularly the Supreme Court, where it was a relevant matter, to take into account the fact that the Constitution said that Quebec was a distinct society. That could mean a shading of interpretation about sections in the Charter at some point, but they would be within the ambit of a constitutional provision about the nature of that society.

As to the argument on the other side, the criticism has been that those who think as I do are saying that the distinct society clause was nothing but pure symbolism and therefore totally unimportant. I think that is quite wrong. A good deal of nationalism, whether it's in Canada or Quebec or Yugoslavia, is a desire by people for recognition as being something that is unique, a special quality and character that is theirs alone. Why is it that we ask what is distinct about Canada? Because we want to be seen not simply as a democracy, a small echo of the United States, but as something that is distinct. I think this sense, this desire and wish on the part of Quebec, is thoroughly comprehensible: they are a distinct society, and our Constitution should say they're a distinct society. This formal recognition could be quite important.

BOTHWELL: These nuances were lost in the translation. In Quebec, Bourassa found it useful to trumpet the Meech Lake accord not as something modest, but as a highly significant and effective achievement. And if something was not in Meech, then Meech was a much better launching pad for the next round of constitutional negotiations, in which Quebec would certainly bargain to advantage. Political scientist Max Nemni argues that Bourassa felt it necessary to dress Meech up in nationalist clothing:

NEMNI: The Meech Lake accord wasn't something that the nationalists wanted, because to them it wasn't enough. So when Rémillard and Bourassa tried to sell Meech Lake they kept hammering on the fact that it was only the first step. It was just the beginning, and Quebec would end up having its traditional demands fully met. These traditional demands had never been specified; no one knew what these famous traditional demands were, except that Quebec wanted more and more and more and more. So

Bourassa and Rémillard both sold the accord as just a first step in an on-going situation, and they were already saying what was going to be the second step and so forth. Obviously, their approach opened the door to a continuous play on 'let us get what we can from the federal government.' And this is another game that Quebec politicians have been playing ever since the Quiet Revolution.

BOTHWELL: Some people outside Quebec considered Bourassa's arguments alarming. Stephen Harper, Reform MP for Calgary West, explains:

HARPER: As bad as the contents of Meech Lake were (and there is very little about the specifics of Meech that I support), the country would have gone along with it if Canadians had really believed that this would solve the Quebec problem. But the statements coming out of Quebec, not from a separatist, but from the proponents of the deal itself, Bourassa and Rémillard, that these were minimum demands and first rounds, et cetera et cetera, this is what really killed it. Those comments reinforced the view that this was not a settlement, but the first step of a path that the rest of the country would find very unacceptable. When some people said that the next step would have been a Triple-E Senate, or other things, that didn't sound very credible when the most important aspect of the first step would have been securing a veto over all these matters. The fact is that the constitutional deal of 1987, the Meech Lake accord, could have been ratified had the government been willing to drop the veto provision. It was the change to the amending formula that made the deal require unanimous consent and that killed it.

BOTHWELL: Those reservations lay in the future. Politicians had to deal with the present, and in June 1987 the present looked rosy. Mulroney's cabinet were surprised and delighted by the Meech Lake deal. Barbara McDougall was then a member of the cabinet:

MCDOUGALL: There was a fair amount of discussion. Most people were pleased: it was very much in keeping with Conservative doctrine. I don't think there was anyone from Quebec or the other provinces who took serious issue with us. There were certainly a couple of ministers from Quebec who would have liked to have seen more for Quebec. But Meech Lake was actually in keeping with what had gone on, not just in the party, but going back to the Victoria agreement that had been signed in the early 1970s.

BOTHWELL: Opposition to Meech Lake was at first scattered and politically insignificant. Former prime minister Trudeau weighed in with a blistering attack on the document in late May. At the time and since, it was pointed out that many of the items in the Meech Lake accord had been agreed to by Trudeau himself. Michel Robert, who represented the federal government in the constitutional cases of 1980-1, considers whether there was a contradiction in Trudeau's position:

ROBERT: Trudeau was willing to contemplate discussions on the topics that found their way in the Meech Lake debate, but I don't think he agreed with the conclusions. Trudeau's basic concept was the equality of the provinces. In other words, he did not believe that Quebec should have a special status in any way, shape, or form, other than the one Quebec had under the Constitution. In some ways, Quebec already has a special status within the existing Constitution. Trudeau is a traditional or classic federalist, and his approach to federalism was very traditional. He disagreed with the conclusion of the Meech Lake accord, but he was certainly willing to discuss all the topics of the debate – and they were discussed.

BOTHWELL: In the short term, Trudeau's vividly expressed opinions firmed up the premiers' resolve to pass Meech Lake and have done with it. That Trudeau spoke for others could, of course, be assumed, but at the time it was also assumed that the others were not many. Michael Bliss, one of the leading opponents of Meech Lake, recalls the mood of the time:

BLISS: I was out of the country when the Meech Lake negotiations were going on. I came back and heard that constitutional unanimity had been reached, and that there was peace in the land. I read the terms of the basic Meech Lake agreement and realized right away that these were fraught with long-term implications, that it was a vague accord. It seemed to be a decentralist set of propositions, and it clearly gave special status to Quebec. I'd heard all those debates back in the 1960s and had listened to twenty years of argument in which it was clear that the idea of special status for Quebec would almost certainly make the continuance of Canada impossible. I guess, without realizing it, I'd been a Trudeauite on constitutional matters. I thought that things had been settled by 1981-2.

When I saw that the whole issue was reopened, and reopened in a way that was, in effect, giving away everything that had been fought against for twenty years, I experienced a sinking feeling. I wrote a letter to the *Globe and Mail* saying these are the implications, and then I found that there were lots of people who felt that way.

BOTHWELL: Soon there were vocal objections to Meech Lake, objections that quickly reached the politicians. Inside the Mulroney cabinet, Barbara McDougall soon felt the heat:

MCDOUGALL: The heat came from interest groups. I don't think that the people in my constituency, which was in central Toronto, were negative about Meech Lake, although some of them obviously were. My first sense of trouble coming was with women's groups. I was minister responsible for the status of women, and there was a request from a group of women to meet with me, with regard to the Constitution and the Meech Lake accord and their impact on women, and the perceived override of the Charter by cultural rights and language rights groups. It was a fairly tense meeting. Lowell Murray came with me to that meeting. It was led by two women lawyers, both of whom I respect a great deal, although I am in profound disagreement that the Meech Lake accord would have done anything to jeopardize women under the Charter. I think we've seen lots of things since that have jeopardized women under the Charter, but nothing to do with the Constitution. And that was really how the opposition built up. It built up through interest groups.

BOTHWELL: The governments that signed Meech Lake bound themselves to accept no amendments and to stand by the terms of the agreements. They had, of course, to pass the document through their legislatures, and the Constitution gave them a three-year time limit to do it. The clock would start running with the ratification by the first legislature, which turned out to be Quebec's, on 23 June 1987. The deadline for the ratification of Meech Lake by all the provinces, and the federal parliament, was thereby set for 23 June 1990.

There was a political flaw in the length of the process. Governments in any democracy are by their nature temporary. Canada, with ten legislatures and a federal parliament, is bound to have an election or two every year, and 1987 was no exception.

The Conservative government of New Brunswick was approaching the end of its five-year term, and was deeply unpopular. Premier Richard Hatfield chose not to bring Meech Lake before his legislature in its expiring days. Instead, he called an election for 13 October, in which he suffered a total defeat. The new Liberal government of Frank McKenna won every seat in the legislature, and McKenna had stated publicly many times that he wanted changes in the agreement. What he would do if he did not get them he did not say.

In retrospect it is obvious that Meech Lake started to unravel from that moment. Michael Bliss explains why:

BLISS: The more that people talked about the Meech Lake accord, the less popular it became. And in a way, the main job of the anti-Meech forces was simply to keep Meech on the table. It was fundamentally a contradictory set of propositions, and as people talked about it the contradictions became very apparent. Bourassa and the Quebeckers were saying this was the greatest gain since the Quebec Act, and people like David Peterson and the other premiers were saying, 'Oh, this is just symbolism; it doesn't mean anything at all.' Clearly, people were talking out of both sides of their mouths and had no consensus about the meaning of this document. It was also clear that the more you got Mulroney to talk about the issue, the more you realized he had very little understanding of Canada's Constitution. The constant danger in the Meech Lake negotiations was that they would slip ratification through so fast that it would be done before there was a chance to understand it. And the mistake they made, obviously, and everybody realizes it now, was that the Meech people ought to have rammed it through all the legislatures right away and had a fait accompli.

BOTHWELL: Brian Mulroney and his provincial counterparts proceeded as if there was not much of a problem. In Ottawa, Mulroney scored another coup when the leaders of the two opposition parties, the Liberals and the NDP, came out strongly in support of Meech Lake. Raymond Garneau was then a federal Liberal MP from Quebec, and Liberal leader John Turner's Quebec lieutenant. The Liberals, at Garneau's and Turner's urging, had already modified their stand on federalism. Meech, according to Garneau, was a logical extension:

GARNEAU: And when Meech came around, it was pretty close to that approach, so I wanted the Liberal Party to support the Meech accord. We had a very long caucus. I don't know how many hours we sat there discussing and trying to iron out our differences. Finally, Turner rose to speak.

Up to that point, I didn't know on what side he would fall, for or against. And he made a speech, probably one of the best speeches he ever made. In about half an hour of addressing the caucus, he gave a short history of his understanding of what Canada was all about. At the end he concluded, 'I think that we the party should support the Meech accord, because it's good for Canada and it's in the spirit of the Canadian confederation. I may be wrong for the moment, but I'm confident that I'm on the good side of history.' And that was it. That was how the caucus decided to vote for the Meech accord, though some members were still opposed.

BOTHWELL: Not all Liberals were comfortable with this position. Robert Kaplan, a former minister in the Trudeau government, was one of those who did not view Meech Lake as the logical culmination of Trudeau's constitutional reforms of 1982:

KAPLAN: I saw a different conclusion to the Trudeau period, because I thought the country was quite happy when the Constitution was repatriated. Even Quebeckers who had not approved of the constitutional package that Trudeau brought forward and who opposed what they called the unilateral patriation, were by and large content. They were well represented in the Trudeau government, and there was a tremendous support for them within the province of Quebec. I thought that the renewal of the federation, which was promised in the package, would mean the kind of cooperation and rationalization of responsibilities that in fact took place after that. I thought that the idea that something grand was needed, like Meech Lake or Charlottetown, was really an invention of the Mulroney government.

BOTHWELL: Strongly urged on by Turner, and by Liberal premiers like David Peterson of Ontario, most federal Liberals joined in the approval of Meech Lake. As some participants in the process argue, it was a very prudent thing to do. Stanley Hartt was deputy minister of finance from 1985 to 1989, and then chief of staff in Mulroney's office in 1989-90. As an English Quebecker, he was not indifferent to the political stakes:

HARTT: Brian Mulroney understood a very simple fact: there was only one opposition party in the province of Quebec, and it was a separatist opposition party. One day or another, people would become fed up with the Liberal administration, for reasons that have nothing to do with nationalism or separatism, would want a change of government, and would elect a

Parti Québécois government. The Parti Québécois would have a sovereignist agenda and would offer Quebeckers another referendum, and in that referendum the federal side would have nothing to say, because it hadn't taken the opportunity when it had a federalist premier fixing the situation.

BOTHWELL: In Hartt's view, Mulroney was haunted by the idea that Trudeau had pledged a renewal of federalism in 1980 in his speech in the Paul Sauvé arena, and that had meant something different from what Trudeau believed:

HARTT: The only problem was that he was the only person in the Paul Sauvé arena who thought that patriation and the amending formula on a Charter of Rights was renewed federalism. The others were looking for the rejigging of constitutional legislative jurisdiction to give them more power, to ensure that Quebec remained a French society. Trudeau hadn't had that delivered. So, what does the prime minister of Canada promise in the second referendum? From Mulroney's perspective, he has to be able to say, 'I did something; I fixed the problem,' because if he can't say that, he's painted into a corner, where people are fed up with talking about the Constitution. They don't want another constitutional reform proposal, and yet the only way to prevent a Yes vote is to offer something other than the status quo.

BOTHWELL: As 1987 turned into 1988, there were other issues on the political agenda. The Mulroney government had its political difficulties between 1984 and 1988. There were scandals, financial problems, and a growing uneasiness among the electorate – the electorate in English-speaking Canada – about Mulroney. Charlotte Gray, an Ottawa political correspondent, observed Mulroney's government during the 1980s. I asked her to characterize Mulroney's approach to government:

GRAY: The easiest way to characterize this is actually in terms of what a contrast he was to his predecessors, the Liberals led by Trudeau and Turner. Trudeau in particular always had a great pride in their sort of intellectual analysis of problems and in their belief in government. Ottawa had a sort of tweedy, provincial, academic atmosphere to it. As soon as the Mulroney government kicked in, it became a city where it was much more a centre of business. In my own view, Mulroney never had a clear ideology, but he clearly had a business mind-set. I remember between 1984 and 1987 the buzz phrase was 'What's the bottom line?' And that was the sort of mentality that Mulroney and his gang brought in.

BOTHWELL: Brian Mulroney was the linchpin in a political alliance between English-speaking Conservatives and the Quebec wing of the party. Without Mulroney, the link probably would not have worked; but with the link, the Conservatives seemed for a time to have a hammerlock on government.

GRAY: The ministers from English Canada, particularly the strong ministers like Don Mazankowski and Michael Wilson, were very traditional Conservatives. They were people who had often spent long years in the trenches and who came from Bay Street. They never professed to know any-thing about Quebec, and they knew that they had only returned to power, they'd only won the election, because Brian Mulroney had managed this wonderful marriage between old-style Conservatives and the Quebec nationalists. So, they were very respectful of everything that the prime min-ister said should be done about Quebec. They left it to him because they didn't feel they had any expertise about it and knew that it was Mulroney's appeal within Quebec that had got them power. As far as the Mulroney ministers from Quebec are concerned, and I'm thinking here particularly of people like Marcel Masse, they were big spenders. They were a quite differ-ent mind-set. They had no roots in the Conservative Party, and their con-servative philosophy was shallow if not absolutely invisible. They were totally concerned with Quebec and not with much else.

BOTHWELL: Mulroney secured a free-trade agreement with the United States, and then ran a federal election in November 1988 on the issue. It proved a popular issue in Quebec, where Mulroney ran with the tacit sup-port of Premier Bourassa, and where he won even more seats than he had in 1984 – seats that were crucial to Mulroney's renewed majority in parliament.

The federal Liberal Party under John Turner opposed the trade deal and found, as a consequence, that most of its votes and seats came from English Canada. English-Canadian nationalists opposed to free trade were crushed to discover that Quebec nationalists did not share their concern. Such nation-alists, especially on the political left, had been traditionally sympathetic to Quebec and its nationalist concerns; after 1988 that was no longer true.

But it was another issue that dominated the headlines in the last month of 1988. In 1985 Bourassa had postponed the issue of language rights in Quebec under Bill 101, because it was being fought out in the courts. On 15 December 1988 the Supreme Court of Canada finally pronounced on the matter. To no one's great surprise, it found that portions of Bill 101 governing the language of commercial signs violated rights to free speech granted under the Charter of Rights and Freedoms.

In Quebec there was an immediate outcry from nationalist defenders of Bill 101. 'Ne touchez pas à la loi 101,' they demanded. There were demonstrations. There might be more. What would Bourassa do? Clifford Lincoln, a cabinet minister in Bourassa's government, recalls the atmosphere in Quebec City at the time:

LINCOLN: Starting halfway through 1988, we started getting rumours that the decision might be coming down at any time. It had been a long time and I guess it was almost like a sort of sword hanging over all of us. It was a terrible feeling; you almost sensed it would happen. It's almost as if you sense there's going to be an earthquake, and you don't know exactly when, but you know that it will change your life very significantly.

BOTHWELL: The news reached Bourassa in the National Assembly. Outside, the press were clamouring for reaction, while, inside, the French-speaking Liberal members realized that the government would have to take a position. What would it be?

After a slight hesitation, Bourassa brought in a new law, Bill 178, which applied the notwithstanding clause to the Supreme Court decision and Bill 101, exempting the law from the provisions of the Charter of Rights. On 20 December, three English-speaking members of the Bourassa cabinet resigned.

LINCOLN: Maybe I was naive; I really hoped that we would find a way out. We had all sorts of different formulas we worked on, but the decision was probably made a couple weeks before to go ahead with this Bill 178. When it came that Bourassa had made his mind up, I went to see him. One thing about him, he's not vindictive and he's very congenial and a nice person. It was in the back of the Throne Room in the National Assembly; he had a little office there. I told him I was going to vote against the Bill. He was extremely cool and never got annoyed. He just said, 'Well, you know, these decisions happen in life.' I remember him saying, 'When you live through Laporte's death, one of your colleagues, somebody reports to you that he's dead in the trunk of a car, after that, everything seems very relative and you just take it.'

So that's the way it happened. In fact, he gave me a slot to speak against it. He agreed that those of us who were voting against it (there were three cabinet ministers) were to resign.

BOTHWELL: Bourassa searched for a precedent that would allow cabinet members to vote against a piece of government legislation, but there was none. In the debate on Bill 178 in the National Assembly, Lincoln spoke of what was at stake:

LINCOLN: I was trying to point out that there are some fundamental values that you cannot shift and reduce and change; they are rights that belong to people in their very essence, in their totality. You can't dissect them, you can't reduce them. It was preposterous to say that tomorrow you could hang a sign on your own lawn that said 'House for Sale' and that this would be illegal. It was against freedom of expression, against freedom of the individual to express himself or herself. How far do you carry it? Do you carry it into spoken communication, or into newspapers? I said that once you start encroaching on rights or abusing them, it sets up a motion of events that certain governments might carry to extremes.

BOTHWELL: 'Rights are rights are rights,' Lincoln said. To the French-speaking majority, however, it remained more a question of protecting their right to a language that they believed was under the persistent threat of disappearance. By comparison, the disabilities imposed on the English were little more than inconveniences. And to Bourassa, it was a question of social peace. He had been marked by the experience of his first term in government in the 1970s: riots, the October Crisis, a general strike. Stanley Hartt witnessed the events of the 1970s and their aftermath:

HARTT: Bourassa fundamentally believed that if the masses ever understood the power that they wield, and tried to wield it, we governments wouldn't have a chance. He had seen it in the streets in various labour protests against his administration, where the avowed purpose of such demonstrations was to bring down the regime. When a handful of separatists demonstrated in the street against something, Bourassa's antennae were up immediately, and he was wary of what the other guys would say. People have asked me, 'Why did he surround himself with separatist-leaning advisers?' The answer is very simple: so he could know immediately. If his own instincts didn't work, which they usually did quite well, he knew how Péquistes, sovereignists, would react to every move he made. He was motivated by fear of civil disorder, and by the use of his own blunders by sovereignists to motivate nationalist unrest.

BOTHWELL: There was one particular problem with the Supreme Court judgment. In the view of Quebec nationalists, it was another case of an English-speaking majority telling Quebec what it could or could not do on an issue crucial to its survival. In Hartt's opinion, Bourassa should simply have thrown the issue back to the courts with a minimal liberalization of Bill 101, banning outdoor signs except in French, while giving the English language slightly greater standing in indoor signs. Bill 178 actually provided for this distinction. Why not set the legal machinery in motion again, and postpone the problem for the couple of years? But Bourassa insisted on the notwithstanding clause.

HARTT: I personally think they could have got away with that. Claude Ryan told Bourassa he couldn't get away with that; there had to be no more court cases, no more risk of the Supreme Court telling Quebec what it could or could not do. To save French, he had to use the notwithstanding clause. Well, from that moment on, the poison had been planted. The day after they signed the informal entente at Meech Lake, for example, the headlines the next day, all over the country, in every single paper, English and French, were absolute euphoria: 'The problem has been solved, just like that, easy as pie, the ten premiers have solved the Quebec problem.'

The big turning point, in public opinion, was when Bourassa said there's 'deux poids, deux mesures,' in other words, two rules. Outside Quebec, you send your kids to French immersion. You all try to become French or French-speaking, and you have bilingual services available to all Canadian citizens where numbers warrant. But inside Quebec, there's only one official language. And it's too bad; it's two different rules. I think that Canadians' sense of fairness was outraged. That was complicated by the fact that Mulroney had in his cabinet, sulking at the time, Lucien Bouchard, who basically said, 'You're not going to come out with a typical Anglo response that this is awful, this notwithstanding clause, are you?' Fundamentally, Mulroney believed that it was awful. But he could only say one half of that. The half that he said was, it was awful that Trudeau had put such a clause in the Constitution. It was a price he paid to rush through patriation. From Mulroney's point of view, such a clause would be incomprehensible to the people who invented the concept of a charter of rights. A lot of people say that Trudeau had something to do with the growth of opposition to Meech; I don't believe it. I believe that Bill 178 was the virus that destroyed Meech Lake.

BOTHWELL: David Peterson, the friendly Liberal premier of Ontario, phoned Bourassa to persuade him not to proceed with Bill 178:

PETERSON: Bill 178 had nothing to do with Meech, but it had everything to do with Meech. I fought with Bourassa all weekend. I remember I was at my farm, we were on the phone all weekend, yelling and screaming and telling him. I told him what was going to happen, that it was going to kill Meech Lake, that it would make everything so very difficult. I guess if you were trying to figure out why he viewed it that way, it was back to the issue of 'social peace.'

BOTHWELL: Bill 178 evoked all the fears, all the misgivings, of critics of the distinct society clause. And it gave particular point to the reservations held by the Liberal Party leader in Newfoundland, Clyde Wells. Wells had been briefly a politician in the 1960s, but had sat out most of the 1970s and 1980s practising law. Among other things, he had represented the federal government in some of its constitutional battles under Pierre Trudeau. More importantly, he had studied the amendment and patriation of the Constitution as a member of a Canadian Bar Association committee at the time.

Meech Lake offended Wells's constitutional beliefs, and he made no secret of his views. This was important, because in Newfoundland another deeply unpopular Conservative government had to face an election in the spring of 1989. The existing government of Newfoundland had already passed Meech Lake, but Wells promised to rescind the province's ratification. He recalls his initial reaction to Meech Lake in the spring of 1987:

WELLS: I remember that I was campaigning for the leadership of the Liberal Party at the time. I was in a small community in the Great Northern Peninsula of Newfoundland, when somebody faxed me the details of the Meech Lake accord. I remember being horrified by what I saw. It had the effect of creating a different quality of citizenship in different jurisdictions of Canada, of essentially destroying Canada as a federal nation, as a federal state.

You can't create a situation where the citizens of one province, or one constituent part in a federal state, have a different quality of citizenship from the citizens of the other: a citizen is a citizen is a citizen. Equally, in a federal state, a province is a province is a province. It matters not what its economic capacity or its geographic extent or its population size is: if you're a province in a federal state, you have the same exclusive legislative jurisdiction as any other province. PEI is as much a province of this nation as is

Ontario; Wyoming is as much a state of the United States as is California.

BOTHWELL: As for the ratification of Meech Lake by the Conservative government in Newfoundland, it was clearly defective, in Wells's estimation.

WELLS: There was no coherent debate. I think there were at least five or six different sessions, debating the Meech Lake accord, over a two- or three-month period. The issues were not at all adequately debated in the province. I took a very strong position; the Liberal Party had opposed it at the time, and I made it clear that if an election intervened, between then and final approval, I would seek to rescind the resolution of approval because I thought it was so wrong.

BOTHWELL: Wells describes how the distinct society clause was especially important in forming his negative judgment of Meech Lake:

WELLS: I had no trouble recognizing that within the province, Quebec is a distinct society. It's distinctly different from any other society in Canada, by reason of its ethnic origin being predominantly French and French-speaking. It's distinctly different by reason of its cultural background and its legal system. For those three reasons – culture, language, and the law – I have no quarrel with making sure that our constitutional structure accommodates those differences. My quarrel was with creating a situation where the legislature of Quebec had a different legislative status, which gave the citizens a different voting and legislative power from other citizens in the country.

BOTHWELL: Meech Lake's deadline was late June 1990. New Brunswick, with a new government elected in 1987, had not yet ratified. Manitoba, with a new government elected in 1988 under the Conservative Gary Filmon, brought the accord to the legislature late that year. But Filmon did not have a majority. Sharon Carstairs, who was leader of the opposition Liberal Party at that time, describes the political climate of the day:

CARSTAIRS: It was only after the Liberal Party was elected in 1988 with a substantial number of seats – not as a government, but with twenty seats – that Meech really became an issue. There's a great deal of revisionist history that goes on in Canada. One story is that I won the election in 1988 on Meech Lake: that's ridiculous. It wasn't an issue in 1988; it became an issue the day after the election when I was asked by a CBC reporter, 'What impact does this have on Meech Lake and is Meech Lake dead?' And I said, 'Yes.' I had tried to make it an issue in the campaign because I thought it was a wrong direction for the country and for the province, but nobody paid any attention.

BOTHWELL: Carstairs believed that only a strong federal government could protect the interests of small and relatively poorer provinces like Manitoba. The restrictions on the federal spending power and the opting-out provisions spelled disaster for Manitoba, in her opinion:

CARSTAIRS: There must be a federal presence in decision-making with respect to the objectives, or the standards more particularly, of many of these national programs. I have spent most of my life living in 'have-not' provinces, Nova Scotia and Manitoba; my one experience of living in a 'have' province, for twelve years in Alberta, led me to believe that those provinces have little or no interest in the protection of people living outside. Therefore, you have to have a federal government that can say there must be equality of standards, there must be equality of service from coast to coast. Only the federal government can do that.

BOTHWELL: Carstairs, like many other Canadians, was also sceptical of Brian Mulroney:

CARSTAIRS: We had a prime minister for whom I have no respect, who wasn't interested in defending the nation; we had a prime minister who was interested in cutting a deal. And the deal was more important to him than the nation, because he wanted to do – ego driven as he is – something that he thought Pierre Elliott Trudeau wasn't able to do. We have this great ego that drives a deal, but we have nobody standing up and saying, 'Hey, who protects Canada in all of this?' Canada is more than the sum of its individual parts. It's got to have a vitality and a concept and a drive all of its own in order for us to sit back and say, 'I'm Canadian before I'm a Nova Scotian.'

BOTHWELL: So Meech Lake was in trouble in Manitoba, too. The provincial NDP held back on the issue so as not to embarrass the federal NDP, which was firmly in support of the accord, but once the federal election of November 1988 was over, all inhibitions were removed. Bill 178 in Quebec was merely the last straw. Facing certain defeat in the legislature, Premier Filmon prudently withdrew Meech from consideration. Newfoundland had not yet rescinded its ratification, but when he became premier, Wells promised it would. By early 1990, with less than six months to go, Meech

Lake lacked the support of three provinces.

As time ticked away, the Quebec government became increasingly concerned. Veiled threats began to be heard from Quebec City. If Meech Lake failed, perhaps there would even have to be a new referendum on Quebec sovereignty. Although Quebec separatists had opposed Meech Lake back in 1987, they now held up its impending rejection by English Canada as proof positive of the chasm dividing French Canadians from English Canadians. Carstairs got a taste of the sentiment when she visited Montreal in 1990:

CARSTAIRS: There is a tendency in the province of Quebec that if you ever disagree with anything, then you are a racist and a bigot. They never understood that my essential disagreements were with a different vision of collective and individual rights, that to me individual rights are paramount. To many in Quebec, collective rights are paramount and they simply reject my position as a basis for formulating a nation. Clearly, we are at odds there. But I am half French; my mother was Acadian. I am not a racist or a bigot, and francophones in the province of Manitoba know that I have been on the forefront of recognizing their rights. So to find yourself in Quebec and to be treated as a bigot and a racist is tough going, because you know that is not where you're coming from.

BOTHWELL: In the spring of 1990 Mulroney constituted a parliamentary committee under Jean Charest, a strongly federalist politician from Quebec. Its task was to find a formula that would enable Premier McKenna of New Brunswick to accept Meech Lake without having to alter any of the existing text. McKenna had already indicated that he was looking for a way out of the constitutional dilemma, and with McKenna leading the way it was possible to hope that the other two objecting provinces would finally swing into line. Stanley Hartt, Mulroney's chief of staff, believed the omens were favourable:

HARTT: The negotiations went on with all provinces, to keep the support of those that had given it and to try to arrange the support of the others. They culminated in 1990 with McKenna's companion resolution; in effect, 'If you do these other things, then you don't really have to change Meech.' That formed the basis of federal strategy thereafter; send that resolution to the Charest committee, get an all-party agreement, and, using that, McKenna would immediately declare that he was on side and maybe he'd start the ball rolling. The timing was also good, because you were not getting so close to the deadline that it was time to speak up, or kill it by silence.

BOTHWELL: McKenna's companion resolution set down conditions or interpretations for the acceptance of Meech Lake – very modest conditions. Perhaps McKenna's modest proposal might have had a chance, in some other year or in some other country. But in Canada in 1990 it had none. To nationalist opinion in Quebec, it was too much. Clearly the other provinces were conspiring to ram change down Quebec's throat. Quebec was about to be humiliated – again, just like Louis Riel, or conscription. Bourassa had been threatening the other provinces with the consequences of failing to accept Meech, and now the consequences were before him, vividly reflected in an aroused and increasingly hostile Quebec opinion. There would be no compromise on Meech Lake, from Quebec at least, and Bourassa supported a PQ resolution in the National Assembly to that effect. Meanwhile, in St John's, Premier Wells had his legislature rescind Meech Lake.

And if Mulroney had his problems with the provinces, he also had his problems inside his own cabinet. There, Lucien Bouchard had become disillusioned with Meech Lake, and with Mulroney's apparent willingness to compromise to save it. This was not what Bouchard had meant when he had Mulroney propose a new constitutional deal that Quebec could accept 'with honour and enthusiasm' – as Mulroney expressed it in a speech at Sept-Iles – back in 1984. Stanley Hartt remembers Bouchard in the spring of 1990:

HARTT: It is clear that Bouchard was not on side with the strategy of endorsing McKenna's companion resolution. He was on side with the strategy of trying to preserve the support of the seven supporting provinces, and to do unspecified things to try to bring along the three opponents. He was on side that we must adopt Meech Lake and ratify it. The fix was so far along, in Quebec, in terms of public opinion, that you couldn't oppose Meech Lake. I remember Parizeau, as leader of the opposition, pointing an angry finger at Bourassa in question period, saying, 'Does the premier intend to make any changes to Meech Lake?'

So, Bouchard couldn't be against Meech Lake. But he also could not have misunderstood that if it was signed, the separatists were out of business for a long time. So, he was on side, with a strategy to try to preserve it and get it adopted, whether willingly or because he knew there was no percentage in trying to state that he was opposed to it. But when the McKenna resolution was proposed and it was determined that the prime minister ought to refer it to a committee headed by Jean Charest, there's no doubt that Lucien Bouchard was not on side. He didn't express his not being on side, because at first he didn't understand what was going to happen. Whenever groups of ministers met to discuss how it was going at the Charest committee, and to have an update given to them by Lowell Murray, he was uncharacteristically quiet. I mean, Bouchard is never quiet in a meeting. He dominates every meeting he goes to. He loves to talk.

BOTHWELL: Jean Charest, who chaired the parliamentary committee on Meech Lake, at first believed that he would have Bouchard's support:

CHAREST: It was a very interesting process. We had a caucus meeting, I think in March, which Bouchard presided over as Quebec lieutenant. It was agreed at that meeting that we would not do anything disruptive until the process had gone its full course; that we would support anything the prime minister tried to do to salvage the Meech Lake accords. That meant that a committee would be put together. Bouchard led that committee and it met at Meech Lake. At the end of the session, Bouchard summed up: there would be a summer caucus meeting held in the Gaspé, and at that time we would take a position. The whole emphasis was on rallying around the prime minister. The caucus was of that frame of mind.

What happened eventually was interesting, because Bouchard was the person who asked me to chair the committee. I remember my reaction when he asked me, because I'd just resigned from cabinet and I'd made up my mind that I would spend more time with my family. My own reaction was to say, 'Well, Lucien, I don't need this.' Obviously, what I was referring to was that I didn't need this as a step to get back into cabinet. I was worried that if I were to do it, I'd be seen as doing it for the purpose of trying to get back into cabinet. But he encouraged me, and the prime minister gave me a call and asked me to do it, and I accepted. I felt that I could probably do the job. It was very new to me, though, and the pressure was very intense.

Throughout the process, I met with Bouchard a few times to brief him on what was happening, so he had a pretty good idea of our approach. At one point I was informed that he would be out of the country; he was going to Europe. Now, we were going to produce a report, and we had very little idea how it would be received. If one of the major players said it was unacceptable, the report would become politically tainted. Given the short time frame, the prime minister would have to set the report aside and do what he felt he had to do to salvage the Meech Lake accord. That's the game; that's politically the way things would unfold, and we knew that. So when Bouchard told me that he'd be in Europe when the report came out, I was very surprised. I called the prime minister and told him he should not authorize Bouchard's trip to an environmental conference in Bergen, Norway, and that it was extremely important that Bouchard be here. The prime minister told me that he would look into the matter, and I don't know what transpired. Bouchard went to Bergen. He was not on government business when the report came out; he was in Paris taking some personal time off. We had tried to reach him with a draft of the report before I signed it, to get his reaction, but I think he quite deliberately decided to attack the report. Somewhere along the way, he made up his mind that he would use the report as an excuse to resign.

BOTHWELL: The Charest committee reported as hoped, on 17 May. Despite its good intentions and its limited recommendations, the report was immediately repudiated by the Bourassa government, acting with the support of Quebec public opinion. And on 21 May, Bouchard resigned from the cabinet.

This left Mulroney with only one option, and he took it. He summoned the premiers for a last-ditch conference in Ottawa on 3 June. Manitoba, without a majority government, sent all three political party leaders, to maximize the chances of an enforceable agreement. For six unhappy, contentious days the first ministers met and met again. It was Mulroney's hope that with a virtually certain crisis in Quebec staring them in the face, the dissident premiers would cave in at the last moment, even though he had nothing tangible to offer them in the way of amendment to Meech Lake. Sharon Carstairs was part of the Manitoba delegation, and she describes the experience:

CARSTAIRS: It was a horrible week emotionally and psychologically; the pressures were enormous to come up with a deal. But there was also a mood there that was very different from what was happening outside Ottawa. I used to go outside the conference and talk to people. They didn't know who I was, and so I would ask them why they were standing there, what they were doing, what their concerns were, to see if I could get a pulse on people; I was, after all, totally removed from the people I represented. It was very clear to me that those people thought that if we did not come up with a deal, the country was going to fall apart. I became convinced that if we didn't come up with a deal, the country would fall apart at midnight, like Cinderella – the whole country would dissolve. Then, to come back to Manitoba on the Sunday and to realize that Manitobans did not feel that way at all was an incredible experience. In Ottawa, you really thought you were talking to Canadians, that you had the right pulse, but you didn't. It was a false pulse, it was fed by media, it was fed by the Prime Minister's Office, it was fed by rumour and innuendo and sometimes outright lies.

BOTHWELL: On 9 June, Prime Minister Mulroney announced that he had secured agreement of a kind. New Brunswick would ratify the accord, and it did, on 15 June. Newfoundland and Manitoba, the other two hold-outs, signed a communiqué promising to use their best efforts to 'achieve decision' on Meech Lake by the deadline, 23 June. It was clear that Wells did not like the agreement, any more than Carstairs, but he would, at least, bring it back to St John's and seek a decision from the Newfoundland House of Assembly.

As for Manitoba, the federal representatives believed that, faced with the fact of Bouchard's resignation, Carstairs had agreed to go along. Hartt describes what happened:

HARTT: What was disturbing was that Carstairs was more or less willing to come on side. I say more or less, in the sense that she had a representative in the Railway Station Conference Centre. That representative became convinced that, rather than face another Quebec referendum, the best possible outcome tactically was to accept the 1990 constitutional amendment. He never believed that it was the best arrangement. Now, I have to say her agreement was never totally procured, simply because the deal was never totally made.

BOTHWELL: As for Clyde Wells, Hartt doubted that he ever intended to let the agreement go through. Mulroney flew to St John's, addressed the Newfoundland House, and left in hopes that he might have raised the odds in a vote. But with the deadline at hand, Wells adjourned the debate on Meech Lake. Hartt condemned Wells's action:

HARTT: I think that Wells had his mind set on defeating Meech Lake from the onset. Everything after that was a tactic. It wasn't pure, and things that aren't pure don't get past Clyde Wells. Practical solutions, politics as they are, the possible preventing of greater disasters by tiny exceptions to your general rules are not in his universe. I believe that he left the conference room not intending to fulfil his promise to submit this to public consultation or legislative ratification, that he made his deal with Filmon to bolster his ability to carry that through, and that he so conducted himself in Newfoundland as to dishonour his signature. He didn't appear to be someone trying to sell what he had signed. Mulroney would have thought of him as a union negotiator going back to the membership to try to obtain ratification. If you sign something, you're supposed to recommend it. There certainly was no recommendation.

BOTHWELL: Newfoundland was, however, only half the story. Manitoba also had to ratify, and there, too, the deal came apart. It came apart in terms of public politics because an NDP member of the Manitoba legislature, Elijah Harper, a Cree Indian from Churchill, refused unanimous consent to expedite action on Meech Lake – consent that was required by the rules of the Manitoba House.

And so, on 23 June 1990, the Meech Lake accord was not ratified and the Constitution of Canada was not amended to meet Quebec's five constitutional conditions. Meech Lake had produced a clear division, not compromise.

Meech Lake originated in a division between those Canadians who believed that the constitutional settlement of 1982 was appropriate and legitimate, and those who believed, for one reason or another, that it was incomplete or even deeply flawed. For the latter category, the outcome of Meech Lake was extremely unsatisfactory. Certainly, many of Meech's Quebec supporters came to conclude that the *beau risque* proposed by René Lévesque and Brian Mulroney was not worth taking, and that it was time to revert to the separatist option.

But here, too, there was division. Canadians across the country had taken the 1982 Constitution to their hearts. They believed that it defined a new equality, while enshrining a fairer way of doing things. For such Canadians, Clyde Wells, Sharon Carstairs, and ultimately Pierre Trudeau were more representative than Brian Mulroney.

As the Constitution of 1982 helped redefine Canadian nationalism, and Canada's sense of nationhood, so Meech Lake would define Quebec's response.

Chapter 11

Preparing for the Second Round, 1990-4

O<small>N</small> 23 J<small>UNE</small> 1990 the package of constitutional amendments known as the Meech Lake accord failed to be adopted. There would be no 'distinct society' for Quebec in the Canadian Constitution. There would be no Quebec veto, no limits on the federal spending power, none of the other changes Meech proposed. But what did it mean? And what would happen next?

The opponents of Meech inside and outside Quebec breathed a sigh of relief. Canada could get on with its real business, free of constitutional sideshows. The existing Constitution, the status quo, would carry on. That came as good news to separatist sympathizers inside Quebec, who viewed the constitutional status quo as political poison for the federalist camp. What, then, did the status quo represent, and was it still strong enough to hold back the tide of nationalism in Quebec?

Many Quebeckers, but also other Canadians, thought not, and over the next four years they debated back and forth what they should do next. The Quebec debate was not held in a vacuum. Quebeckers were not the only Canadians to be discontented, and certainly not the only ones to question how the country was governed or the assumptions on which it was founded. The coincidence of these two phenomena gave the debate over Canada after Meech Lake a particular sharpness.

The years around 1990 saw profound changes in the rest of Canada, changes reflected in Canadian politics. There was a sharp and bitter economic recession. Unemployment rose, incomes fell, and governments bickered over what to do. In Canada since 1945 governments had reached into deep pockets in good times and bad, ladling out money to citizens in need. But in the 1990s the deep pockets developed holes. Vast debts and the growing burden of interest charges were matched by rising taxes and a political inability to respond to discontent.

The status quo was not, therefore, something that Canadians necessarily desired, even if they could not agree on anything else. In Quebec, it was not clear that Canada offered as many advantages as it once had. Could the central government still respond to Quebec's concerns in an age of diminishing expectations? In the far west, British Columbia and Alberta, many people wanted to change the agenda of the central government. The central government, as many westerners saw it, was really the government of central Canada. Rather than withdraw from the central government, they wanted to realign it, to make central Canadians take the west and its concerns more seriously.

In Quebec, however, there was a sense of a monumental rebuff. On 22 June Premier Robert Bourassa stood up in the National Assembly and stated: 'English Canada must clearly understand that, no matter what anyone else says or does, Quebec is today and forever a distinct society, free and able to undertake its destiny and its development.' He was characteristically ambiguous. He might have meant that Quebec would now undertake its destiny by preparing for independence. Or, since Quebec was already a distinct society, perhaps it could give federalism yet another chance.

Admittedly, the support for such an option was not what it had been. Economist Pierre Fortin took the view that Quebec had already given Canada quite a few chances and had been rejected:

FORTIN: What the Quebec people feel they've done in the last fifteen years is to say twice, 'We love you,' to the rest of the country, 'We love you and we want a nice deal.' The only thing we want is to make sure that you believe that French culture and language is an asset to the country and not a liability. You understand that our feeling is that we're a cube of sugar in a gallon of coffee, and if we have free trade in language and culture, then one of the two is going to melt into the other and it's quite clear which one. We want an absolute rampart against the destruction or deterioration of the French language and culture in North America. For this we want some constitutional safeguards.

BOTHWELL: Alain Dubuc, editor of Quebec's largest newspaper, *La Presse* in Montreal, describes the reaction to the failure of Meech Lake:

DUBUC: There were two of them. The first was rage. People were incensed when Meech didn't pass. And this tells us something: people would have liked Meech to be passed, and it was a very soft solution to Quebec problems; there were very few concessions from the rest of Canada. If people were so outraged, it obviously meant that most Québécois would have liked to have found a solution to stay in Canada, to be in Canada. So, there's something important here, which is that Québécois, if they have the choice, would prefer to stay in Canada. The other reaction is that since this small solution didn't pass, it gave rise to the idea of an unchanging Canada. It's seen only as a dream. Generations of Québécois have been federalist because they thought that this regime, which they didn't like, could be changed. And this is obviously not possible, so it forced Québécois to choose the status quo. And we'll have this debate in the next months where we'll say, 'What is the status quo? Can it be changed?' Basically, people know that if they choose to stay in Canada, they are not sure that it is possible to change this country, so it helps the sovereigntists. And it creates a kind of cynicism and desperation in those who will not switch to sovereignty.

BOTHWELL: In Ottawa, the failure of Meech Lake plunged the Mulroney government into profound gloom. The Conservatives' star minister in Quebec, Lucien Bouchard, had already defected. Now, separatism was on the rise, and the alliance between moderate nationalists and federalists in the province, not to mention the political future of the Conservative Party, was seriously threatened. Barbara McDougall was minister of employment and immigration in the Mulroney cabinet; she recalls the reaction inside the cabinet room. The Quebec ministers, led by Benoît Bouchard, were deeply affected:

MCDOUGALL: They'd worked very hard on the Meech Lake accord. We were all in the cabinet room the day Newfoundland failed to vote, we were all watching it on television, and Benoît Bouchard burst into tears. It was just very sad. Everybody in that room was really heartbroken and at that point, it was a moment of great closeness. We all felt for each other.

BOTHWELL: June 24 is Saint-Jean-Baptiste day in Quebec, though in an increasingly irreligious society it is now more often referred to as the Fête Nationale. June 24, 1990, saw an outpouring – of people and emotions. Lucien Bouchard and Jacques Parizeau marched proudly at the head of a flag-waving crowd in Montreal. That day seemed to be an affirmation that Quebeckers not only saw themselves as a nation, but as a sovereign people already separate in spirit from the rest of Canada.

In Calgary, David Bercuson watched the demonstration and decided that the Quebec he was watching no longer had a place in Canada:

BERCUSON: The moment for me was the aftermath of Meech, the demonstrations in the streets of Quebec, the utter disdain for Canada, the complete inability of Quebeckers to understand why Meech had gone down the tubes, the feeling that Canada somehow was an oppressor nation which was attempting to destroy or to undermine the culture and the traditions of French Canada. I just felt that this great country of ours does not need a class of people who feel that way about it, and who are going to act on their feelings politically and constitutionally for the next generation or so.

BOTHWELL: Canada had entered the post-Meech period, but the players on the political and constitutional teams were virtually the same as before. Indeed, the post-Meech period was defined by the tenure of two of its survivors, Brian Mulroney and Robert Bourassa. Mulroney had won a general election in November 1988, and he remained prime minister until his resignation in June 1993. Bourassa had won a provincial election in September 1989, and remained premier until January 1994. Both men produced short-lived successors, Kim Campbell and Daniel Johnson, but both these politicians were an apostrophe tacked on the end of the main political event.

The events of the early 1990s were therefore closely linked with what had gone before – with the perceived failures and deficiencies of the regimes that had produced the grand fiasco of Meech Lake in the first place. Mulroney in particular enjoyed, if that is the word, a personal unpopularity unparalleled in Canadian history. Observers in Quebec like Alain Dubuc found Mulroney's low reputation curious:

DUBUC: In the case of Mulroney, there was something that we didn't see in Quebec, because we don't understand English Canada well enough. The whole problem of Meech was to sell this thing to the rest of Canada, and

Mulroney was not able to do that. A lot of French Québécois see Mulroney as a Québécois, and sometimes just as a francophone. They don't see the English Canadian in him. It's strange, because Trudeau was also a French-speaking Québécois, but people never saw him as a Québécois, only as a Canadian. So, maybe we're right, Mulroney is not exactly Canadian and has problems understanding Canada.

BOTHWELL: Bourassa was also widely mistrusted in English Canada, especially but not only among nationalists, for his language legislation, for his support of Mulroney's free-trade pact in 1988, and for his role in Meech Lake. Mistrust is the natural reciprocal of ambiguity, which was Bourassa's characteristic political style. By attempting to please everyone, he ran the risk of failing to satisfy anyone. His record appears much clearer in retrospect than he ever allowed it to appear at the time.

DUBUC: Bourassa believed that Quebec should stay in Canada, and he did what he could to defuse the crisis that there was after Meech. Of course, it's manipulation of public opinion, but I think he did it because he believed somewhat in Canada.

BOTHWELL: 'He believed somewhat in Canada.' It's an apt phrase, but not exactly inspiring. But Canadians believed neither in Mulroney nor in Bourassa. This was especially ironic in the case of Mulroney, who initially drew on tremendous support outside as well as inside Quebec. John Harvard, since 1988 a Liberal member of parliament from Winnipeg and a former CBC public affairs journalist, describes Mulroney's impact on Manitoba:

HARVARD: Manitobans realize that we don't have a big province, we're not a big player in confederation, and we need the other provinces and the federal structure to survive. I think Manitobans in the main are modest and moderate, and they're fairly comfortable in federalism. They were left quite bewildered and of course concerned when Mulroney came along with his agenda to change confederation, to change the balance of federalism. It was quickly seen that he was playing up with the nationalists and the separatists in Quebec, and that he would only weaken our structures.

BOTHWELL: In Manitoba, Mulroney's political goose was cooked early, when a contract to refit Canadian fighter planes was withheld from a Winnipeg firm and given to a Montreal company by the federal government.

HARVARD: That really hit us, when you feel you're playing the game fairly and the prime minister of Canada – who is prime minister of all Canadians, not just Quebec or Manitobans or Albertans but all Canadians – comes along and says he's got a different agenda to follow and you're not going to win that contract, even though you won it fair and square. That happened before I went into politics and I was working for the CBC as a journalist. I did many stories on it, and I have some idea of how that really got right to the core of us. The Manitoba federal Conservatives never survived that.

BOTHWELL: Mulroney founded his government on his ability to appeal to traditional Conservative support in the West while adding Quebec nationalists to the Tory camp. There was always the risk that in appealing to the one he would irritate the other, especially since western Canadians were already suspicious of 'central Canadian' policies like official bilingualism.

Tom Flanagan, a former research director for the Reform Party of Canada, describes how traditional western resentments became attached to Mulroney's government:

FLANAGAN: A lot of western voters shifted away from the Conservative Party to the Reform Party, because they felt that the Conservative Party had sold out to Quebec, and sold out to bilingualism. This has a lot to do with Mulroney's political strategy to gain support in Quebec, which worked for him for a couple of terms, but there was a backlash to it.

BOTHWELL: Ironically, in the West Mulroney came to carry much of the political baggage of his great antagonist Trudeau. The chief western complaints were the Official Languages Act and the National Energy Program of the early 1980s, which attempted to recoup much of the profit of the oil bonanza for the federal government and away from western Canada. This was a profoundly important political event that shifted the basis of politics in the West. It underlay western demands for constitutional reform, to prevent or inhibit a government based on a central Canadian majority from ever again raping and pillaging western resources. Flanagan explains:

FLANAGAN: Brian Mulroney, by the end of the 1980s, had pretty much replaced Pierre Trudeau in the West as a symbol of Quebec domination. It's one of these great curiosities, although it's easily understood that Mulroney's political strategy was to make an alliance of Quebec with the West. The two great pillars of the Conservative caucus were the members from Quebec and the members from the western provinces. But that was a balancing act that required him to make political concessions to both sides, and the more he made concessions to Quebec, the more these were resented in the West, particularly when they appeared to be direct losses for the West, such as the CF-18 affair. Mulroney tried to be too many things to too many people. He tried to satisfy the constitutional demands of Quebec for greater provincial autonomy, and that led to Meech Lake and Charlottetown. He might have been able to sell that in the West, if he had not simultaneously attempted to embrace the cause of Trudeau-style official bilingualism. He could have sold greater power for Quebec in the West if he had framed it as a new approach to the contemporary reality of Canada.

In retrospect, I'm not sure that Mulroney's project was impossible. He carried it off for a few years, but he failed to make the tradeoffs that would have been necessary to sustain it. The result was that Mulroney came to occupy, in the western imagination, the sort of demonic role that Pierre Trudeau had.

BOTHWELL: Stephen Harper is not so sure that Mulroney's Quebec objectives and his western support were really compatible:

HARPER: The blatant alignment that Mulroney made, not with Quebec interests, but specifically with nationalists and even separatists, was not compatible with western interests. Although there are vague similarities between some of the concerns and demands of alienated westerners and alienated Quebec nationalists, Mulroney got on to questionable ground in many issues – the constitutional issue obviously, but also on ordinary governance issues. Westerners have never demanded a bigger share of the pork; rather, they've been demanding an end to the pork system. That was a very different perspective from Mulroney's approach to politics, and for him to come out and say that westerners were getting a bigger share of the pork under him only alienated people.

What has always struck me about Mulroney's constitutional position was not its specifics, but the degree to which it endorsed the PQ mythology about 1981-2. It accepted the argument that the Constitution was not just bad, or mistaken, but that Trudeau was the bad guy and that Lévesque had been the good guy. Of course, Trudeau was never popular here, nor was his constitutional deal, but that sort of perspective is completely alien: that Quebec really was shafted.

BOTHWELL: To Stephen Harper, a central problem with Mulroney's style of government, and his approach to the Constitution, was the assumption that the most important Canadian affairs are best managed by a small group of premiers, the so-called first ministers – what has come to be called 'executive federalism':

HARPER: I don't know how many Canadians understand what is meant by the term executive federalism, but what most voters will tell you is they don't like the system whereby they elect a bunch of people who get together in secret meetings, and then stage almost ritualistic debates in the legislature and pass bills on a script. This is how our parliamentary system is functioning in this country, and very few people believe that is how it should work.

BOTHWELL: There is an easy assumption that provincial premiers represent the entire population of their province, or even that the prime minister represents the population of all of Canada. This is not necessarily true, as the history of Canada's constitutional negotiations shows. David Elton of the Canada West Foundation in Calgary observes:

ELTON: One of the lessons is that first ministers, in addition to representing the population of their provinces, also represent cabinets, bureaucracies, and governments. Their ability to differentiate between their role as premier and head of a government, and their role as spokesperson for a group of people (their province), is sometimes difficult. This dual role is abused and misused by people at different points for different purposes; it's simply a natural expectation that when you ask somebody to wear three or four hats, he'll wear the wrong hat on the wrong day from time to time, because he hasn't made the transition as the people who elected him thought he should. There are many occasions where the citizens of any province take a look at their premier and say, wait a minute, he's not speaking for me on this one, because he may well be speaking for another segment of the population, or be speaking primarily as the head of a government rather than as an elected public official who's supposed to be concerned about the best interests of his constituents.

BOTHWELL: In responding to the failure of Meech Lake, Bourassa had made it plain that it would not be business as usual between Quebec and Canada. Any new constitutional initiative would have to be different, in kind and presumably in substance. Above all, it would have to represent the considered opinion of what was coming to be called the Rest of Canada – ROC. It was Mulroney's job to find out what that was, while Bourassa himself plumbed the views of the province of Quebec.

Both Mulroney and Bourassa had to contend with a new political situation. Lucien Bouchard, Mulroney's former cabinet colleague, had recruited a separatist party in the House of Commons, the Bloc Québécois or BQ, composed of former Conservative and Liberal MPs. Bourassa was characteristically ambiguous on the subject of the BQ, perhaps viewing it as yet another means of putting pressure on the rest of Canada by confronting it with a real, live separatist threat right inside parliament. It was, at any rate, the first organized separatist party actually to sit in the House of Commons (there had been a solitary separatist MP in the 1960s).

Mulroney and Bourassa got parallel consultations under way. If the problem with Meech Lake had been too little participation, then there would be hot-lines, polls, hearings, submissions, focus groups – all the paraphernalia of contemporary public opinion research, and all with an eye to shaping as well as expressing opinion for the next round. Constitutional authority Alan Cairns thought the process excessive:

CAIRNS: In one of Mulroney's speeches, either just before Meech Lake finally foundered or after it was clearly dead, he said, 'Next time I'll consult and I'll consult and I'll consult and I'll wear the Canadian public out. I will not leave one voice unheard.' This was said with Irish blarney, but also with some bitterness.

BOTHWELL: Mulroney was, of course, in ultimate charge of the federal position. But Mulroney was handicapped by a startling unpopularity in English Canada, an unpopularity which, in the opinion of some observers, masked and even negated his real qualities. Marcel Côté, as Mulroney's director of policy and communications at the time, observed the prime minister up close:

CÔTÉ: Mulroney unfortunately has a face you want to knock. You want to punch him. He looks like a liar. He talks like a sweet talker. And he doesn't come across well on TV. He has a lot of faults – he's vain and all that. But he's also a man of principle. On questions of government, on the major questions this country faced, he was a man of principle. The free trade negotiation might have been a foolish thing to do, but he did it. On matters of principle he conducted to the end. He always supported his minister of finance, and he supported the Bank of Canada, which did things that were very unpopular. And even I myself, when I was there, was against that.

BOTHWELL: Mulroney put first Keith Spicer, a colourful and very senior federal official, and then Joe Clark in charge of the federal consultation exercise. Spicer was the John the Baptist of the new reformed federalism, prophesying the golden mean that would lead to agreement between Quebec and the rest of Canada. Joe Clark was removed from his job as external affairs minister in 1991 and told that he would have to supervise Canada's internal diplomacy instead. His new job followed on Spicer's public consultations and was supposed to build a consensus of the nine majority English provinces, not forgetting the Aboriginals and the various special-interest groups. Spicer was the essential preliminary, followed by a series of regional conferences designed to bring Canadians together to react to ideas about the Constitution. Jean Charest compares the experience to rebuilding a bridge:

CHAREST: The bridge had been blown apart. We tried to rebuild it in different ways, and we weren't sure how. The Spicer Commission finally invited everyone in, to give a hand. What we found is that they all arrived at the site, and rather than try to build the bridge they wanted to hold an inquiry on who had blown it up, and why this had happened, and why we let it happen. Then we tried to move beyond that into putting some blueprints together for a new bridge we can build somewhere.

BOTHWELL: Cairns tends to agree – Spicer helped Canadians let off steam:

CAIRNS: The Spicer report was probably viewed as, and might have accomplished, a kind of catharsis. You allowed a lot of people to get bad feelings about the episode we had just gone through out of the way. Then there were the regional conferences and the separate Aboriginal one. Some attention was paid to them; they were not just lip service to the idea of consultation. Some things that were in the original package definitely got blown out of the water in those regional conferences.

BOTHWELL: Unlike Meech Lake, the government decided to consult with and, as far as possible, involve the Aboriginal peoples.

CAIRNS: There was a separate consultation process for Aboriginal peoples. They were given $9 million and all the major Aboriginal organizations made separate consultations with their constituencies. The Assembly of First Nations produced a very interesting report called *Back to the Source*, which then fed into the joint parliamentary committee. It was probably the most systematic statement of status Indian philosophy about their role in the future of Canada we have seen. In that sense, it got more information out to all of us.

BOTHWELL: *Back to the Source* was an uncompromising view of the history and goals of Native people in Canada. It did not, however, prevent Native organizations from consulting, negotiating, and ultimately joining in a constitutional dialogue. But for all the complexity and ultimately the inclusiveness of the federal consultations, they risked falling on barren ground. For Quebec, too, was having its consultations, a grand national inquiry into Quebec's constitutional prospects. It was designed to exclude nothing. Separatists and federalists both participated, and a separatist, Jean Campeau, co-chaired the inquiry with a federalist, Michel Bélanger: collectively the exercise was known as Bélanger-Campeau. Federalists are harshly critical of Bourassa for establishing the commission. Historian Michael Behiels considers it another example of the premier's poor judgment:

BEHIELS: There was a meeting of minds between Mulroney and Bourassa, reinforced by people like Rémillard and academics like Léon Dion who said, 'You must put a knife to the throat of English Canada, otherwise you're not going to do anything; you must push them to the precipice. That's the only way you're going to get anything out of them. You must use blackmail tactics, otherwise they're simply not going to move.' Through lack of better judgment, Bourassa fell into that trap and he was the author of his own demise and the demise of the Meech Lake accord, even in its amended form, the Charlottetown consensus report. He put the Campeau-Bélanger operation on the road, and the Quebec government paid millions of dollars for that, giving the soap-box to the separatists. Under tremendous pressure, Bourassa always crumbled.

BOTHWELL: Ron Graham, a journalist and historian with a particular interest in Quebec, followed the Bélanger-Campeau phenomenon:

GRAHAM: The Bélanger-Campeau committee hearings had a sort of voguish fascination. They were very popular, and people were paying attention. This commission was meant to go around and find out what Quebec really wanted, and it had a lot of press. It was broadcast live, and it had a kind of cathartic effect at a time when people were feeling high emotions. So it was an important stepping stone on the way to separation. It was all part of a separatist strategy. You could convince even middle-of-the-road federalists that the system didn't work any more, that it wasn't worth trying to save. Basically, that was their bottom line; they came out with a long list of things, and they said, 'If we don't get this, then we advise leaving.'

The fact that somebody like Bélanger, a banker, was signing it and that a lot of Liberals were on it seemed to have a real effect. It was seen as the voice of the people, the will of the majority, in a very Rousseauian way. You couldn't get the majority in English Canada to agree about anything, so the fact there was an agreement here was amazing. Yet the agreement was only for a referendum. It actually didn't agree on anything.

Also, the result was rigged from the beginning. Federalist voices weren't invited, Aboriginal voices weren't invited, ethnic voices weren't invited, and if they were invited they were put on at two o'clock in the morning when nobody was watching. There was a real mood of hostility, when someone like Chrétien came in and gave a strong pro-Canada speech, in terms of the questions and the media reaction. All of which made you feel that there was a real problem here that something really profound had snapped.

BOTHWELL: The Bélanger-Campeau commission had a dual importance. Its process exposed Quebeckers to a largely negative analysis of federalism and to a positive endorsement of the prospects of a separate Quebec. Political scientist Stéphane Dion describes the climate on which the Bélanger-Campeau discussions drew:

DION: Not only economists but some business people now support the idea that secession might be a good idea; they think that the federal government is useless, costly, and is only doing duplications. The provinces are able to do the job at a low cost. So why do we need two governments? One is enough, we don't need two governments.

You have a leftist nationalism, but you have a rightist one, too. The leftist will say that with an independent Quebec, we will have more solidarity, more capacity to govern in a partnership between the unions, the government, the social movements, and so on. And the rightist will say, now we have the free market, we don't need the protection of the federation any more; we have the GATT rules, we have the Free Trade Agreement.

BOTHWELL: Bélanger-Campeau's conclusion ran straight up the middle between continued federalism of some kind and separatism: issued in March 1991, it offered the rest of Canada a stick and a carrot. The stick was the threat of a Quebec referendum on sovereignty, to be held no later than 26 October 1992, unless the rest of Canada came up with an acceptable offer on the Constitution. This proposal was adopted and legislated by the Bourassa government.

But Bourassa went a little further. A Liberal Party commission, chaired by Jean Allaire and made up entirely of people who until then had counted as federalists, produced a report proposing a drastically decentralized version of federalism. The commission could barely be persuaded to agree to the continued existence of an elected federal parliament with the power to tax; it limited federal jurisdiction as closely as it could, conferring a scant six exclusive powers on a future federal authority, as compared with twenty-two for a future Quebec. This report, the Allaire report, was then debated and adopted at a Liberal Party convention in Montreal.

The Allaire report produced much controversy. One prominent Liberal minister, Claude Ryan, threatened to resign, and had to be appeased by a parallel pro-Canada resolution at the convention. Robert Bourassa was, of course, ambiguous. While the Allaire commission was reaching its conclusions, Bourassa was frequently absent from Quebec, being treated for cancer in the United States. He could plead illness as an excuse for inattention, but it is also true that in 1990-1 Bourassa on a number of occasions found it useful to turn up the heat on English Canada by allowing others to put forward radical propositions about the future of the province and the country.

Dion believes that Bourassa's strategy of threatening ambiguity was mistaken:

DION: Bourassa had a very strange strategy: in order to have bargaining power and to keep the streets quiet, he suggested that he might say 'maybe' or even 'yes' to sovereigntists in Quebec. It was a very bad strategy. Before Meech, Bourassa did not have the right to say, if Meech collapses, we may secede. After Meech, it was important for him to state clearly that he would never suggest secession to Quebeckers. Quebec might not be satisfied with the way Canada is managed today, but there will be other occasions to make a constitutional deal. He would have had problems with the secessionists and sovereigntists, but support for secession would never have come so high if he had had a clear strategy at the start.

BOTHWELL: Others take a milder view of Bourassa's performance. Kenneth McRoberts, author of a major study of modern Quebec, considers that Bourassa was both skilful and successful in his strategy:

MCROBERTS: In terms of the larger objective of keeping Quebec within the country, he bought time and succeeded in avoiding any decision on Quebec sovereignty until much of the sense of humiliation had disappeared. For people who are committed to sovereignty, there must have been an enormous sense of frustration, for clearly in the wake of the accord's collapse, he could have led Quebec out of the country in 1990 or 1991. It's not quite accurate to see him as having been a trickster in the sense that he openly endorsed an objective and then went out of his way to undermine it. There's a kind of consistency throughout his whole career and his actions, and his ultimate commitment was to keep Quebec within Canada.

BOTHWELL: The rest of Canada now had a deadline – a knife at the throat, to use Léon Dion's phrase. It was not exactly a phrase calculated to win hearts and minds in the rest of Canada, though it did, certainly, express the impatience of many Quebeckers with the endless process of constitutional bargaining.

The rest of Canada, federally and provincially, now had to come up with a response. It came up with many, in provincial studies and federal studies, parliamentary reports and special commissions. In a time of recession, there was certainly one area of growth and prosperity in Canada: the constitution industry. Senator Gérald Beaudoin, co-chair of a parliamentary committee on the subject, remembers the experience of taking the Constitution to the people:

BEAUDOIN: Speaking for myself, I was of the opinion that we should consult the people of Canada, we should hear the people of Canada. But we cannot draft the Constitution with 27 million people around the table; it's impossible. Even the Americans didn't do that. So when people are talking about consultation and not hiding behind closed doors, I have some reservations.

BOTHWELL: In March 1992 Joe Clark, as minister responsible for constitutional reform, convened a multilateral ministerial conference on the

Constitution. Nine provinces, two territories, and Native organizations all took part, alongside the federal government. Their task was to formulate an offer acceptable to Quebec, one that would meet Quebec's requirements, before the October deadline.

Rather to the surprise of the prime minister, Clark had by July 1992 succeeded in cobbling together an agreement. The sticking point was a commitment to a Senate with equal representation from each province; on that point Ontario, which along with Quebec had the most to lose, finally agreed. But would Quebec? As July moved into August, Quebec's position was once again unclear. Quebec did not like an equal Senate, but without an equal Senate there could be no deal with Alberta or with five other provinces. Quebec would not negotiate, but it would attend non-negotiating meetings. There was, finally, a negotiating session in Ottawa and, at the end of August, a meeting in Charlottetown. There ten premiers, one prime minister, plus Native and territorial leaders, agreed on a deal – the Charlottetown accord. It was not an easy package, including as it did something for everyone – for Quebec, for Alberta, for Native peoples, even for the territories. A final text was not ready, just an agreement in principle. That had to do, for the Quebec deadline was by then only two months away.

Alberta, next to Quebec, was the driving force behind the constitutional debate in 1991-2. In that province, Conservative premier Don Getty was heading an unpopular government that suffered from its alignment with Mulroney and the Ottawa government. Preston Manning, son of a former Alberta premier, was leading the new Reform Party, which threatened to decimate the Conservative Party at the next federal election. Manning during 1992 was therefore in many ways the key Alberta political figure. Tom Flanagan was at that time director of research for the Reform Party, and he describes how important Quebec was in getting the federal government to address western issues:

FLANAGAN: Preston Manning said that Quebec was the only player with the power to 'crack,' to use his phrase, the Constitution open, and once it was open, that would be the opportunity for the West to satisfy its own demands. That was Manning's original conception of strategy, when the Reform Party was still a western party.

To some extent, that's also been true of the provincial government in Alberta, although, I would say, inconsistently. As late as 1987, Don Getty was prepared to let Meech Lake go through and to put off Senate reform until a hypothetical second round. He paid a big price for that, politically. Getty was not aggressively trying to hitch a ride on the Quebec chariot, and his agenda changed in the next round. Getty made the Triple-E Senate a virtually non-negotiable demand for his support for Charlottetown, and he did finally get some sort of semblance of a Triple-E Senate. So, in the late 1980s, he was trying to ride the Quebec tiger.

BOTHWELL: Triple-E, equal, effective, and elected, had its origins in western frustrations with the Trudeau government. The West's problem was that its population, and therefore its weight in the Canadian political system, did not guarantee that its concerns would always be addressed at the centre. David Elton of the Canada West Foundation in Calgary explains:

ELTON: It was a recognition that even at first ministers' conferences, with the four western premiers joining together, they couldn't obtain the kinds of things that they thought were in the best interests of their citizens. So they said, 'Well, maybe we're going to have to reform the central government in meaningful ways,' and the only meaningful way they could identify that they thought was doable was through Senate reform. Of course, most of us recognized that Senate reform was something that Canadians had been trying to attain for well over one hundred years and that nobody had done it yet. It's much more difficult to reform than any of us would have thought, because the effort that was put into that over a thirteen or fourteen year period was phenomenal, yet the Senate remains the same today as it was before all this began. And there's nothing on the horizon that would suggest that it's going to change.

BOTHWELL: Native groups had won admission to the constitutional table with some difficulty. In 1981 they had not been at the table at all, and their representation thereafter was occasional, not regular. The grand chief of the First Nations, Ovide Mercredi, had been a major figure at Charlottetown, and he was especially pleased with the accord's provisions for Native peoples:

MERCREDI: Our approach in the Charlottetown accord was not just about political liberation. We never even used the word 'liberation.' We chose to use the term 'inherent right of self-government.' Canadians understand what self-government is, and they know that an inherent right derives from the people, or maybe comes from the creator. The whole concept of inherent rights is something that's acceptable to the Canadian people.

In the end we got recognition that we were distinct peoples. In my opinion that's even more powerful than recognition of a distinct society. Some commentators in Quebec, shortly after the Charlottetown accord was negotiated, came to the same conclusion – that what we negotiated in terms of the Canada Clause was stronger than what was there for the province of Quebec, and some people were upset with that.

BOTHWELL: Roy Romanow participated in the reform of the Constitution as Saskatchewan attorney general in the early 1980s and as premier of the province at Charlottetown. He reflects on the differences between the two episodes:

ROMANOW: In 1992 we had matured as a society, and the leadership of the Aboriginal community also was prepared to speak now with some effectiveness and a clear voice on the principles. This was a substantial difference, because you had now another order of government in addition to the provincial and the federal orders.

The one negative I have about Charlottetown, although it turned out all right, was that, unlike the late 1970s and 1980s in the first round, there was a relatively limited, detailed analysis of the various provisions of the accord. In the first round there was a moving from city to city in a detailed study of various provisions. Charlottetown did not have that; as well, the chemistry was not as good.

There were tensions between Clark and Mulroney, for example, in the period leading up to the Charlottetown accord. The rest of us as premiers were not quite sure whom we should listen to. At the end of the day, there was substantial compromise by Bourassa, especially considering the history and the historical demands of Quebec premiers, and a big compromise by the other premiers: the 25 per cent floor for representation of Quebec in the House of Commons, for example, was a major compromise; reform of the upper chamber, the Senate, was a big compromise by Ontario and Quebec. It was a much more pan-Canadian agreement. I have held the view, and I still do, that Charlottetown will go down in history as one of our finest acts of compromise, of accommodation of our competing interests. It would have maintained the strong central government, and strengthened and modernized the federation. If the public had voted for it, the accord would have put to bed for quite some time the issues surrounding national unity.

BOTHWELL: Why did Bourassa decide in favour of the Charlottetown accord? Marcel Côté, who was Prime Minister Mulroney's director of policy and communications, explains:

CÔTÉ: It was part of the process, and it was the federalist process. He went forth, he tried to get a deal out of it, and he got caught in it. At the end, everybody realized they ended up with a big spaghetti, but it was too late.

BOTHWELL: In an ultimate act of consultation, Charlottetown would be referred to the people in a referendum – or rather two referendums, for there was one in Quebec and another in the rest of Canada. The question, however, was the same: Did you approve (or not) of the Charlottetown accord?

Patrick Boyer, a Toronto MP, had promoted a Canada Referendum Act and piloted an amendment to the act through the House of Commons, establishing a permanent legal mechanism for popular consultation. The Charlottetown accord was its first test:

BOYER: Direct democracy through voting in a referendum or a plebiscite is not an alternative to representative democracy; it's a complementary process; it works in harmony with it. The last Canada-wide direct vote that everyone would remember, for example, the Charlottetown accord in 1992, was a process that was started by parliament passing the Canada Referendum Act, setting out the framework and the ground rules through which the vote would be conducted. Next it was parliament that adopted the wording of the ballot question that Canadians would be asked to answer. And if the Charlottetown accord had been approved by a majority of Canadians in that referendum, then it would have been parliament and the legislatures that would have enacted various measures to implement the results.

BOTHWELL: Boyer considers that the Charlottetown accord had its problems as a referendum package. It was large and complex, even though the basic question was simple:

BOYER: On one level, the Charlottetown accord was the simplest thing you could imagine. It was a whole package of proposals to deal with the Constitution, and Canadian voters were being asked, 'Here's the package: Do you want the governments to proceed to implement it? Yes or No?' Is the light green or is the light red? On that level, it was very straightforward.

However, once you looked at the package, you found that, within it, there were seven or eight major subjects, each of which could have been the subject of a national referendum: Aboriginal self-government, an elected Senate, recognizing Quebec as a 'distinct society within Canada,' the devolution of many powers such as job training from the government of Canada to the provincial governments, the whole idea of how we define ourselves through the Canada Clause, and so on. As Canadians delved into that, as they got behind the simple question, they began to realize that there was too much there to change all at once, that it was better to be cautious and to say no, not so much so fast. The willingness of Canadians to evolve (we are a dynamic country and our Constitution has evolved dramatically on an incremental basis over the past 130 years) was certainly reflected in the fact that half the Canadians voted for the accord. But the desire to be progressive on one hand was countered by an instinct to be conservative on the other hand, a voice saying 'If in doubt, don't.' The end result was better than we ever could have dreamt of, because the result of the defeat of the Charlottetown accord was that seemingly unstoppable process of constitutional discussions in Canada, which saw more and more of our country's political issues being 'constitutionalized' rather than being addressed in parliament – a constitutional locomotive – had at last been derailed. And it happened without the country splitting along regional or linguistic lines.

BOTHWELL: The Charlottetown accord was put to the vote on 26 October 1992. The result was a *No*. It was not a resounding *No*, but in a referendum 50 per cent plus 1 is sufficient. It was *No* in British Columbia, *No* in Quebec, *No* among Native peoples. It was a narrow *Yes* in Ontario.

Peter Russell observed Charlottetown closely and ruefully. He reflects on the experience:

RUSSELL: Charlottetown was simply a pot-pourri – a little bit of something for everyone, but not enough for anyone. Everyone's got a little bit of their Canadian vision in there, but nobody's got their vision clear, coherent, and straight on the rocks. We know that we shouldn't try to do it again. The idea won't work, that if we had one more go at it, and put in a little bit more for the West and not so much for Quebec, we might get it right. That whole approach was ridiculous. It was a learning experience. I hope people can learn what they cannot do, and we should not do that again, unless we're forced to.

BOTHWELL: The referendum of October 1992 was in a sense Brian Mulroney's swan song. Not long afterwards he announced his intention to retire, and in June 1993 he was replaced as Conservative leader and prime minister by Kim Campbell, the minister of national defence. Campbell's was a brief eminence: she and all but two of her followers were erased in the general election of October 1993. The Liberals under Jean Chrétien returned to power in Ottawa; but the separatist Bloc Québécois under Lucien Bouchard became the official opposition in the House of Commons.

It was, Bouchard proclaimed, round one in the final defeat of federalism and the separation of Quebec. Round two, the defeat of the Quebec Liberals, would follow; and round three, the separation of Quebec from Canada via a referendum, could be seen on the horizon.

Chapter 12

Where Do We Go from Here?

Iɴ 1965 the Royal Commission on Bilingualism and Biculturalism informed Canadians that this country, without being entirely aware of the fact, was in the greatest crisis in its history. No one could possibly make that claim today. Canadians are aware, all too aware, of a crisis.

In 1995 Canada is entering the thirtieth year of its political and constitutional predicament, centred on the province of Quebec and the place of French-speaking Canadian citizens in Canada. 'What does Quebec want?' used to be the question in English Canada. That was a question that presumed there was an answer, and in fact there were many answers, none of which could be said to represent the majority of Quebeckers. Because there is no agreed answer, Canadians have been tempted to ask another question: 'What does Quebec not want?' That would seem to be a more appropriate inquiry as we approach Quebec's third decade in the spotlight and the second referendum on that province's place inside, or outside, Canada.

If the basic question varies, so too does its context. In the 1960s, when English Canadians began to ask the question, they hoped that the answer would be something they could and would accept. In 1995, they are not so sure.

John Honderich, publisher of the *Toronto Star*, has for some years studied and written about the Quebec problem. He describes the evolution of
English Canadians' views of Quebec:

HONDERICH: They think of Quebec in various ways. English Canada in the
last two or three decades has gone through an evolution, particularly in
Ontario. In the 1950s and 1960s there was a sense of guilt towards Quebec,
that all the big Quebec firms were run by English-speaking executives and
that French-speaking Quebeckers couldn't get ahead. There was the sense
that the system wasn't working well for Quebeckers. When Trudeau brought
about the Just Society and introduced bilingualism, there was a basic acceptance of the fact that French Canadians were a founding people and French
was a founding language, so we had to create structures and systems in the
federal government that reflected that fact.

We're beyond that now. What's happening is that, with the evolution of
Quebec in terms of its provincial politics, its language, and its cultural policy, people have seen a strong, vibrant Quebec emerge, within the existing
structure. So, people say to themselves, Quebec has basically got what it set
out to accomplish, and there is no longer any need to feel guilty that the system isn't working for French-speakers. What they want now is something
totally different from what we want. What you hear is more a sense of, Okay,
Quebec, it's time: take it or leave it.

BOTHWELL: Take it or leave it. To people using the argument, it may appear
irrefutable. Leaving it, leaving Canada, has seemed like a drastic act. In 1980,
when Quebeckers last confronted that question, they decided against leaving, because to some Quebeckers, at least, leaving seemed so much like the
worse alternative. But does it today? Western economist Paul Boothe reflects
on this question:

BOOTHE: People are much more aware that the transfers they get from the
federal government are supported in large part by borrowing. With the
transfers they get today come a future claim on their income and future
taxes. People are not under any illusion about the fact that they're going to
have collectively to pay back a good deal of this money in the future. That
said, it's also true that the benefits that flow to Quebec on a per capita basis
are substantially less than they were before. The net transfers to Quebec in
1982 were in the order of $890 per person and, using comparable dollars in

1991, they were down to about $405 per person. We have seen a substantial reduction in the magnitudes of the flows of income towards Quebec.

BOTHWELL: The transfers referred to by Boothe range from unemployment insurance to regional development schemes. In Canada since the Second World War the federal government has taken the lead in social policy of all kinds even though, under the Constitution, the actual jurisdiction or responsibility for these fields lies with the provinces. Since 1974 the federal government has also been running a deficit, which has meant that the federal government has been borrowing money and transferring it to the provinces to spend on programs that were originally designed in Ottawa. Along the way something seems to have been lost.

BOOTHE: One of the problems with these programs is that we don't have a set of clearly defined goals at the beginning against which we can measure our performance to see how well we're doing in terms of reaching our goals. Until we have these benchmarks, we're not going to make the judgments about these programs that we should. Instead, what's happening right now is that the lack of funds for the federal government to continue financing these programs is really what's driving the agenda.

BOTHWELL: The federal government, after running twenty years of deficits under both Liberal and Conservative governments, now faces considerable financial problems. Its financial miseries are familiar to Canadians from coast to coast, including Canadians in Quebec. Whatever the federal government may have been or have done in the past, it isn't today what it used to be. Ken Norrie explains why leaving Canada seems acceptable or even attractive to some economists in Quebec:

NORRIE: If you did the old-fashioned balance-sheet kind of stuff, Quebec almost certainly has been a net beneficiary in terms of fiscal transfers, interregional redistributions, and spending through tariffs. Most economists would argue that as part of Confederation, in the postwar period at least, Quebec has been a beneficiary through the operation of the unemployment insurance scheme and some of the regional developments schemes. What Quebec economists are now arguing is a much more subtle point. This traditional system was fine – then. This is now and this is a different world, a world that requires a lot more investment in human capital and in research and development, a lot more international presence on the world stage, and a flexible dynamic state, in the way that the private sector has to be flexible and dynamic. Their argument is that in this new world, notwithstanding whatever the case was in the past, Quebec is being dragged down by being part of a confederation that's slow and ponderous. It's difficult to get going, and there is overlap and duplication. If the Quebec state were free to act in an innovative, flexible way, the same way they see some of their leading businesses acting, and to be a presence on the international stage, they would be better off. They want full control over trade, over manpower and immigration, and over taxation, industrial subsidies, and so on, and they don't want to have to negotiate with Ottawa and the other provinces.

BOTHWELL: Quebeckers are not alone in making the point that the federal government is an encumbrance. In the mid-1990s Canada's indebtedness abroad has reached a very high level. Economist David Laidler outlines the problem:

LAIDLER: Canada is a country with a very small population and lots of resources, and it has always borrowed heavily for economic development purposes. There's no particular reason to be concerned with that, or to think that was a bad thing. What Canada has been doing over the last twenty years has been borrowing abroad to finance domestic consumption of government services: primarily health and education. If you want to put it in a cheap way, Canada's got the highest quality of life in the world, according to the United Nations, but it's provided for itself with borrowed money.

BOTHWELL: In terms of the Canadian debt, Laidler considers whether it would be fair to say that we are already in a crisis of fiscal federalism:

LAIDLER: We're just in a crisis, a fiscal crisis. The debt-to-GDP ratio is enormously high. We're in the same league as the Italians and the Belgians. Our foreign debt is about 50 per cent of the year's GDP net. That's an enormously high figure. I think that among developed countries, Italy is next, with about 15 or 16 per cent. We're in a fiscal mess already, without the Quebec situation coming in on top of it.

BOTHWELL: In 1980 participation in Canada meant sharing the prosperity of a transcontinental economy rich in resources. By 1995 the economy, and the assumptions we make about the economy, have changed considerably. The free-trade pact with the United States and the 1988 federal election that ratified it have had six or seven years to work through the economy.

In 1988 Ontario was divided on the issue of free trade: its opponents were many, including the Liberal-leaning *Toronto Star*. John Honderich comments on Ontario's trading links:

HONDERICH: With free trade and what has developed, the market for Ontario is no longer the West. The market for Ontario is the Midwest of the United States: New York, Pennsylvania, Ohio, and so on. That's our market all of a sudden.

BOTHWELL: As far as Ontario was concerned, trade had already taken a significant turn in the 1960s, when free trade in automobiles and automotive parts was established between Canada and the United States – the Autopact of 1965. Bernard Landry, vice-premier of Quebec and a professional economist, views the Autopact as a precedent and a foundation for freer trade:

LANDRY: You must not forget the Autopact, which was the ancestor of free trade, and the evidence, through its tremendous success, that the movement of trade would have to be rearranged north/south instead of east/west, which was the old national policy of the John A. Macdonald pattern. That was quite obvious. Without the Autopact, Canada would be a miserable place in terms of industry. So, if it was true for automobiles, why not for the rest?

BOTHWELL: While Ontario's trade with Quebec and with the rest of Canada continues to be valuable and significant, it is not quite as important as it used to be. It is not just Quebec or Alberta or British Columbia that looks inquiringly at the state of Canada.

Nevertheless, even if economic links have diminished, compared with twenty or thirty years ago, they remain significant. Lloyd Atkinson, a prominent Toronto economist, notes that trade flows are not the only measure:

ATKINSON: In the first instance, there are the obvious trade ties. You have interlinked companies, and it really is to a large extent an Ontario-Quebec story. Where you have production, financial, and other service entities that have offices in both Montreal or Quebec City on the one hand, and in Toronto or London on the other, those ties are quite extensive. What is interesting is that we can only now estimate what the magnitude of the trade flows are: the last official data was 1989, so all you can do is infer. But what you do infer is that there is a huge amount of trade and financial activity that takes place between Quebec and Ontario in particular.

BOTHWELL: Economics and economic management are only a few of the issues currently on the table as Canadians in all parts of the country reappraise where they stand, or should stand, in case of Quebec's separation. There is another important factor closely involved with economics, a factor that has shown itself to be inextricable from the political debates over language or equality or self-determination. That is the question of the make-up of the Canadian population.

In the most recent census, that of 1991, French-speakers constituted 6.5 million people, roughly 25 per cent of Canada's population; there has been a slow descent from almost 30 per cent in 1941. The bulk of French-speakers, 5.5 million, are concentrated in Quebec, where they form more than 80 per cent of the population. In Quebec, the French-speaking population has risen slowly in absolute numbers and as a proportion of the population. Why so slowly? David Foot, an economist specializing in demography, explains:

FOOT: Because fertility rates are lower in Quebec than in the rest of the country, you have less augmentation of the population from births. If you've got fewer younger people, then, by comparison, you've got more older people, and I'm talking about people in their thirties and forties, not necessarily seniors. The average age of the population goes up as fertility goes down. Immigrants tend to be in their twenties, and, to the extent that immigration has contributed to the growth of the Quebec population, it's making the Quebec population younger, not older. But the number of immigrants compared with the number of births is not even close: about 80,000 births to maybe 25,000 immigrants. Still, immigration is helping to ameliorate the aging trend coming from lower fertility. At the other end of the age spectrum, people in Quebec don't live as long as those in the rest of the country. There's lower life expectancy in Quebec. Perhaps because, on average, they smoke more than the rest of us, they don't live as long.

BOTHWELL: Immigration into Canada has been running at about 250,000 a year and, according to Quebec's 1990 immigration-sharing agreement with Ottawa, Quebec should have received about 60,000 of those – 25 per cent. But immigration does not flow to Quebec. Instead of 25 per cent, Quebec takes 10 per cent of immigration, a phenomenon that is likely to diminish

Quebec's political and probably economic importance further relative to the rest of the country. At 30 per cent or even 25 per cent of the total population, Quebec had a plausible and even crucial claim on Canada's attention. But at 20 per cent or even less? At that point the special position of French and French-speakers might be expected to erode. While Bill 101 might solve Quebec's internal language problem, the balance of languages inside Quebec, it could do nothing for Quebec's external language problem, the position of French in Canada as a whole.

There is already a feeling that French is no longer special in Canada, but just one foreign language among many in an English sea. Here the problem, from the point of view of Quebec nationalists, is Canada's multicultural policy, adopted by the Trudeau government and confirmed by Trudeau's successors. If Canada is or becomes a mosaic of languages and cultures, what then becomes of French Canadians as a 'founding people' or 'partner in Confederation'? What will happen to the hope, common among Quebec nationalists, that Quebec could be or would be an equal partner in a Canadian confederation? But is multiculturalism really as dominant a characteristic of English Canada as some suppose?

Tom Flanagan assesses how firmly multiculturalism is embedded in the political culture of western Canada:

FLANAGAN: Multiculturalism has had its supporters. The thing is, it means different things to different people. To some people it just means that you're tolerant of difference, and so there are those who support it for that reason. For various ethnic communities it means specific benefits and grants to their communities, so they support it. Initially, multiculturalism was also seen in the West as a rebuff to bilingualism, so it may have been popular in western Canada because it was thought to prevent the West from coming under the French domination that would be entailed in bilingualism and biculturalism. There were different attitudes towards it and different threads in it. The earlier reaction that it was a rebuff to biculturalism has been forgotten, except in Quebec. So now your views on multiculturalism are a kind of litmus test on whether you're a member in good standing of the intellectual class, and the spiritual church of which that class is the leading element.

BOTHWELL: Ironically, both in the West and in Quebec, multiculturalism is inextricably tied to the name of Pierre Trudeau. To Ken McRoberts, who has studied contemporary Quebec closely, that is no recommendation in the minds of Quebec nationalists:

MCROBERTS: The Trudeau vision of Canada hasn't taken root in Quebec. It's taken root in the rest of the country. There's an irony there that a vision of Canada that was based on bilingualism, multiculturalism, the charter, and a particular kind of federalism, one that was fashioned to counter nationalism within Quebec in the hope that it could sway francophones to identify with all of Canada, hasn't had the desired impact in Quebec, but has altered the way in which many English Canadians see Canada.

BOTHWELL: Lise Bissonnette, editor of *Le Devoir*, agrees that multiculturalism must be seen as part of Trudeau's legacy:

BISSONNETTE: Trudeau believed in the state, and the state he believed in was Canada. He was building from the top all the time, and he imposed his theories on Canadians, even bilingualism and multiculturalism. The way he worked at it was always to say, 'Well, this is the truth. Look at it and I'm going to tell you that you should live by that.'

BOTHWELL: English-Canadian critics have sometimes suggested that Quebec's coolness towards multiculturalism implies a vision of a racially pure and necessarily separate Quebec. Some Quebeckers presumably think in this manner, but such views are probably not in the majority. According to Bissonnette, the older variety of linguistic nationalism has been replaced by a territorial identification:

BISSONNETTE: The sense of nation is changing very much in Quebec. We have consciously decided that we are not going to be a nation based only on language, culture, a shared sense of history (that of Nouvelle France), and a view of the future in terms of French-speaking people who have resisted. Over the past twenty, but particularly the past ten years, there has been a conscious decision that the nation is not only that; concurrently, there has been the birth of what we call territorial nationalism – that everyone who lives in Quebec and wants to live there is part of this 'country,' which, because it's still not a country, is only a sense of being there. So, you have to change your definition to understand why there is still a sovereignist movement if the traditional nationalism is going away. What you are witnessing is a sense that you don't belong to Canada, and you don't see how you are going to connect with the world through Canada; therefore, it makes more sense to connect through Quebec, through the Quebec government and Quebec institutions. You don't need to have a close relationship to Canada in order to participate in the larger world. That's what I see emerging, especially among the young people.

BOTHWELL: Instead of concentrating exclusively on language, the Quebec government since the 1970s, under both the Liberals and the Parti Québécois, has generated its own mini-multiculturalism. The difference is that in Quebec the majority, the alternative, language is French, not English. Political scientist Max Nemni sees a considerable irony in the situation:

NEMNI: What most Quebec nationalists claim today is not an ethnic nationalism, but either a territorial nationalism or an open kind of nationalism. They'll define a Quebecker as someone who lives in Quebec. They want a multi-ethnic Quebec nationalism. Fundamentally, what they want is their own state, a state in which the French language and culture will be dominant, but in which there will be room for all others to do what they want. In other words, they want to rebuild a Canada on their own level. They are living a contradiction in a way, because if it isn't an ethnic state that they want, if it isn't a French state, they have a multicultural state, and it's called Canada.

BOTHWELL: Multiculturalism is a relatively recent development in Canadian history. Relations with the Aboriginal nations predate the existence of Canada. Through most of the nineteenth and twentieth centuries, the Aboriginal inhabitants of Canada were pushed aside and marginalized both politically and economically. Only in the last twenty years have they returned to the political stage, to assert a political standing that is older than the country itself. Ovide Mercredi, grand chief of the Assembly of First Nations, defines the main points of contention between the First Nations and the government of Quebec:

MERCREDI: There are a number of contentious issues. The first has to do with who has rights and what these rights are – to land, to resources, and to self-determination. When we made representations to the legislative assembly in Quebec, the message we gave them was this: that we're not opposed to the development of their political goals, to the assertion of their self-determination, and that there's a lot of parallels to be made between what they want to do and what we want to achieve ourselves. However, what they propose to do they can't do without our consent. In other words, they can't secede from Canada unilaterally, take all the land and all the resources, and with that take our sovereignty, too. That's the primary issue between the First Nations and people in the province of Quebec; there are others, though, that are just as important.

BOTHWELL: Ghislain Picard, the regional chief of the Assembly of First Nations, Quebec and Labrador, is just as emphatic:

PICARD: We stated that this is Quebec's process with the rest of Canada, it's their choice to make. But is that choice, or is the process, legitimate? As we know it today, it involves more than just cultural or linguistic specifics, including the notion of a distinct society or distinct nation for Quebec. We know that it involves the territorial integrity of this province, as they claim it. And we've already stated publicly that we question that, because we have our own territorial integrity to protect.

BOTHWELL: Nor would it be a simple case of handing over a federal responsibility, a federal jurisdiction, to a successor government, in this case an independent Quebec.

PICARD: Quebec claims that once it becomes independent, an independent state, then all the responsibilities that used to flow from the federal government to the provinces would automatically become provincial jurisdiction. That might be true in certain cases, such as airports or ports. But when it comes to people, it just cannot happen; you need the consent of those people to be transferred from one jurisdiction to the other. What if those people want to remain in their own jurisdiction? There seems to be no provision for that, and that's what we're contesting. Now that the French and the English want to settle their differences, it is time for us also to stand on our own two feet, with what we claim is ours. The understanding of our people is that whatever obligations the present federal government has, and indirectly Quebec has as a province, come from treaties that were signed with the Crown, the English regime.

BOTHWELL: Picard argues that the federal government can't be released from those obligations without the consent of the First Nations:

PICARD: It's a two-way street. It's been confirmed over and over with a Royal Proclamation, it's been confirmed with the latest Canadian Constitution in 1982, and we feel that it is only up to us to decide when that obligation ends.

BOTHWELL: In Picard's view, a Quebec referendum would simply not involve the province's First Nations, nor would the Quebec government's timetable for independence some time in 1996 have any effect on them:

PICARD: It can't be our timetable, because we won't take part in any of the processes that are linked directly to the sovereignty of Quebec. Our feeling is that we've agreed on a common declaration among ourselves on where we stand as First Nations of this territory. We've agreed that we have our own territorial integrity to uphold, that we live among Quebeckers, and that we need to maintain peaceful coexistence with the people who surround us. That's really what we need to assert, and we will do it, in a timely fashion, regardless of any calendars that might be there, which are really of little concern for us. What we need to do is respect the common declaration we all agreed on, and determine our own calendar for the benefit of all the communities we represent.

BOTHWELL: The Native communities do not feel bound by decisions of the Quebec government regarding sovereignty, or even by a Quebec referendum. While this does not mean that they would refuse under certain circumstances to recognize or cooperate with a sovereign Quebec, they believe that it must be done, if at all, on their terms.

Marcel Côté, Brian Mulroney's former director of policy and communications and currently president of Secor in Montreal, argues that the Aboriginal nations have a crucial role to play in how, or whether, the sovereigntists approach separation:

CÔTÉ: They know what they want. They have a vision of their country, their land. They know that it's their land, and they want to stake their land. There's no way they're going to be traded like baseball players from one country to another one. The white man doesn't have that power anymore. And I don't care how many constitutional lawyers will come to committees and do their role about the rights of this and the rights of that, and what the king said and what the queen said. All these things are going to be solved in thirty-second clips on the 7 o'clock news. And the rest of the world will side with the Aboriginals, and won't have to give heed to what they want.

What they want probably is the status quo on our agenda, and movement on their agenda. And they have a veto right on our agenda, to the extent that it affects them. They did it with Meech. And I think they'll do it again. So don't think that Parizeau can separate northern Quebec out of Canada, because the Aboriginals say this is not what they want to talk about. And so that's another major obstacle. I think Parizeau realizes it.

It's not a question of economic advantage, it's one of dignity, one of being recognized: recognize that it's their land, recognize that they have rights which are as important as our rights. They have a first claim on that land, and it's a new generation of Aboriginal. They don't recognize the treatment that we've given them, and they recognize that it's first and above all their land; we might use it, but only if we get their permission. So it's a total reshaping of our attitude towards the land mass of this country, and the use of the land mass, the use of the resources, and the redistribution of income generated from that land mass.

BOTHWELL: The history of Canada began with the interaction of whites and Aboriginals; the wars of the French and the British continued the process; and now the quarrels between Québécois and English Canadians have raised the issue again.

John Honderich assesses how important the Native issue is to Canadian public opinion, and what effect it might have on Canadians' attitudes towards the possible separation of Quebec:

HONDERICH: If there is to be a flash point, in any eventual separation or division of this country, I am convinced it will be over the Aboriginal people. They have made it perfectly clear, the Cree in northern Quebec, that they want to stay within Canada. They have a defined territory; depending on your interpretation of the historical maps, they can point to an area which they can say is 'ours.' What happens if Quebec declares sovereignty and separates, and these Native groups appeal to the Canadian government for help? I think that would create a very strong emotional response. I think by any doctrine of self-determination a strong legal case could be made that they have legitimate legal rights in this matter, and, as a group within a well-defined territory forming a majority within that territory, they have the same right to self-determination as do the people of the province of Quebec. They would make not only a strong legal but a strong moral argument, which would be well received in English Canada.

That raises the question, What would we do about it? Would we send in the troops? One hates to think of the consequences, but it's certainly something I've thought about. I think that's the flash point, rather than the West Island of Montreal or Akwesasne. Those areas might well try and make other distinctions, but it's the people in northern Quebec who are the ones that really cause the most concern. I don't know at this point whether I would send my son to fight for northern Quebec. That's what it would come down to, and that's a pretty frightening thought.

BOTHWELL: Aboriginal questions are not confined to Canada or Quebec. The treatment of Aboriginal peoples is followed outside Canada and affects how Canada is perceived. The largest impact is in Canada's southern neighbour, the United States, which shares much of Canada's history on Aboriginal issues.

It takes considerable provocation to cause Americans to take much interest in what goes on in Canada. On the subject of Quebec independence, as Joseph Jockel points out, there is not much particular knowledge, though what there is tends to be both reserved and sceptical:

JOCKEL: There is no enthusiasm for Quebec independence here, and there really isn't much knowledge about it. In encounters with Americans, such as US congressmen with Lucien Bouchard in 1994, a reassuring chord was struck when Bouchard said that an independent Quebec would want a defence relationship with the United States, and would want to continue the FTA [Free Trade Agreement] and now NAFTA, and would want to join NATO. It's reassuring, but not ultimately convincing. The best that can occur under such circumstances is for US officials to come out and say, 'Well, we still don't think it's such a good idea, but if they really want to do it, they really want to become independent, well, that's okay too.'

BOTHWELL: Quebec independence might be achieved through negotiations with the rest of Canada, and with the Aboriginal nations scattered around the province but concentrated in northern Quebec, where Natives form a majority. Or it might not, in which case Quebec's legislation on sovereignty following a *Yes* vote in the referendum calls for a Unilateral Declaration of Independence, called UDI for short.

JOCKEL: If there's a unilateral declaration of independence on the part of Quebec, if there's a *Yes* in the referendum, and negotiations break down between English Canada and Quebec, and there's UDI, the US government will turn to a set of criteria that it usually uses for deciding whether to recognize a new state. And one of the criteria is effective control of the territory. If the Aboriginals in Quebec say *No*, the Quebec government doesn't control northern Quebec, or pieces of Quebec, and that could be a factor in the simple legal advice provided to the administration on whether to recognize UDI. Similarly, the Aboriginals are a wild card, in general public opinion and perception.

Americans don't know much about Quebec, or don't know much about Canada in general. Given our history and our strong presumption for national unity, and given the tendency to compare what's going on in Quebec with linguistic developments in the United States, there isn't much support for Quebec and for the French language here in general. In the presence of an effective Aboriginal public-relations campaign surrounding both James Bay and now Quebec independence in general, and because of the links between the environmental movement in the United States and Aboriginals in Canada, and because of the presence of Aboriginal groups here in Washington who have links to Aboriginals in Canada, I think Aboriginals in Quebec really are the wild card for public opinion in the United States. They can significantly affect public opinion in the United States towards Quebec independence.

BOTHWELL: There are, then, three direct parties to the Quebec-Canada political crisis, and a fourth, an onlooker, but a very close onlooker. The two principal parties, however, are the separatist forces in Quebec and the federalist forces inside that province and in the rest of Canada.

There are varieties of separatism, as there are varieties of federalism. On the separatist side, there is independence pure and simple, the position generally associated with Jacques Parizeau. Independence might mean, but would not have to mean, treaty links with the rest of Canada, as well as membership in the NAFTA and the GATT. Quebec would use the Canadian dollar. And Quebec would strive for a division of federal assets in the year before its unilateral declaration of independence took effect. But none of these things, except independence, would have to happen, and need not happen.

Softer separatists propose a confederal regime, in which a sovereign Quebec would be linked with the rest of Canada through common but equal institutions, which would exercise minimal powers but would, presumably, furnish some kind of order and psychological reassurance. This confederal association merges imperceptibly into the softer federalist position, in which the central authority would be denuded of considerable jurisdiction, but some kind of central elected body would be retained. Finally, there is the federalism of the status quo, in which a recognizable federal government, with real powers, would continue to exist.

Support for confederalism is not confined to Quebec. Michael Walker of the Fraser Institute in Vancouver argues that fiscal pressures are likely to force a change in Canadian government in any case:

WALKER: I think Alberta, Ontario, and British Columbia are in due course going to want a disempowerment of the federal government, a devolution of powers to the provinces, and application of the principle of subsidiarity in the allocation of powers within the federation so that everything is done at the lowest level at which it can be done. If that's what Quebeckers want, and let's hope that's what they want, then we should be accommodating to them in every way we can, and not take positions of intransigence, because it's not in our interest to do so. We can't compel them: if they want to have this devolution of powers, they will get it, one way or another, and so from our own rational and informed self-interest we should negotiate with them, on a basis that takes into account our own interests and those of our children, and make a deal.

Do I think it's likely we're going to do that? Unfortunately, I have to say no. It's highly likely that this is going to be emotional, cantankerous, bitter, acrimonious. It's going to be like most divorces, to use an analogy, and there's going to be vindictiveness and an attempt to make up for past assumed or perceived wrongs. We should try to be as rational as we can under the circumstances, and try to avoid the kind of confrontation that Parizeau may want to bring about on issues of the debt or on anything else.

BOTHWELL: In the summer of 1994 Gordon Gibson published a closely reasoned pamphlet that he called 'Plan B' – the future of the rest of Canada. In it he argued for a Canadian confederal state as the only position likely to command decisive political support within Quebec:

GIBSON: If you look at Parizeau's strategic position, he is able to say to his electors in the province of Quebec, in effect, you are in a box. The box has only two exits: one exit is status quo, and the other is separatism. I'm going to make you choose between those two exits. Given his control of the public purse and his ability to institute those studies he thinks are right, to time the referendum, to be provocative, and, if he wishes, to follow the general game plan of the separatist leader in Slovakia which brought Czechoslovakia from a unified country to a dismembered country within a couple of years, he can manipulate the situation. He has a good shot at winning, as long as there's only those two exits to that box. If there's another exit we can construct, which is called significant decentralization, in my opinion most Quebeckers want to go through that door. And that preserves Canada.

BOTHWELL: The example of Czechoslovakia has been raised. That country enjoyed an existence of just over seventy years, an existence marked by war and by communist rule. Czechoslovakia had two principal components, the Czech lands of Bohemia and Moravia, centred on Prague, and Slovakia, to the east, centred on Bratislava. Generally speaking, industry and advanced development were a feature of the more populous Czech lands; and although the Slovaks did have some industry, they were regarded as more rural if not backward.

When Czechoslovakia finally freed itself from communist rule in 1989, in the so-called Velvet Revolution, few people inside or outside Czechoslovakia would have thought that the country would split apart; but it did, and within three short years. Robert Young, who has studied the break-up, describes what happened:

YOUNG: The Slovaks were more rural, more conservative, more Catholic, and more deeply traditional than the Czechs, who were one of the cosmopolitan groups of eastern Europe. They certainly saw themselves that way, and Prague was one of the great centres of learning and culture in the entire region. But under the communists, the Slovaks had made enormous progress. Education rates advanced and economic growth accelerated, often with massive communist-type industrial installations. Slovak participation in both the republican bureaucracy and the federal bureaucracy expanded substantially, and, by the time of the Velvet Revolution, the standards of living in the two areas were comparable.

BOTHWELL: Once liberated, the Czechoslovak government decided to convert the country to liberal capitalism in short order. State ownership and controls were dismantled as soon as could be, and liberalization became the order of the day. This caused strains between Czechs and Slovaks, but possibly not crucial ones.

YOUNG: Some commentators would have it that the economic changes associated with a free market were more severely felt in Slovakia, and that this caused resentment. There's certainly some truth to this argument. Slovak politicians claimed that many of the new modernization plans, the privatization, were designed to favour Czech interests; they were more suited to the Czech economy than to the Slovak economy, which was dominated by agriculture and by very large industrial enterprises. Unemployment was higher in Slovakia than in the Czech republic, and opinion polls showed that fewer people in Slovakia supported the liberalization program.

But another part of the explanation is simply that some politicians were prepared to stand on national issues and to attempt to garner political support from them. Politicians are in competition and they always try out platforms and programs. Slovak politicians tried nationalist programs and nationalist thrusts, and they met with success.

BOTHWELL: In Slovak politics, the momentum in 1990-2 seems to have been towards the nationalist extreme. Exploiting grievances, real or fancied, with the central authority or with the majority Czechs paid political dividends at home. Better still, it caused resentment and reaction in the Czech lands, where certain powerful politicians, especially finance minister Vaclav Klaus, came to view the Slovak nationalists and their leader Vladimir Meciar as obstacles to what they considered a sensible economic regime.

Part of the frustration was finding out what the Slovaks actually wanted. The Czechoslovak president, Vaclav Havel, condemned the situation.

YOUNG: Havel said that work on the constitution was complicated by the fact that Slovak positions held yesterday were no longer held today, and no one could say whether positions held today would still be held tomorrow. And so proposals and demands that at first appeared marginal or absurd were suddenly taken seriously and defended even by those who until recently had rejected them, and who now adopted them as their own. Unfortunately, they did so not out of conviction, but for fear of appearing too half hearted in their championing of Slovakia's interests. Havel saw himself as negotiating with a moving target.

BOTHWELL: The question became: Should the federal government in Prague exercise significant powers, significant control, over the economy, or should Czechoslovakia become a loose confederation, with most sovereign power reserved for separate Czech and Slovak republics? Czechoslovakia became enmeshed in a cycle of action and reaction which made sense in terms of political gain and rewards, but which proved fatal for the structure of the country as a whole. Young describes what happened:

YOUNG: In the Czech-Slovak case, the centre was paralysed by the magnitude of the tasks it had and by institutional difficulties in making constitutional changes, or in fact in making policy at all. As it became clear that the Slovaks were working towards some sort of confederal system, the politicians in the Czech republic began to make plans. They took more initiative in the negotiation around the constitution and they laid out contingency plans for what would happen in the event of separation, as some powers were decentralized.

The critical event occurred after the 1992 elections, when Klaus declined to take the office of prime minister at the federal level and instead became premier of the Czech republic. When that happened, a very weak central caretaker government was set up, and Klaus in the Czech republic and Meciar in Slovakia squared off against each other. Both of them shared a common interest in destroying the centre and having two sovereign independent states.

BOTHWELL: Once the decision was made to break up the country, it happened with amazing speed. Within six months, two new republics were established. Both states pledged to keep an economic union, including a common currency.

YOUNG: The Czechs and Slovaks agreed to form a common market – not to impose tariffs on each other's goods, to have a common external tariff, and to arrange for the free flow of labour, capital, goods, and most services within the common economic space. This agreement had already been forced upon them by the European Union, since the EU would not maintain a relationship with the two republics unless the level of economic integration between them was at least equal to that in the rest of Europe. Nevertheless, although the two sides had signed a treaty to maintain the common currency, this broke down within six weeks of the formal separation. It was simply impossible to maintain it when speculation occurred and there were runs on banks, especially in Slovakia; people were trying to get their money out, fearing that Slovakia would be forced to establish a separate currency. So the currencies separated, the Slovaks devalued theirs slightly, and trade relations between the two countries declined sharply right after the separation. Trade levels went down to 50 per cent of what they were before, before bouncing back.

BOTHWELL: The Czech and Slovak example shows that it is indeed possible to wrench apart a previously viable country and to replace it with two separate, smaller, but viable states. It shows, too, that economic arrangements can be made, especially in the first flush of optimism, but that those arrangements can equally well be set aside as necessity or convenience dictates. Treaties are, in the final analysis, less enforceable than common domestic legislation.

In Canada, discussion of the technicalities of separation begins with the federal debt – $500-billion-plus of obligations owing outside and inside Canada. William Robson of the C.D. Howe Foundation in Toronto has studied the question of the division of the debt:

ROBSON: Essentially, the only solution that stands a chance of being accepted by the person on the street, on either side of the border, is one that divides the debt by population, so Quebec ends up taking more or less a quarter. That's a political problem. Whether it's resolved in a tidy way really depends on the amount of good will, and willingness to seek a constructive solution, that's evident on either side. When it comes to how you actually go ahead with that division of the debt, then a whole host of other problems arise.

Most people who have lent to the federal government tend to think that they've made a contract with Ottawa, and that's the way they'd like to keep it – that they get cheques from Ottawa when the debt has to be serviced and when it comes due. That's a problem for the rest of Canada, because, although Jacques Parizeau has said he'd be happy to have a system where Ottawa continues to service the debt, and Quebec regularly mails cheques with its share, a lot of things can go wrong. The most obvious problem is that it gives Quebec a gun to the head of the rest of the country. And the threat has already been made by Parizeau that, if negotiations in other areas aren't going well, he might see fit to hold back, delay some of his payments, or maybe even make smaller payments than was originally intended. Obviously, that's a problem.

BOTHWELL: The same consideration of short-term political advantage that characterized Czechoslovak politics applies in Canada. The question of a future Quebec currency is unsettling, even in Quebec, where it signifies a leap into the unknown. As Robson observes, it is not to the separatists' advantage to worry the electorate about this aspect of the future:

ROBSON: One of the ways that separatism has to be made more palatable to the population is by holding out the hope that somehow the economic arrangements that make Quebec and Canada such prosperous societies right now will stay in place in the wake of separation. One of the most critical aspects of this relationship, from the point of view of the ordinary citizen, is the currency. After all, it's a physical thing you carry around in your wallet. Your pension savings, all the contracts you have in place as you carry out your daily life, are denominated in Canadian dollars. It's profoundly unsettling to think that one of the things that might happen in the wake of separation would be a redrawing of all those contracts, a re-denomination of your pension savings into a separate currency. So, from the point of view of the separatist cause, there's no up side whatsoever to making a statement in favour of a separate Quebec currency. It's something that people in Quebec, as people in the rest of Canada and the rest of the world, would view with profound suspicion.

The difficulty from the separatist point of view is that, although the commitment to maintaining the currency union is one that they are willing to make, and that they may well be quite confident of in their own minds, the lack of confidence that the rest of the world and individual Canadian citizens have in that commitment is likely to cause a movement of capital out of the country. And as that happens, the quality of that commitment, the steadiness of that commitment, is going to come into question, and the possibility that Quebec won't be able to use the Canadian dollar will become much more front and centre in the debate.

BOTHWELL: That is a question of intergovernmental relations, a political matter. But decisions on the economic future are not limited to governments. Governments may set events in motion, but they have difficulty either predicting or controlling the consequences, as Lloyd Atkinson suggests:

ATKINSON: There are two issues here, one of which could make its impact known in the short run. The question whether there would be developments on the political front could have a huge negative effect on investor confidence. While everybody gets concerned about the foreign investor, I'm equally concerned about you and me, because if we really thought there was a confidence problem, if we really thought the Canadian dollar was going to take a knock, all of us, foreigners as well as Canadians, would love to park our Canadian dollar assets in US dollars for a while.

BOTHWELL: The stakes are considerable, and public chaos cannot be segregated from private discomfort. There have already been consequences in the dispute over Quebec's future, and there will be more.

Can Canada survive without Quebec? Should Canada survive without Quebec? David Bercuson, co-author of a book called *Deconfederation: Canada without Quebec*, gives his opinion:

BERCUSON: We basically say that the Canadian experiment in dual nationalism, if you want to call it that, or multi-nationalism on the one hand and singular ethno-nationals on the other, has failed; that the long-run costs of ending this arrangement will be less than the short-run costs; that there is no chance of building a viable nation in this country as long as Quebec and Canada stay together, because what Quebec wants and what the rest of us want at the end of twentieth century is very different; that we might as well face the facts that there is no compromise with Quebec nationalism, that either Quebeckers are serious about getting out or they're not. If they're not serious, then separatism is a threat, and if it's a threat, then it doesn't dignify a reply. If it's a goal and if it's an objective, stop threatening to do it, just go ahead and do it. You can't have a viable nation when one partner, as in a bad marriage, has bags packed at the door. Obviously, there are some problems to which there will never be solutions. As a historian, I know that process is the way things work, that everything evolves. It doesn't matter if we have ongoing constitutional talks and developments with Quebec for the next hundred years, as long as the existence of this nation is taken as a given. But we lost that battle back in the 1960s when the federal government refused to say that. And Trudeau didn't say it, either.

During its term in office the Progressive Conservative Party declared the right of the Quebec people to self-determination. This was the party of Macdonald and Cartier, the governing party of the country at the time! I asked myself, what sort of cuckoo clock land has this country become? We're at the point, now, where we've lost that fight, so how can you resolve this problem? The only way you can resolve it, in my opinion, is to say: 'Look, Quebec, go and make your country and we'll remake ours, and then it'll probably be in our interest and in your interest to develop trade relations and all kinds of other things afterwards, but, basically, once you're gone, you're gone, and I relate to you the way I relate to Afghanistan. You're a foreign country, and that's the way I'm going to relate to you.' The challenge is to keep the country together, without Quebec, and it won't be an easy challenge. But if the people of Canada have the will to do it, then they will do it; and if they don't have the will to do it, then they don't deserve it.

BOTHWELL: What can that future hold? I asked political scientist Guy Laforest in Quebec City:

LAFOREST: I'll start with something that I find troubling – the fact that it is quite possible to imagine that Quebec and English-speaking Canada understand that it would be in their best interests to organize themselves politically in the northern half of North America so that they can resist and withstand, not for two years but for a long period of time, the force of the colossus to the south. They could understand that and they could devise a political system that would be supple enough, though with central powers, to give sufficient room for the particularity of Quebec in North America. In the best of all worlds we should be able to do that, and it should be our first choice, our priority.

Unfortunately, we do not live in that world, and, despite the generosity of a number of English-Canadian intellectuals in their approach to Quebec, what we have is a system that is log-jammed, that is blocked completely. That is the system that Trudeau, with his own negative obsessions, gave us in the early 1980s. That's his legacy, and we're more or less the prisoners of that project.

BOTHWELL: And yet, for more than two hundred years, the descendants of two antagonistic colonial powers have been able to live together more or less harmoniously.

LAFOREST: This is something that people should be proud of and that could be part of a common vision. Unfortunately, we're deprived of such a possibility by the current circumstances, but in the best of all worlds the country would be called Canada-Quebec. It would be called that because the idea of a Canadian nation has been more or less appropriated by the heirs of

Trudeau, and I don't think that Quebeckers can ever be reconciled with that. Canada and Quebec are also Native names, not English or French names: they come from the Native tradition, which is part of our common heritage. So calling a country Canada-Quebec would open the road towards the future, a future different from the kind of confrontation that we cannot seem to avoid.

BOTHWELL: Confrontation: in the opinion of Guy Laforest, that is the Canadian reality from which Canada and Quebec must escape, in Quebec's case by becoming independent.

Other Quebeckers do not share that perception. Jean Charest, MP for Sherbrooke and interim leader of the national Progressive Conservative Party, argues that the fundamental political fact about Quebeckers is that they want to maintain what he calls the Canadian link:

CHAREST: The polling over the last twenty years has been interesting in this regard. If you ask Canadians and Quebeckers whether they want to maintain the Canadian link, they have consistently said *Yes*. The issue of their identity within Canada has really been at the heart of it. That's what's sad about the Meech episode – the missed opportunity to do that.

For the federalist side to win the referendum, we have to keep the onus on the shoulders of the Péquistes and the Bloc. They're the ones who are proposing the break-up of the country. They have to tell us what it means, what advantages that will give them, and what the consequences are. On the federal side, though, we have to be cautious. We can't just say the onus is only on their shoulders. There has to be a light at the end of the tunnel. There has to be some significance in a federalist victory, something that brings Canadians together, that enables us to move forward. That's where we probably come together in this country, in the freedoms that we have not only through charters (free speech, free religious beliefs, and so on, all protected by rights or by laws) but through the freedom to speak two languages, to see the world in a different way, to move around in a vast land, to pursue work and interests. Perhaps Canada will pursue love, with all these anglophones and francophones that marry. We have also acquired great freedoms over several generations, through our parents and our grandparents, to travel the world and be Canadians; by virtue of being Canadians, we have more freedoms than any other citizens in the world. These are things that are intangible, but they're the great freedoms that countries fight for. They're the freedoms that immigrants seek when they come to this land. Maybe that's the approach we have to take. We also have to try to give all Canadians, including people in Quebec, a sense that change is possible and that we can do things differently. We have to enable them to express their nationalism, which by definition is dangerous, and enable Quebec nationalists to express themselves in a Canadian context. We have to have a modern vision, one turned towards the next century, not the last. That's the challenge, and we must convey that openness and express that vision during the referendum campaign.

BOTHWELL: The outcome of the referendum, like the ultimate shaping of Quebec's shared history with Canada, remains uncertain. Within Quebec and within Canada, there are many views and many opinions of the province's association with the rest of Canada. Which one will prevail, no one can say.

On the separatist side, it is argued that Canada and Quebec have proved their incompatibility. In that perspective, the history of Quebec within Canada is a standing reproach, certainly to English Canada, but also to Quebec's leaders in earlier generations who preached accommodation and even cooperation. To even a moderate separatist, Quebec can only find itself by losing its Canadian connection. The birth of a new nation, an independent Quebec, means more gain than loss. And recently, in the rest of Canada, there have been those who agree: Quebec's departure will benefit English Canada, whether or not it advances Quebec.

Not everyone agrees – and indeed most do not agree, in the rest of Canada at least. To many, perhaps most, Canadians, including Quebeckers, Jean Chrétien still expresses the opportunity of Canada. Chrétien throughout his long political career has preached the cause of Canadian unity, and never more so than now. In summarizing his own experience, the prime minister recounts his own discovery of Canada, back in the early 1960s:

CHRÉTIEN: Of course I expected to have problems, but as I wrote in my book, like any person in Quebec educated completely in French, the historians or the professors of history in the schools tended to talk more about the negative than the positive element of the history, so you became very self-centred. Like everyone else, that was my problem until I had a discussion one day as a young lawyer. One of my friends was a judge who had lived in New Brunswick, and in this discussion he defended Canada and I defended Quebec. And he said, 'Jean, I'm surprised, you've never been out of Quebec, you've never even been out of Shawinigan and Quebec City, in your life. Yet you talk like that. I've been around, and I know you're talking through your hat. You are prejudiced. I cannot accept some of your statements, because they're sheer prejudice.'

I was pretty mad at him. When I drove home that day – from Trois-Rivières to Shawinigan is twenty-five miles, half an hour – the first five minutes I was mad at my friend, and the next five minutes I was asking, Is it possible that he hit the right note, or he hit something that's true? By the end of the drive I had concluded that it was better for me to know more about the rest of Canada.

Today, I am very comfortable with that. Nobody doubts from one ocean to the other that I'm a francophone and that I'm a Quebecker. I am very proud of my province, of my language, of my valley, the St Maurice Valley, and my home town. Everybody knows who I am, and I have no problem with my own identity. My province is Quebec and my country is Canada, my language is French, and nothing is incompatible.

BOTHWELL: It is far too easy, Chrétien observes, to be negative. But in the event, he believes, there is too much at stake, too much to lose, to give up on Canada:

CHRÉTIEN: We tend to look negatively, and the media tend to be negative. It's a fact of life. Good news is not news. A dog biting a man is not news, but a man who bites a dog would be big news. So it's a fact of life. For me, we have to work with that and we have to talk positively. We are backed by a history that proves that Canada has been a fantastic experience, and we shall continue to be an example to the world.

BOTHWELL: Whether Canada is a good example, as Chrétien believes, or a bad one, as Parizeau and the separatists argue, is at bottom a question of history. But which history? There is the long history, of French-English rivalry in North America, and what that has meant for the descendants of the French and English settlers and the Aboriginal inhabitants of North America. There is the shorter history, of French and English cohabitation in the northern part of North America, in the territory that is contemporary Canada. There is the political history of Canada, of compromises made and accommodations grudgingly tolerated – a mixed history of rivalry, jealousy, and cooperation, too. There is the demographic history of Quebec, in which the population of Quebec steadily rose between 1760 and 1960, to meet a declining birthrate in the 1960s and after. There is the social history of Quebec, the history of a rural and religious people that became urban in the course of the twentieth century. In urbanizing, French Canadians also replaced and sometimes clashed with the English-Canadian inhabitants of the cities. There is an ideological history, of disputation between those French Canadians who hoped for a common future with the rest of Canada, and those French Canadians who accepted Canada as, at best, a necessary evil.

There is also a history much closer to the present. Quebeckers and the rest of Canadians are divided among themselves about the meaning of Canada's recent history. What does Quebec want? Dignity, accommodation, and acceptance, some say, symbolic gestures that recognize Quebec as a 'nation' – an equal nation in association with the rest of Canada. What does Quebec want? The survival of the French language, through legitimate legal safeguards that place the defence of Quebec in the hands of Quebeckers, and Quebeckers only. Does Canada truly understand and include Quebec, some ask, when the Canadian Constitution was revised in the early 1980s without Quebec's consent? Did Canada understand Quebec, critics ask, when it rejected the Meech Lake accord that would have brought Quebec into the Constitution, as Mulroney put it, 'with honour and enthusiasm'?

These are powerful questions, but they are not the only way of approaching the issue of Quebec's recent relations with Canada. It was, after all, a French-speaking prime minister of Canada, Pierre Trudeau, who defeated Quebec separation in the provincial referendum of 1980. It was the same Pierre Trudeau who reformed the Canadian Constitution and, in a compromise with the English-speaking provinces, isolated the separatist government of Quebec. It was the government of Quebec, not the people of Quebec, that rejected the new Constitution, and polls show that initially Trudeau's constitution, including his Charter of Rights and Freedoms, was well accepted in Quebec as elsewhere.

In this reading of Canada's recent history, it was irresponsible politicians, especially Brian Mulroney and Robert Bourassa, who reopened the constitutional question and then proceeded to put Canada at risk through tactics of brinkmanship, tactics that ultimately backfired in the defeat of Meech Lake in 1990 and, later, of the Charlottetown accord of 1992.

Trudeau's constitution, according to its supporters, offered the best hope of breaking the pathological cycle of Quebec politics, one that rewarded confrontational nationalism and discounted the less spectacular common achievements of French- and English-Canadian politicians. Under the unskilful ministrations of Bourassa and Mulroney, Quebec separatist nationalism got a glandular transplant, rather than the political euthanasia that Trudeau had made possible.

What does Quebec want? The question is misguided. What, rather, do Quebeckers want? And what, too, do English Canadians want? The answers given are too often a projection of the present, a natural but besetting sin among forecasters – academic, journalistic, or political. It is possible that the answer will be 'more of the same,' but since there is no common agreement on what 'the same' may be, that seems to be a political cul-de-sac. The three years since the 1995 referendum have not found a way out, as the following postscript shows.

Postscript

THE QUEBEC GENERAL ELECTION of September 1994 brought to power the Parti Québécois under Jacques Parizeau. It made inevitable a provincial referendum on sovereignty, which Parizeau was determined to bring on as soon as possible.

Among separatists, Parizeau was known as *pur et dur,* hard-line and uncompromising. His experience in government stretched back over thirty years. Well-educated, fluently bilingual, he had been considered for senior federal appointments back in the 1960s. Like many of his generation, he believed in strong and effective government, coming to the conclusion that Canadian federalism could not hope to work well. Canada's fate was to be polarized between an English-speaking majority centred on Ottawa and a French-speaking majority centred on Quebec City. The decentralizing compromises fashionable in the 1960s and 1970s would actually make matters worse. A weakened federal government would no longer be able to act, but strengthened provinces would not be able to step into the policy vacuum. Canada's governments would fall into a state of perpetual contradiction and probable confrontation, with no one able to make the decisions necessary for the proper direction of the state. In Parizeau's opinion, Ottawa lacked the political support in Quebec to impose a pan-Canadian policy in that province; but the result of that uncomfortable circumstance would be no policy at all because the government of Quebec lacked the jurisdiction in the Canadian federal system. To acquire jurisdiction and escape from political paralysis, Quebec would have to free itself from Canada. And so, as Parizeau famously recalled, he reasoned himself into separatism in the course of a train trip from Montreal to a conference in Banff in the late 1960s.

Parizeau joined René Lévesque's Parti Québécois and was eventually elected to the Quebec National Assembly in November 1976. He became minister of finance in Lévesque's government and as such was a participant in the gradualist – and unsuccessful – referendum strategy to which the PQ was committed. Parizeau also directed a notably stringent austerity program that slimmed down public salaries in the aftermath of the PQ's referendum defeat in May 1980. Under the circumstances – the recession of the early 1980s – the austerity was unavoidable, but it harmed the Lévesque government's standing among its most militant supporters in the trade unions and civil service. Parizeau, too, became disaffected at Lévesque's turn toward compromise with Canadian federalism in 1983 and resigned from the government in 1984.

At that point the sovereigntist dream looked very distant indeed. Lévesque was on his last legs politically and resigned as premier. His successor, Pierre-Marc Johnson, held office for less than a year before being defeated by Robert Bourassa and the Liberals in December 1985. Public interest in separation fell off the political charts, and for a time it was possible to claim that Quebec did not have even one separatist party. But Johnson fumbled and faded, and when he finally resigned as PQ leader Parizeau was there to pick up the pieces and re-establish separatism as a political option. Success depended less on Parizeau's abilities – he was admired for his abilities but not loved for his personality, as Lévesque had been – than on the Liberal government's mistakes. He was better liked within his party than without, and he carried with him always the appearance *un grand bourgeois,* a hint of the upper crust. No one could accuse Parizeau of being a populist. Nevertheless, Parizeau believed he had learned from the mistakes of an earlier period. His separatism was unconditional, not tied to an agreement or association with Canada. It would follow a single referendum victory, avoiding entanglement in a second plebiscite.

Such was Parizeau's platform in the 1994 provincial election, and as he afterwards said, he was careful not to commit himself to any hint of a postreferendum pause or compromise. His government immediately began to lay the groundwork for a referendum in 1995. Immediately problems began to appear. First, there was the state of the economy, sluggish and mired in high unemployment. The government's priorities had to accommodate economic housekeeping at a time when the tendency in the rest of Canada was to contract the public sector and slash welfare entitlements. Quebec was not immune to these trends. Second, there was the state of public opinion. It was not as favourable to separation as it should have been. French Quebeckers, it was true, did favour separation, as they had ever since the Meech Lake fiasco. But they did not like it enough. To win, Parizeau had not only to carry the French-Canadian vote but to carry it massively – by

60 per cent or more. That figure, if achieved, would also take care of any lingering problems of legitimacy, because the Quebec *nation,* the French-speaking inhabitants of the province, would have spoken so decisively that their conclusion could not be ignored.

There was another problem. Even if French Quebeckers could be induced to vote for sovereignty, what would they mean by the word? Apparently not independence pure and simple, if public opinion polls were to be trusted. They wanted what Lévesque had once promised – sovereignty-*association.* To Parizeau this meant shackling his project to an English-Canadian veto, for he believed, realistically enough, that English Canada would not be in a mood for generous partnership. But this 'soft' option had its proponents, especially Lucien Bouchard, the leader of the Bloc Québécois in the federal House of Commons.

There followed a period of internal struggle in the separatist movement. Parizeau could not ignore the probability that his decisive version of sovereignty would lose and that sovereignty-association could win. Indeed, Bouchard was more popular than Parizeau among Quebeckers. Trapped by this dilemma, Parizeau eventually gave way and signed a pact with Bouchard and with the twenty-five-year-old Mario Dumont, leader of the small but potentially decisive Democratic Action Party, which stood somewhere between pure sovereignty and weak federalism. The three clasped hands and promised ... what? That a referendum victory would confer on Parizeau and his government a mandate to declare independence within a year at the longest. Quebec would offer to negotiate terms with the rest of Canada, but what Quebec would or could accept was quite limited: a Council of Ministers constituted on a fifty-fifty basis, with each side retaining the right of veto, a consultative assembly of parliamentarians with no decision-making powers, and a treaty that would regulate the common economic space of the two future partners, Canada and Quebec. An economic tribunal would regulate trade and other questions, while a new bureaucracy would run whatever administration resulted from the new relationship. In fact, on any question, Canada and Quebec would be free to go their own ways, and any coincidence of policy would be purely voluntary. The pact of 12 June was not a model for effective government and it is hard to believe that Parizeau in his heart really took it seriously. Perhaps he relied on the common sense of Canadians outside Quebec to reject the Quebec terms out of hand. But if this unworkable proposition could scoop up the 15 per cent of voters who subscribed to the semi-separatist vision of Dumont and the Action Démocratique, then it would serve its purpose.

Not surprisingly, the referendum question, debated and passed in the National Assembly late in the summer, was notably obscure. The English version was: 'Do you agree that Quebec should become sovereign after having made a final offer to Canada for a new economic and political partnership within the scope of the bill respecting the future of Quebec and of the agreement signed on June 12, 1995?' The date of the referendum was fixed for 30 October.

In the referendum, Parizeau had some assets. Unlike in 1980, the federal prime minister, Jean Chrétien, was unpopular in his home province. The provincial Liberal leader, Daniel Johnson, though more popular than Chrétien, was neither an inspiring speaker nor a master strategist. The memory of Meech Lake haunted and divided the federalist camp. The time was ripe for political opportunism of a kind that would further undermine the federalists, so the separatist leaders decided. They formulated the referendum question in a manner so obscure that it could hope to draw in everyone from hard separatists of the Parizeau stamp to the ambiguous ex-Liberals who marched under Dumont's banner. *deliberately vague*

After debate and passage of the referendum legislation in the National Assembly, the great date was set. Almost immediately things began to go wrong for the separatists. Opposition groups sprang up. Polls plummeted. By the last week of September, it seemed that sovereignty would not only lose, but also lose big, by more than the 60-40 margin that had occurred in 1980. If that happened, then separatism would be dead for a generation and possibly forever.

That, apparently, was a prospect the majority of French Quebeckers was unwilling to contemplate. Beginning in late September, they began to drift back to the separatist camp. Meanwhile a desperate Parizeau appealed for help to Lucien Bouchard, who, he said, would handle the postreferendum negotiations with English Canada. Bouchard then became the principal spokesman for the pro-sovereignty forces *before* the referendum and bombarded the electorate with his particularly effective brand of oratory. Don't be afraid of the future, Bouchard told French Quebeckers. Separation was a 'magic wand' that would banish the gloom and compromise and mediocrity of federalism. Crowds began to swell, the polls reversed themselves, and panic began to spread in the federalist camp.

If the first stage of the referendum campaign had highlighted the weak-nesses of the separatist leadership and platform, the second stage, in October, emphasized the federalists' problems. The federal Liberal Cabinet seemed to have no plan for a reversal of fortune. Worse, there were real dif-ferences between federal and provincial Liberals, which only the prospect of victory had served to obscure. The federal cousins tended to believe that the Canadian constitution was fine as it was and that there was in any case no realistic possibility of changing it. The provincial Liberals, children of Meech Lake and heirs of Robert Bourassa, believed that it must be changed along the lines of the 'distinct society' once promised by Brian Mulroney.

Chrétien, against his better judgment, finally agreed to do what he believed to be unwise – he promised to try to secure a 'distinct society.' Orators, organizers, and ordinary Canadians poured into Quebec. The fed-eralists scheduled a monster rally in downtown Montreal on 27 October, and by bus, plane, and train non-Quebeckers arrived to tell their fellow cit-izens that they were loved and would be missed. In some senses the rally was a big success. More than 100,000 people thronged the streets of downtown Montreal under the biggest Canadian flag ever manufactured. There was tremendous publicity nationally and internationally. The polls reversed themselves once again, just enough to allow the federalist side to squeak out a victory the following Monday.

Voter turnout was very high on referendum day; more than 94 per cent of the electorate cast ballots. The federalists carried the centre and west of Montreal, Western Quebec along the Ottawa River, the fringes of the Eastern Townships, and a few scattered constituencies elsewhere in the province. That was just enough for the 'no' side to prevail, but not by much: 50,000 votes and a margin of 50.6 per cent to 49.4 per cent. One commentator afterwards calculated that if votes had been weighted by wealth or property the result would have been 80 per cent to 20, obviously in favour of the 'no.' It was assumed that non-French Quebeckers would vote overwhelmingly 'no,' and, nearly unanimously, they did as expected. To vote 'yes' one was almost certain to be 'old stock' Quebec and French speaking. (In fact, 61 per cent of francophone Quebeckers voted 'yes' and 39 per cent voted 'no.') Like all gen-eralizations these have their exceptions, yet the vote came perilously close to one in which origin and language were infallible predictors – a vote of race.

The victory was not all it seemed on either side. The separatists cried foul, claiming that Quebec's referendum process was polluted by the presence,

influence, and money of outsiders. As Parizeau himself pointed out to a ref-
erendum-night audience, most French Quebeckers voted for sovereignty;
only the 'ethnics' and 'money' had not. Federalists for their part asserted
that the poll had been anything but fair. In federalist areas – meaning especially non-French parts of Montreal – the number of 'spoiled' ballots'
rejected by electoral officials hit record numbers. (These accusations were
never satisfactorily proved because election officials refused to do the necessary, very extensive, investigation that would have been required.)

Parizeau announced his resignation the next day. It would take effect in
January 1996, after his inevitable successor, Lucien Bouchard, had been
anointed by the PQ. It was not a happy outcome for Parizeau, who believed
that he had come so close to his ultimate goal only to be cheated of his
prize. How close, people only afterwards learned. Parizeau himself publi-
cized his postreferendum plans in a book in the spring of 1997 (*Pour un
Québec souverain*, Montréal, vlb éditeur). With the referendum over and
won, the Quebec National Assembly would have been reconvened to pass a
declaration of sovereignty. Negotiations with Canada could then have been
undertaken, but with the issue or outcome of independence removed from
the table. Quebec would have become a separate country not within a year
but within weeks. Parizeau had drawn on provincially controlled resources
to set up a $17 billion fund ready to stabilize the Canadian dollar, which
would have faced immediate downward pressure in the event of a pro-
sovereignty vote. Parizeau claimed that such action was well within the
meaning of his pact with Dumont and Bouchard, but his strained interpretation was not what his referendum question actually said and not what
some, at least, of his voters were gulled into supporting.

Quebec would have sought international recognition immediately. The
French government, Parizeau believed, had promised just that. Given the
character of the French government of the day and the general trend of
French politics, that seems to have been a safe bet. Parizeau also later
claimed that French recognition would have led the Americans to offer the
same thing. This part of his strategy was probably delusory. For one thing,
the Americans had a great deal more at stake than did the French, such as
the consideration of real political instability on their northern frontier for
the first time since the War of 1812. For another, the American government,
in its political and diplomatic aspects, does not like the French and is more
likely than not to be in a state of contradiction with Paris.

There is not much doubt that the Quebec government would have moved to isolate and recruit that part of Canada's military located on Quebec soil. A Bloc MP in Ottawa even sent round a circular requesting support from French-speaking soldiers in the aftermath of a separatist referendum victory. Though this escapade received a certain publicity in the months after October 1995, the Liberals in Ottawa eventually buried the matter, fearing to alienate even more the disaffected majority of French-speaking Quebeckers. This papering-over of what was surely a disquieting incident did little to guard against its repetition when and if there is another referendum.

Meeting his federal Liberal caucus after the referendum, Prime Minister Chrétien burst into tears. He believed that he had done his best, and it had not been enough to secure a decisive victory. Instead, Canada had got a reprieve, after which another referendum was virtually certain. There was certainly no reason to believe that Chrétien could hope to carry that future day any more than he had carried the one just past. It was with a sense of deep unease that Chrétien and his followers faced the future.

True to his desperate referendum promise, Chrétien put recognition of the 'distinct society' through Parliament. He did more. His Constitutional Amendments Act restored Quebec's right of veto while conferring it, eventually, on Ontario, British Columbia, the Prairie provinces, and the Maritimes as well. Introduced at the end of November 1995 and passed in February 1996, the Act raised more questions and controversy than it laid to rest. It certainly did not reconcile separatists in Quebec, and it is doubtful it had much impact on 'soft' nationalists. Naturally, the government of Quebec did not like it, and the Bloc Québécois voted against it. The provinces, whose consent was necessary for any constitutional amendment to take effect, were unenthusiastic if not unforthcoming. After a flurry, the 'distinct society' ploy quietly died as far as public opinion was concerned.

The 'distinct society' manoeuvre and an attempt generally to conciliate postreferendum Quebec by accommodating its demands over such issues as job training were known by politicians and the public alike as 'Plan A.' There was also a 'Plan B,' which, strictly speaking, was not a plan at all. It expressed an approach to a future, notional, independent Quebec in which everything was up for negotiation. Quebec, in the world of Plan B, could not have its independent cake and eat Canadian subsidies too. Plan B had no fixed definition but included from time to time a refusal to accept a mere majority (fifty plus one) in a future referendum, suggestions that federalist regions of Quebec could separate from a separating province, and demands that the Cree and other First Nations be allowed to separate and take their lands with them. Plan B promised no special deals with a separated Quebec: no association, no common market, and so forth. Some commentators inside and outside Canada went further and suggested that with Quebec gone the rest of Canada should consider joining the United States. An unspoken assumption of such arguments was that 'the rest of Canada' did not have enough in common, or enough of a shared agenda for the future, to hang together. There was much speculation about whether the federal government supported Plan B and whether, if it did, such an attitude of tough love would carry much weight with 'soft' nationalists. In a public exchange of letters with Quebec vice-premier Bernard Landry, federal minister Stéphane Dion drove home the point that an independent Quebec might not be able to count on Canadian good will and cast doubt on the Parti Québécois claim that independence was a matter for Quebeckers alone, to be resolved in a unilateral act. To judge from public opinion polls, Dion's assertions did not drive more Quebeckers into the separatist camp; indeed, in the fall of 1997 federalism enjoyed a modest resurgence in the province.

Chrétien tried to strengthen Quebec representation in his Cabinet through the appointment of three high-profile ministers: first Lucienne Robillard and then in January 1996 Pierre Pettigrew and Stéphane Dion. They undoubtedly improved Quebec's representation and contributed to the quality of Cabinet debates, but they were not in themselves political powerhouses. Robillard added little to the referendum campaign, while Dion and Pettigrew had never before held public office.

The federal government then returned by mid-1996 to its principal agenda, the restoration of Canadian credit through reduction of expenditure and eventual balancing of the federal books. Sustained by a dwindling deficit and the affection of the banking community and assisted by the weakness of the opposition parties, the federal Liberals achieved re-election on 2 June 1997. The election campaign was dull though not entirely uneventful. The traditional leaders' debate showcased the debating talents of the federal Conservative leader, Jean Charest. Observers concluded that if only Charest had had something to say, he might have done better. Handicapped by his party's platform and by the deep and abiding unpopularity of his predecessor, ex-prime minister Mulroney, Charest made some inroads in Quebec and the Maritime provinces but failed to surpass the western-based Reform Party of Preston Manning.

The 1997 election therefore did not restore Canada's traditional party system. The Conservatives remained far in the rear, the fourth party in the House of Commons. Charest had tried desperately not to offend and had succeeded only in blurring what his party stood for. The emptiness of his rhetoric could be masked by his oratorical skills as long as he was exploiting the vacant medium of television, but it was not enough to make a difference in the competition for space and time in the House of Commons or on the national news. Worse, the Conservatives lost, with retirements, their majority in the Senate and thus the capacity to obstruct the Chrétien government. Finally, given the opportunity to perform as the official opposition in Parliament, with privileged status in the daily Question Period and before the media's microphones, Reform increasingly took the place of the Conservatives as Canada's alternative party, the government in waiting.

The Bloc Québécois, the separatist party in the House of Commons, did not have a good year in 1997. The departure of Lucien Bouchard for Quebec City in January 1996 left the BQ adrift and prone to infighting. Its performance in the federal election campaign was at best uninspiring and at worst comical (as when its leader was photographed wearing a silly hat during a factory inspection). Premier Bouchard's attempts at rescue may have stemmed but did not reverse the party's downward slide. In a lighter than usual electoral turnout it dropped ten seats, which were picked up by the Liberals and Conservatives. Those parties for their part made inroads into French-speaking Quebec, diluting though not negating the BQ's claim to represent the French majority in that province. Though hardly a sign of rude health, the improved performance of the federalist parties in Quebec suggested that opinion had not gelled on the separatist side, confirming the indications of earlier polls. Polls also showed that Quebeckers thought rather well of Jean Charest, whose popularity in the province surpassed that of Chrétien and of Gilles Duceppe, the BQ leader.

The Liberals and Conservatives were not the only federalist parties with a position on 'the Quebec question.' The Reform Party also had its views, summarized as equality of citizens and equality of provinces. Reform leader Preston Manning argued that all Canadians, including Quebeckers, should be offered a serious devolution of federal powers to the provinces. With much greater powers, the provinces could then be equal, and Quebec's demands for autonomy would be satisfied. Manning also let it be known that he would accept a separation vote of 'fifty [per cent] plus one.' There would be no special deals thereafter.

The premiers of nine provinces – all but Quebec – met in Calgary in September 1997 and issued a declaration recognizing 'the unique character' of Quebec, a gesture that was well received by some in that province. Public opinion polls that month showed support for separation down and for Canada up. No one was quite sure whether these results represented a recognition that separation was a tougher proposition than previously believed or a positive response to the 'Calgary declaration,' or both.

The history of Canada and Quebec by early 1998 lacked either a happy climax or a dismal conclusion. Quebec remained a province of Canada, though the majority of French Quebeckers were apparently discontent. Yet they did not seem to be ultimately dissatisfied. Polls suggested that most French Quebeckers would still settle for 'reformed federalism.' But what did that mean?

'Reformed federalism' could mean anything from transferring federal programs in provincial jurisdiction firmly into the hands of the provinces all the way to restricting the powers of the federal government so that Ottawa could not move without provincial consent. Over the years in Quebec it has been assumed that 'reformed federalism' is closer to the latter than to the former. This position has had some echoes elsewhere, from ambitious provincial politicians to various regionalist commentators. Baldly put, they propose to save Canada by castrating or even abolishing its central government. Since nobody thereafter could possibly object to anything Ottawa did – it could do nothing – there would be no reason for any part of Canada to secede.

There are, of course, milder versions of this prescription, just as there are varieties of 'reformed federalism.' But they all have in common a significant degree of devolution of power from the centre to Canada's many peripheries. The Chrétien government, short of cash and concentrating on restoring Canada's drooping credit rating, has reduced some federal programs and transferred others wherever possible. Job training, which the federal government ran for many years, has been assigned to Quebec as an indication of how reasonable and flexible Ottawa can be. Flexible, certainly. Reasonable remains to be seen.

The Reform Party in the 1997 federal election proposed to go further still, as did Jean Charest's Progressive Conservatives. Preston Manning, arguing that Canadians could hardly accept inequality in citizenship, proposed to restrict the meaning of that citizenship by massive transfers of jurisdiction from Ottawa to the provinces. He plausibly argued during the election campaign that this would give Quebec all it could reasonably want. And if jurisdiction were all that was required that would be true.

At bottom, the issue of Quebec separation is about power, not powers. It is about the language of daily life, not the words of statutes. It is a question of psychology as much as it is a question of history, or philosophy, or law. It is a contest between an outward-looking Quebec and a defensive Quebec, both equally and strongly rooted in the province's history. It is also a race with time, and with the fatigue the rest of Canada feels as it contemplates, one more time, the 'never-endum' of Quebec. Jacques Parizeau, in one of his better metaphors, compared Quebec's presence in Canada to that of an aching tooth. How much simpler, how much pleasanter, to get it pulled.

If the 'never-endum' were to continue with a separatist victory and the independence of Quebec many, perhaps most, Canadians would find Dr. Parizeau's prescription tempting. To date, though, their mood is of weariness rather than despair, and there is still a healthy sense of dread of Parizeau's 'the sooner, the better,' approach. Canadians, including Quebeckers, still sense that separation would not be the end of their troubles but a beginning.

Bibliographic Note

THE HISTORIOGRAPHY of Quebec is vast. This note deals for the most part with works translated into English or written in English in the first place. Thanks in part to interest among book publishers and in part to subsidy, many French-language works are accessible to English-speaking readers.

There are, to begin, a number of general studies of the province. Brian Young and John Dickinson have produced a general survey, *A Short History of Quebec: A Socio-Economic Perspective,* 2nd ed. (Mississauga: Copp Clark 1993), which ranges from pre-history into the 1990s. It treats society and economy from a rather left-wing perspective; as for politics, its treatment should be supplemented by Mason Wade's hoary but still (alas) unequalled *The French-Canadians, 1760-1967* (Toronto: Macmillan 1968). For the period since 1867 the standard text, with useful bibliographical notes, is Paul-André Linteau, René Durocher, Jean-Claude Robert, and François Ricard, *Quebec: A History,* 2 vols. (Toronto: Lorimer 1983, 1991).

In terms of French-English relations and perceptions of Quebec's place in Canada, Arthur Silver's useful and imaginative *The French-Canadian Idea of Confederation, 1864-1900* (Toronto: University of Toronto Press 1982) should be consulted. Robert Bothwell, Ian Drummond, and John English, *Canada 1900-1945* (Toronto: University of Toronto Press 1987), and Bothwell, Drummond, and English, *Canada since 1945,* 2nd ed. (Toronto: University of Toronto Press 1989), trace the history of federal-provincial relations and the development of the Canadian economy in the twentieth century. Michael Behiels, *Prelude to Quebec's Quiet Revolution: Liberalism versus Neo-Nationalism, 1945-1960* (Montreal and Kingston: McGill-Queen's University Press 1985), is a handy guide to its subject, as, from a different perspective, is Kenneth McRoberts' very thorough *Quebec: Social Change and Political Crisis,* 3rd ed. (Toronto: McClelland & Stewart 1988).

The national question in Quebec and the question of English-French relations have been frequently examined. Ron Graham, *The French Quarter: The Epic Struggle of a Family – and a Nation – Divided* (Toronto: Macfarlane Walter & Ross 1992), treats Quebec history through the prism of the author's own family, French and English. William Johnson, *A Canadian Myth: Quebec, between Canada and the Illusion of Utopia* (Mont-real and Toronto: Robert Davies 1994), discusses the twists and turns of Quebec nationalist thought from a very sceptical point of view. (Johnson, it should be noted, raises the hackles of Quebec nationalists of all stripes.)

All the above books treat Quebec's relations with the rest of Canada to some extent. For a closer look at the constitutional problem, there is Peter Russell, *Constitutional Odyssey: Can Canadians Be a Sovereign People?* (Toronto: University of Toronto Press 1992), which covers the subject since the 1860s in a mercifully brief form. On Meech Lake, there are, among many others, Patrick Monahan, *Meech Lake: The Inside Story* (Toronto: University of Toronto Press 1991), and Andrew Cohen, *A Deal Undone: The Making and Breaking of the Meech Lake Accord* (Vancouver: Douglas & McIntyre 1990).

The indefinite future has naturally stimulated a very considerable literature. Philip Resnick, *Toward a Canada-Quebec Union* (Montreal and Kingston: McGill-Queen's University Press 1991), was one of the first to suggest a looser but at the same time defensive relationship between Quebec and the rest of Canada. Robert Young, *The Secession of Quebec and the Future of Canada* (Toronto: University of Toronto Press 1995), examines the very complicated details of a possible separation, based on his study of the separation of Slovakia from the Czech Republic. For the Parti Québécois view of this event, see the translation of its plan by Robert Chodos, *Quebec in a New World: The PQ's Plan for Sovereignty* (Toronto: Lorimer 1994).

Participants

Christopher Armstrong Professor of history, York University
Lloyd Atkinson Economist, Toronto
Louis Balthazar Professor of political science, Université Laval
Gérald Beaudoin Conservative senator
Michael Behiels Professor of history, University of Ottawa
Réal Bélanger Professor of history, Université Laval
David Bercuson Professor of history, University of Calgary
Lise Bissonnette Editor, *Le Devoir*
Michael Bliss Professor of history, University of Toronto
Paul Boothe Professor of economics, University of Alberta
Patrick Boyer Former Conservative MP, Etobicoke-Lakeshore
Alan Cairns Professor of political science, University of British Columbia
Sharon Carstairs Liberal senator; former Liberal leader, Manitoba
Gretta Chambers Chancellor, McGill University; journalist
Jean Charest Interim leader, Progressive Conservative Party of Canada
Jean Chrétien Prime minister of Canada
Ramsay Cook Professor of history, York University
Marcel Côté Former adviser to Brian Mulroney
Olive Dickason Professor emerita of history, University of Alberta
Stéphane Dion Professor of political science, Université de Montréal
Alain Dubuc Editor, *La Presse*
Ron Duhamel Liberal MP, St Boniface
William J. Eccles Professor emeritus of history, University of Toronto
David Elton President, Canada West Foundation, Calgary
John English Professor of history, University of Waterloo; Liberal MP, Kitchener
Douglas Fisher Columnist, Toronto *Sun*
Tom Flanagan Professor of political science, University of Calgary
David Foot Professor of economics, University of Toronto

Claude Forget Former Liberal minister, Quebec

Pierre Fortin Professor of economics, Université de Québec à Montréal

Jean Fournier Retired Canadian diplomat

Graham Fraser Washington bureau chief, *Globe and Mail*

Raymond Garneau Former Liberal minister, Quebec

Jean-Robert Gauthier Liberal senator

Gordon Gibson Former Liberal leader, British Columbia

Allan Gotlieb Former undersecretary for external affairs; former ambassador to the United States

Ron Graham Journalist and author

Jack Granatstein Professor of history, York University

Charlotte Gray Ottawa correspondent, *Saturday Night*

Allan Greer Professor of history, University of Toronto

David Hall Professor of history, University of Alberta

Stephen Harper Reform MP, Calgary West

Stanley Hartt Former chief of staff to Brian Mulroney

John Harvard Liberal MP, Winnipeg-St James

Jacques Hébert Liberal senator

Alfred Hero Former director, World Peace Foundation

Peter Hogg Professor of law, York University

John Honderich Publisher, *Toronto Star*

Joseph Jockel Professor of political science, St Lawrence University

William Johnson Columnist, Montreal *Gazette*

Richard Jones Professor of history, Université Laval

Robert Kaplan Former Liberal minister

Guy Laforest Professor of political science, Université Laval

David Laidler Professor of economics, University of Western Ontario

Marc Lalonde Former Liberal minister

Bernard Landry Parti Québécois vice-premier, Quebec

Clifford Lincoln Former Liberal minister, Quebec

Eric Maldoff Former president, Alliance Quebec

Barbara McDougall Former Conservative minister

Kenneth McRoberts Professor of political science, York University

Ovide Mercredi National chief, Assembly of First Nations

J.R. Miller Professor of history, University of Saskatchewan

Dale Miquelon Professor of history, University of Saskatchewan

Jacques Monet President, University of Sudbury

Ken Munro Professor of history, University of Alberta

Lowell Murray Conservative senator; former Conservative minister

Blair Neatby Professor of history, Carleton University

Max Nemni Professor of political science, Université Laval

Ken Norrie Professor of economics, University of Alberta

Fernand Ouellet Professor of history, York University

Doug Owram Professor of history, University of Alberta

Alex Paterson Lawyer, Montreal; former chancellor, McGill University

David Peterson Former Liberal premier, Ontario

Ghislain Picard Regional chief, Assembly of First Nations, Quebec and Labrador

Maurice Pinard Professor of sociology, McGill University

Scott Reid Author and Reform Party researcher

Michel Robert Former president, Liberal Party of Canada

Gordon Robertson Former clerk of the Privy Council

William Robson Director, C.D. Howe Institute

Roy Romanow NDP premier of Saskatchewan

Peter Russell Professor of political science, University of Toronto

Daniel Salée Professor of history, Concordia University

Mitchell Sharp Former Liberal minister and senior bureaucrat

Arthur Silver Professor of history, University of Toronto

Roger Tassé Former federal deputy minister of justice

Arthur Tremblay Retired Conservative senator

Rodrigue Tremblay Former Parti Québécois minister, Quebec

Michael Walker Director, Fraser Institute

Clyde Wells Liberal premier of Newfoundland

Robert Young Professor of political science, University of Western Ontario

Index

Set in Minion with Centaur display
Printed and bound in Canada by Friesens
Copy-editor: Rosemary Shipton
Proofreader: Jacqueline Wood
Designer: George Vaitkunas